Literary Modernism, Queer Temporality

Kate Haffey

Literary Modernism, Queer Temporality

Eddies in Time

Kate Haffey
University of Mary Washington
Fredericksburg, VA, USA

ISBN 978-3-030-17300-5   ISBN 978-3-030-17301-2   (eBook)
https://doi.org/10.1007/978-3-030-17301-2

© The Editor(s) (if applicable) and The Author(s), under exclusive license to Springer
Nature Switzerland AG 2019
This work is subject to copyright. All rights are solely and exclusively licensed by the
Publisher, whether the whole or part of the material is concerned, specifically the rights
of translation, reprinting, reuse of illustrations, recitation, broadcasting, reproduction
on microfilms or in any other physical way, and transmission or information storage and
retrieval, electronic adaptation, computer software, or by similar or dissimilar methodology
now known or hereafter developed.
The use of general descriptive names, registered names, trademarks, service marks, etc. in this
publication does not imply, even in the absence of a specific statement, that such names are
exempt from the relevant protective laws and regulations and therefore free for general use.
The publisher, the authors and the editors are safe to assume that the advice and
information in this book are believed to be true and accurate at the date of publication.
Neither the publisher nor the authors or the editors give a warranty, expressed or implied,
with respect to the material contained herein or for any errors or omissions that may have
been made. The publisher remains neutral with regard to jurisdictional claims in published
maps and institutional affiliations.

Cover illustration: © Alex Linch shutterstock.com

This Palgrave Macmillan imprint is published by the registered company Springer Nature
Switzerland AG
The registered company address is: Gewerbestrasse 11, 6330 Cham, Switzerland

To Jessica,
my past, present, and future

ACKNOWLEDGEMENTS

Like many first books, this one has been a long time coming. Its construction has spanned so many years that parts of it have been written in seven different states, at four different universities, and alongside a menagerie of different pets. As such, there have been many people who have contributed to the shape that this book has taken, perhaps too many to remember, and I owe each of them a debt of gratitude.

First and foremost, I would like to thank Jane Gallop. Jane was the person who first introduced me to queer temporality back in 2005 when I told her about my interest in the intersection of sexuality and time at one of our first meetings about my dissertation. Little did I know then the huge impact that she would have on my work and on my sense of myself as a writer and scholar. From the beginning, Jane offered me guidance, support, constructive criticism, and companionship over the many years it took me to finish this book, even well beyond my time as her student. Her excitement about my work helped me through times when I though I had been derailed. From Jane, I learned what it means to be a mentor, a scholar, and a close reader. I hope to be for my students what she was for me. This book would have been impossible without her.

I would also like to thank José Lanters and Andrew Kincaid for the wonderful comments they provided me on early drafts of this project, which enabled me to fine-tune my attention to literary texts as well as attend to big picture issues. I thank Jason Puskar for his willingness to help with my project even before he was officially a reader on my committee and for the insightful comments that guided me through years of revisions. I thank Cary Costello for his difficult questions about queer studies and for his careful reading of my work. My thanks also to those scholars who provided me with guidance at various stages in my research and writing. To Ellen McCallum and Caroline Levine for pointing me in the direction of authors whose work enriched my understanding of queer temporality and narrative time. To Kathryn Bond Stockton for help in framing my project. To James Phelan and Jean Wyatt for their thoughtful comments on my second chapter.

To those good friends and colleagues who read various drafts and offered comments, copyedits, and criticisms, I offer my deepest thanks. Special thanks to Michael MacDonald, Jessica Ulstad, Shereen Inayatulla, Cara Ogburn, Carrie Wadman, and Jessica Ugarte. Thank you also to those who offered advice about navigating the process of revising and publication: mentor extraordinaire Mara Scanlon, Will Mackintosh, Gary Richards, Antonio Barrenechea, Chris Foss, Shumona Dasgupta, Ben LaBreche, Colin Rafferty, Maya Mathur, Andi Smith, Emily Kazyak, James Brunton, and Jason James.

Thank you to The Graduate School and to The Center for 21st Century Studies at the University of Wisconsin, Milwaukee, for providing me with the funds that allowed me to work on this project. To John Carroll University for support as I worked on the book proposal, both through funds to attend conferences to get feedback on my work and through connecting me with a most excellent research assistant, Claire McBroom. Thanks to the College of Arts and Sciences at University of Mary Washington for supporting this project through various grants. Sections of this book have been published elsewhere. I am grateful for the permission to republish that work here. An earlier version of Chapter 2 appeared as "Exquisite Moments and the Temporality of the Kiss in *Mrs. Dalloway* and *The Hours*" in *Narrative* 18.2 (May 2010). A small portion of the introduction was published as "'People must marry': Queer Temporality in Virginia Woolf and Katherine Mansfield" in *Woolf and Her Female Contemporaries: Selected Papers from the 25th Annual International Conference on Virginia Woolf,* edited by Julie Vandivere and Megan Hicks and published by Clemson University Press in 2016.

Thank you to my colleagues and friends at John Carroll University and Gettysburg College for your support during the writing process, especially Tim Lin, Lynn Burke, Sammie Flores, Katie Batza, Kerry

Wallach, John McBratney, Debby Rosenthal, Anna Hocevar, Katie Horowitz, Alissa Nutting, and Emily Butler. A big thanks to my colleagues in the English, Linguistics, and Communication Department at UMW, who have welcomed me into the department and provided me with everything I need to be successful, especially Susie Kuliasha, the heart and soul of ELC.

A special thanks to my students, past and present, who make the ups and downs of academia worthwhile.

To Sean Grattan, our conversations in Gettysburg, in Montreal, in Utrecht, in Canterbury, have reorganized my thinking on dozens of subjects. I love talking nerd with you.

To my family, both biological and chosen, I thank you for providing me with the confidence to undertake this task, the emotional support to keep going, and the fun times we had together when I would take a break: Mom, Dad, Neil, Dan, Helen, Jodi, Conor, Sean, Aidan, Kara, Chris, Julia, Izzy, Joey, Tommy, Beth, Dee, Juliet, Jason, Gracie, Sam, Brandon, Madelynn, and Jean. To my friends, who recharged my battery and gave me the strength to keep working, I offer my deepest thanks: Shereen Inayatulla, Amy Daroszeski, Amanda Henes, Emma Grey, Jessica Ulstad, Molly Tennessen, Michael MacDonald, Adam Helt-Baldwin, Megan Helt-Baldwin, Drew Anastasia, Tim Lin, Barbie Curatolo, Ryan Brazell, Ted Lewis, Elena Brooks-Perkins, Alex Brooks-Perkins, Jessy Ohl, Maggie Yancey, Marissa Patsey, Elizabeth Stiles, Mindy Peden, and Emily Wilson.

To Jessica, I thank for your patience and understanding during the whole long process and your help in editing and indexing. You showed up during the first chapter and stayed to the last, and I am grateful for every second.

CONTENTS

CHAPTER 1

Introduction: Queer Moments and Eddies in Time

In the foreword of her 1993 collection of essays, Eve Kosofsky Sedgwick makes the claim that "queer is a continuing moment"—that "something about *queer* is inextinguishable" (p. xii). While Sedgwick's collection is not about time per se, its foreword, titled "T Times," which begins with reference to the 1992 gay pride parade in New York, reflects on the temporality of queerness at a moment defined both by gay and lesbian rights beginning to gain political traction and by the "deathly silence" produced by the losses of the AIDS epidemic (1993, p. xii). While Sedgwick was one of the few addressing issues of time in early queer theory, her work might very well have ushered in a new generation of queer theorists particularly attuned to issues of temporality. Indeed, since the early 2000s, there has been a dramatic increase in the number of queer theorists who have turned their attention to issues of time. Their work has shown the various ways in which sexuality and temporality are enmeshed, from the life schedules deemed healthy for child rearing to the bildungsroman structure that charts the passing of time as a progression from childhood through adolescence to mature adult heterosexuality. Their writings have also pointed us toward a variety of queer temporalities that stand in clear opposition to these normative time frames. As Jack Halberstam has claimed, queer temporality is about the future reimagined "according to logics that lie outside of those paradigmatic markers of life experience—namely, birth, marriage, reproduction, and death" (2005, p. 2). For a number of scholars of queer temporality, the AIDS crisis stands as a pivotal moment, a protracted historical event that

© The Author(s) 2019
K. Haffey, *Literary Modernism, Queer Temporality*,
https://doi.org/10.1007/978-3-030-17301-2_1

produced new relations to time. For those living through the epidemic, the future no longer stretched out like a limitless horizon. The AIDS crisis thus allowed for a "rethinking of the conventional emphasis on longevity and futurity" (Halberstam 2005, p. 2).

Though the AIDS epidemic represents a clear example of a historical moment that facilitated a rethinking of time, I believe that we need to go back a bit further to uncover some of the foundations of what has come to be known as queer temporality. In 1927, Wyndham Lewis wrote *Time and Western Man*, a polemic that attempted "to contradict" the work of those writers he described as representing a "time-cult." His text paints a picture of modern literature that is above all else obsessed with time. He takes on a number of prominent philosophers, novelists, and poets of his day, including Bergson, Proust, Joyce, Pound, and Stein. These and other authors' unconventional use of time is a generally accepted component of what defines modernist literature. What might be less recognized, however, is the role these temporalities, developed nearly a hundred years ago, have played in framing much of what has become central in our contemporary discussions of queer temporality.

Literary Modernism, Queer Temporality: Eddies in Time is about the relation between modernist narrative and the more recent work on queer temporality. In this book, I argue that queer theory's work on time owes a debt to modernist literary experimentations. Many of the descriptions of queer temporalities published in the past fifteen years bear a striking resemblance to configurations of time that emerged as part of modernist critiques of conventional narrative. Part of my project is to examine modernist narrative in direct relation to queer temporality. The work in this field allows us to see how modernist experiments with narrative were perhaps always enmeshed with issues of sexuality.

This book approaches queer temporality from a few different angles. One of its central goals is to identify and examine modernist temporalities that can best be described as queer. Because much work has been done in examining the ways in which modernist temporalities break conventions, I will show why particular modernist temporalities are most fruitfully examined through the lens of queer theory. Many of the temporal configurations I examine here have been looked at previously through different critical frameworks. Therefore, my focus will be on the new insights that are gained from framing the issue as a queer one.

A second goal for this book centers on what we might call "the persistence of modernism." Madelyn Detloff's book by this same name has shown the "persistence of modernism in contemporary responses to war, terror, and trauma" (2009, p. 3). I am interested in the persistence of modernist time-senses in the realm of queer theory. I seek to demonstrate how modernist experiments with temporality and narrative have been taken up by a number of authors writing several generations later. As many queer scholars have claimed, the AIDS crisis has served as a flash point for the explosion of new ways of thinking about temporality. Novelists writing in the decades following the crisis thus had these new temporal configurations available to them. And yet, as these temporalities made their way into contemporary literature, they seemed to be deeply inflected with the marks of modernism. What I find notable about many of these texts is their reuse (whether directly or indirectly) of modernist temporalities as a response to contemporary issues or as a defining part of their own narrative projects.

The final, and perhaps most important, goal of this book is to analyze the narrative consequences of queer temporality. If part of what queer temporality does is to jam the mechanisms that produce conventional narratives that reinforce traditional social relations, then queer temporality has much to contribute to theories of narrative in general. There are a whole host of questions we might be able to ask about narrative once we've seen how queer temporality operates in conjunction with narrative structures. For example, nearly every definition of narrative includes the criteria that narrative constitutes a succession of events. But what happens when succession itself becomes a normative convention that is systematically dismantled? And what is the connection between succession and the institutions that regulate sexuality? If succession is at the very core of what narrative is, then queer temporality's interaction with it can help us begin to see the stakes involved here. In many ways, texts that dabble in queer temporality discard much of what, in the conventional sense, makes a narrative a narrative. Given this, the consequences for narrative in general stretch beyond even what I am able to describe within this book.

THE PERVERSE TURN: QUEERING COHERENCE

In the spring of 2007, *GLQ* released a special issue dedicated to Queer Temporality that included a roundtable discussion between some of its most prominent scholars. In the midst of the back and forth between these scholars, Halberstam put forth a definition of queer time that mirrored claims he had made a few years earlier in his book *In a Queer Time and Place*. He writes: "Queer time for me is the dark nightclub, the perverse turn away from the narrative coherence of adolescence–early adulthood–marriage–reproduction–child rearing–retirement– death, the embrace of late childhood in place of early adulthood or immaturity in place of responsibility" (Halberstam 2005, p. 182). Halberstam's definition locates us in a bar, a queer space seemingly outside the institutions of marriage and the family. He sees the bar as embodying a particular temporality, a space where time flows independently of those conventional milestones that make sense of a life. Halberstam's definition presents queer time as an alternate timeframe for individuals, as the space occupied by those who eschew the idea that one must grow into a particular kind of mature adult.

But Halberstam's imagining of queer time as "the perverse turn away" from particular types of "narrative coherence" also takes it beyond the realm of life stories and into the realm of narrative structures. If queer time can be defined as a turning away from narrative coherence, then we must begin to bring into the conversation those structures upon which narrative coherence relies. Halberstam points us to a few. For example, the movement through "adolescence–early adulthood–marriage–reproduction–child rearing–retirement–death," a bildungsroman-like narrative, has often defined just want counts as a life, both within literature and outside of it. Beyond this, however, we might think of a number of other structures that make narrative cohere: the chronological movement of time, the sequencing of events, the progression through conventional narrative stages (exposition, rising action, falling action, climax, resolution) in which meaning comes into focus in a conclusion, the sense of closure produced by an ending, a consistent point of view, and character development, to name just a few.

If part of what defines queer temporality is a turning away from narrative coherence, then we must consider its specific indebtedness to modernist literature, literature known for its tendency to think against the grain of dominant narrative conventions. In Virginia Woolf's well-known and often quoted essay "Modern Fiction," for example, she imagines modernist literature as literature that turns away from much of what has defined fiction up to that point. She describes how the author has been subservient to "some powerful and unscrupulous tyrant who has him in thrall, to provide a plot, to provide comedy, tragedy, love interest," and speaks of the need for narrative to lay stress differently. The Moderns, as Woolf calls them, place their emphasis "upon something hitherto ignored," and as such "a different outline of form becomes necessary." The result of this shift in emphasis, according to Woolf, is often narrative incoherence. "Let us record the atoms as they fall upon the mind in the order in which they fall," she says, "let us trace the pattern, however disconnected and *incoherent* in appearance" (my emphasis). Modernist literature is in some ways a literature of incoherence, a literature that continually breaks the rules that make narrative cohere. For Woolf, in "Modern Fiction," there is a significant connection between coherence and convention. Texts become incoherent when they break convention, when they rearrange or ignore the patterns of accepted narrative.

It is notable, perhaps, that much of Woolf's fiction turns away from exactly the type of narrative coherence that Halberstam mentions. Though Woolf sometimes sets up a bildungsroman-like structure or shows characters organizing their own experiences through such structures, these conventions often serve as the frameworks that her central characters turn away from. In *To The Lighthouse*, for example, Mrs. Ramsey's "mania" for marriage, as Lily Biscoe calls it, is pitted against the "enormous exultation" that Lily feels when she realizes she "need never marry anybody" (1927, pp. 175–176). For Lily, this social convention is inextricably tied to aesthetic convention. In the same moment that she realizes she "need never marry," she also decides that she will move the tree to the middle of her painting and recalls her friend William Bankes's shock at "her neglect of the significance of mother and son" (1927, p. 176). Lily's art, like Woolf's and like Woolf's description of "modern fiction," lays the emphasis elsewhere, showing readers the expected convention and then purposely turning away from it.

Elsewhere in *To the Lighthouse*, we get examples of those normative temporalities that Halberstam describes. As Paul Rayley walks back to the Ramsey's house after proposing to his future wife, the scene is described thus: "the lights coming out suddenly one by one seemed like things that were going to happen to him—his marriage, his children, his house; and again he thought, as they came out on to the high road, which was shaded with high bushes, how they would retreat into solitude together, and walk on and on, he always leading her, and she pressing close to his side (as she did now)" (1927, p. 78). Paul Rayley imagines his life through those paradigmatic markers that Halberstam mentions: "marriage–reproduction–child rearing" and so on. This is the life that Mrs. Ramsey wants for him, the life that she wants for Lily. But this is also the temporality that Woolf is consistently interrupting, not only through characters like Lily who reject such paths as the only viable ones, but through her very narrative method, a method that focuses almost exclusively on moments that have little effect on plot, a method in which progressive movement through life stages takes a backseat to a past that interpenetrates the present.

While Woolf's narrative project probably comes the closest to embodying Halberstam's definition of "queer time," she is far from the only modernist writer whose work is operating along such lines. As has been well established in modernist criticism, experimentation with narrative time was a central aspect of the work of a number of prominent modernists, and part of this experimentation included the dismantling of chronological temporalities in which characters progressed through a series of life stages. Even as we move beyond Halberstam's definition and into other recent discussions in queer theory, a clear affinity can be discerned between "queer temporality" and these modernist literary experiments.

QUEER/MODERNIST/TEMPORALITY

Halberstam's work, while foundational, presents only one way of understanding queer temporality. Over the past two decades, dozens of theorists have added their own voice to this conversation. As such, there are several elements central to any articulation of queer time. At this point, I would like to discuss those elements of queer temporality that are not only essential to its definition but also which form the backbone of my own analysis of the topic.

At the heart of much work on queer temporality is a desire to question, and perhaps even dismantle, notions of linear time. This purpose is echoed by a number of critics writing on different topics and within different disciplines. Medievalist Carolyn Dinshaw, for example, describes her project as "a refusal of linear historicism" (Dinshaw et al. 2007, p. 178). Dinshaw is just one of many critics writing under the banner of what is sometimes called "queer historicism," a body of work that is critical of some of the seemingly foundational assumptions of history. Jonathan Goldberg and Madhavi Menon have coined the term "unhistoricism" to describe the work that they are attempting to do in the area, dependent as it is on debunking "teleological productions of queerness" (2005, p. 1609). One of the goals of these historically grounded projects is to critique those notions connected to linearity like progress, teleology, and closure.

One particular linear temporality often critiqued by queer theorists is the temporality ruled by marriage and reproduction. In his groundbreaking book *No Future,* Lee Edelman uses the term "reproductive futurism" to describe the temporality that positions the child as the symbol of the future. For Edelman, this understanding of time is the one that rules political discourse and shuts down any attempt at opposition. Who, after all, Edelman asks, would take the side against the children? Edelman's analysis of reproductive futurism also demonstrates how this temporality conceives of "history as linear narrative (the poor man's teleology) in which meaning succeeds in revealing itself—*as itself*—through time" (2004, p. 4). Edelman's construction here shows the ways in which theorists have often connected notions of normative time (like the temporality of marriage and reproduction) to linear time or linear history. Indeed, a term like "straight time," used by both Tom Boellstorff (2007, p. 228) and Valerie Rohy (2009, p. xiv), seems to combine these two concepts by using straight to mean both linear and heterosexual.

It is important to note, however, that "reproductive futurism" is not the only normative form of time and that not all normative temporalities are necessarily heterosexual. As Nguyen Tan Hoang notes, "there is also a homonormative time line" (Dinshaw et al. 2007, p. 183). Outside the mandates of marriage and family (or sometimes within them), LGBT individuals create their own normative temporalities. As Hoang says, "we pity those who come out late in life, do not find a long-term partner before they lose their looks, or continue to hit the bars when they are the bartender's father's age" (Dinshaw et al. 2007, p. 184). Recalling the past ten years, as the fight for same-sex marriage took center stage in LGBT rights movements, it is easy to see the way in which "reproductive futurism" has come to function not only as the rhetoric of conservative political movements but also as the rhetoric of gays and lesbians who desire inclusion in institutions like marriage.

Queer critiques of linear time have also led to critiques of certain developmental sequences. Developmental narratives often depend on linear time as they log individuals' movement through a series of stages. Halberstam, as mentioned earlier, describes how "we chart the emergence of the adult from the dangerous and unruly period of adolescence as a desired process of maturation" (2005, p. 4). Within this framework, individuals progress through different stages of development, stages structured by the societal conventions of a normal life, including marriage, reproduction, and retirement. Halberstam's work examines temporalities that exist outside those various institutions that structure time along this trajectory.

Kathryn Bond Stockton uses this developmental framework to examine the figure of the queer child. She shows how the concept of "growing up" is an inappropriate metaphor for the growth exhibited by queer children. If growth is recorded when children move through certain stages, queer children might not grow up at all, but may, to use Stockton's term, grow "sideways" (2009, p. 13). Stockton thus examines the "unruly contours of growing that don't bespeak continuance" (2009, p. 13). The idea of a queer child also poses a conceptual problem for the logic that imagines sexuality as specifically adult; the queer child seems too adult to fit the category of child (2004, p. 283). On the flip side, the grown homosexual is often figured as a child because she has not reached maturity (since such a concept often depends upon heterosexual coupling). The discourse of arrested development rears its head here as queers are conceptualized in a state of halted growth, forever frozen in an immature stage of development.

As queer theorists seek to deconstruct linear time and development narratives, they have often worked to reconstruct and reconceptualize the present in new ways. If the present is not merely one link in the temporal chain, then a whole plethora of conceptual metaphors become available. One particular concept—a view of the present in which the past persists—arises in a number of different ways across theorists of queer temporality. Carolyn Dinshaw, for example, rejects the present as "singular and fleeting," and instead imagines "a kind of expanded now in which past, present, and future coincide" (Dinshaw et al. 2007, p. 190). Dinshaw insists on "the present's irreducible multiplicity" (2007, p. 190) and believes in the possibility of "touching across time," an idea she comes to by way of Roland Barthes (2007, p. 178). In Dinshaw's framework, the present is a time touched and affected by other moments. Similarly, Carla Freccero discusses the "affective force of the past in the present, of a desire issuing from another time and placing a demand on the present in the form of an ethical imperative" (Dinshaw et al. 2007, p. 184). Freccero sees "living with ghosts" as one way to conceive of an ethical relationship with history (Freccero 2006, p. 78). This image of the ghost is a quite common one within the scholarship on queer temporality, perhaps because the ghost is a temporal image. A ghost is a remnant from a previous time that should not, but does, exist in the present. "Living with ghosts," for Freccero, means acknowledging that the present is haunted by the past (2006, p. 80). In both Dinshaw and Freccero, we are presented with an image of the present as heterogeneous and as nonchronological. To see the present as a space "in which past, present, and future coincide," to use Dinshaw's words, chronological timelines must be put aside.

The concept of the present developed by these two authors also bears a striking resemblance to Eve Sedgwick's work in *Tendencies*. While Dinshaw and Freccero specifically theorize their sense of the present, Sedgwick's emerges as she talks about high rate of suicides among "queer teenagers" (1993, p. 1). Sedgwick speaks of how scholars of gay and lesbian studies are "haunted by the suicides of [these] adolescents" (1993, p. 1). She describes also the ways in which she and other scholars of queer studies attempt to "keep faith with vividly remembered promises made to [themselves] in childhood," a kind of work that seeks to keep alive the child within the adult. Seemingly, the introduction to *Tendencies* is itself haunted, haunted by the suicides of queer teens, haunted by those who have died of AIDS, and haunted by the ghostly childhood selves of those who write queer theory. As Sedgwick pieces together the various parts of her introduction, her writing seems to be engaged in the type of "living with ghosts" that Freccero would describe more than a decade later. As Sedgwick herself acknowledges, part of what is at work in her life and in her writing are identifications that cross "the ontological crack between the living and the dead" (1993, p. 257). Indeed, as readers, we get a sense of a present moment, or what Sedgwick will theorize as a "queer moment," in which multiple times come into contact: the dead adolescents remain present if only as ghosts, and the child is kept alive in the adult if only in the form of promises made across time.

Unlike the present conceived of by Dinshaw and Freccero, which seems primarily centered on the recognition of the present as riddled with remnants from the past, Sedgwick's queer moment also reaches out into the future. Specifically, Sedgwick describes queer as "a continuing moment," as a moment that is somehow "inextinguishable" (1993, p. xii). The queer moment that Sedgwick describes is almost contradictory in its placement of the adjective "continuing" as a descriptor for "moment." A moment is generally understood to be an instant; it is that which, by definition, does not continue. As Barber and Clark say of the queer moment, "This present tense, forwarded into an unknowable future, remains" (2002, p. 19). Sedgwick thus conceives of a form of time in which the present is preserved, perhaps anachronistically, in the future.

There is a clear connection between the way these contemporary queer theorists discuss temporality and the aesthetic experiments occurring in the work of several canonical modernist authors. In queer temporality's critique of linear time, we can see a similarity to modernism's critique of linear narrative, a similarity that plays out in authors like Woolf, Faulkner, and Stein who were of often writing in response to the narrative structures of the realist novel. Virginia Woolf, for example, speaks in *A Room of One's Own* about breaking the narrative sequence. When writing about the work of Mary Carmichael, she claims that Carmichael "is tampering with the expected sequence. First she broke the sentence; now she has broken the sequence" (1929, p. 85). Woolf critics have pointed out that she is in some ways referring to her own writing here, to her tendency to write novels that do not use plot development in expected ways. This is a quality of her writing that she is continually critiqued for by realist authors like Arnold Bennett, who found quarrel with the lack of "ordered movement towards climax" in her novels (1975, p. 190). Woolf's aesthetic experiments with narrative time are a response to those literary conventions that she finds restrictive. In her prose, she seeks to disrupt what she sees as the dominant temporal mode of the novel. Such tactics can be seen in my earlier example from *To the Lighthouse*, but they occur across many of Woolf's novels and essays.

Perhaps one way to deal with narrative conventions that require an "expected sequence" is experimentation with styles like "stream of consciousness." To mimic the brain in thought is to produce temporalities not ruled by clock time, temporalities not organized by an "ordered movement toward climax" (Bennett 1975, p. 190). Of course, this style was used by a number of modernists, including Woolf and Faulkner. While Woolf employs "stream of consciousness" to represent temporalities that could not be presented in a more realist novel, Faulkner often seems to be writing under a different burden: genealogical time. Genealogical time in Faulkner is not unlike the "reproductive futurism" that Lee Edelman describes. Like "reproductive futurism," genealogical succession is teleological, and it relies on a chain that stretches endlessly forward, a chain that projects the past into the future. Faulkner's use of "stream of consciousness" deals with the weight of this realization while attempting to create pockets of temporality that are not ruled solely by genealogical time.

Gertrude Stein's work also is invested in throwing off the chains of linear succession. In her *Narration* lectures, Stein resists the idea that all things are given meaning through succession. From her point of view, the early twentieth century is the period in which writers began to break out of the idea that narratives had to progress through a beginning, middle, and end. "The narrative of to-day," she writes in 1935, "is not a narrative of succession as all the writing for a good many hundreds of years has been" (1935, p. 20). Stein's words here could describe the work of many modernist writers, including her own. Stein's own way of resisting "narrative of succession" is the production of what she calls the "continuous present," a form of time that allows her writing to break away from these conventional frameworks.

Stein's reconfiguration of the present as a way to imagine time outside succession or linearity sounds quite similar to the projects of queer theorists like Dinshaw, Freccero, and Sedgwick, who see the reworking of the present as essential for thinking about queer time. And yet, Stein is not the only modernist to explore alternate ways of understanding the present. Virginia Woolf's "moments of being" in "A Sketch of the Past" and T. S. Eliot's analysis of the "eternal present" in the *Four Quartets* serve as additional examples. Indeed, in Dinshaw's description of "a kind of expanded now in which past, present, and future coincide," we might hear a faint echo of Eliot—"all time is eternally present" (1941, "Burnt Norton" line 4).

In the early twentieth century, modernist texts did much to explore and explode various normative temporalities. In recent years, strikingly modernist understandings of time have reemerged, energized to do a new kind of work. This book seeks to explore the strange connection between these two times, that long moment of literary modernism and the recent critical turn to queer temporality. While modernist writers were reacting to "the tyranny of plot" in literature, to use Susan Stanford Friedman's phrase (1989, p. 162), scholars of queer temporality are illuminating the ways in which individuals are seeking to live lives that flow in new directions, that move in strange and perhaps aberrant ways. Modernist experimentations with narrative temporalities in literature, which at the time perhaps seemed unrealistic because fictional, have actually come in handy to analyze the real-life narratives of individuals who live outside the institutions of marriage and reproduction. These literary temporalities thus offer us a framework for theorizing queer temporality (just as the work on queer temporality offers a new way to look at literary modernism).

In this sense, queer temporality and literary modernism seem to make appropriate bedfellows.

The connection between queer theory and modernism has not gone unnoticed by literary scholars. In a 2009 *PMLA* article, Heather Love asked: "Is queer modernism simply another name for modernism?" (2009, p. 744). Love's question gets at the way in which queerness might in fact be at the heart of modernism itself. As she says, "perhaps what makes queer and modernism such a good fit is that the indeterminacy of queer seems to match the indeterminacy, expansiveness, and drift of the literary—partly the experimental, oblique version most closely associated with modernist textual production" (2009, p. 745). Love's statement locates modernist literary practices themselves as space in which queerness resides. Love explores this concept herself in her 2007 book *Feeling Backward*. Her focus is on modernist texts that "turn their backs on the future" and instead orient themselves toward the past. Love sees this backward glance as a key aspect of the temporal movement of modernist texts as well as a mechanism that helps to negotiate the losses within the literature of the period.

Love's book is only one more recent example of a series of texts that explore the connections between modernism and queerness. Since the late 1980s, there have been several articles and books examining what is often termed "Sapphic Modernism" or "Lesbian Modernism."[1] Taken together these texts examine the ways in which criticism had often failed to take lesbian and bisexual female sexuality into account in its descriptions of literary modernism. As Joanne Winning has claimed, lesbianism appears as "a shadowy figure whose fragmentary form disrupts and reforms modernism's master narrative of heterosexuality" (Winning 2000, p. 7). As such, these books have been central to the redrawing of modernism's contours, in what Winning has called "the new modernist critical studies" (2010, p. 17). Authors like Shari Benstock, Laura Doan, Elizabeth English, Robin Hackett, Erin G. Carlston, and Winning have shown how central Sapphic modernism has been to the shaping of modernism itself (Hackett 2004, p. 13).[2] This is not only because of the nonnormative sexualities practiced by many women modernists, but also because "there was a profound and indelible link between lesbian sexuality and aesthetic experimentation" (Winning 2010, p. 224). This connection between form and content has allowed those who analyze Sapphic or Lesbian Modernism to reexamine some of the key conventions of literary modernism in innovative ways. Indeed, it is the fragmentary, disconnected techniques of modernism that often allowed queer desire to be articulated in ways that were indirect or ambiguous (English 2015, p. 14). Though these works of lesbian, queer, or gay modernism rarely addresses issues of time, the tools of analysis developed by these critiques have been helpful in my own analysis of the relation between modernist literary techniques and queer time.

The past twenty years has also produced a growing collection of works that might fall under the rubric of "Queer Modernism." Texts I would place in this category are often less concerned with specific identity categories than they are with analyzing nonnormative forms of desire or deconstructing normative readings of canonical modernist texts. In these texts, as Laura Doan and Jane Garrity have claimed, theorists use some of "the insights and principles pioneered by the proponents and practitioners of 'Sapphic modernism' by focusing upon the text's latent content – upon what is not explicitly named but, rather, potentially inferred – as a way of extracting a queer reading that is not, often, immediately apparent" (2006, p. 544). These texts include Joseph Allen Boone's *Libidinal Currents* (1998), Anne Herrmann's *Queering the Moderns* (2000), and Michael Trask's *Cruising Modernism* (2003). While books like Alan Sinfield's *The Wilde Century* (1994) and Joseph Bristow's *Effeminate England* (1995) specifically explore effeminacy and the formation of gay male and queer identities in the modernist era.

While most of the books that explore lesbian/Sapphic, queer, or gay modernism only deal with issues of temporality in passing, there is one clear exception among the books I have mentioned that I would like to explore in further detail: Joseph Allen Boone's groundbreaking *Libidinal Currents: Sexuality and the Shaping of Modernism*. Boone's book offers a cogent exploration of the relationship between modernist textual practices and "the erotics of narrative" (1998, p. 3). Boone's text is one of the few that explores the intersections of modernism, sexuality, and narrative, and as such it has set the standard for much of what has followed. *Libidinal Currents* concentrates on "those novelistic fictions whose attempts to construct new forms to evoke the flux of consciousness and the erotics of mental activity also invite a reexamination of the literary and sexual politics of modernism" (1998, p. 4). As such, the book focuses much of its attention on forms of "interior representation" like stream-of-consciousness and is able to consider the narrative effects of these conventions, including those related to the presentation of time. Boone's work is especially adept at analyzing the various "currents" that its readings unearth, showing how "a temporal present [...] that, in its unfolding, simultaneously becomes indistinguishable from the past" (1998, p. 18). While much of Boone's book focuses on making interventions into the study of sexuality through psychoanalysis, his analysis of these key modernist narrative conventions makes it clear that the temporalities produced through these conventions inextricably intertwined with the queering of sexuality.

Given the ways in which modernist textualities have been connected to queerness, it is perhaps not surprising that Elizabeth Freeman begins *Time Binds*, her own 2010 book on queer temporality, with a modernist poem. Freeman reads Robert Graves' poem "It's a Queer Time" against the grain of historicist readings that would organize its "various temporal schemae into temporal sequence" (2010, p. xi). Freeman develops an alternate reading that pays special attention to the "nonsequential forms of time" that inhabit the poem. Though *Time Binds* is not specifically a text about modernist temporalities, Freeman uses Graves' poem to provide the initial framework for her readings of queer time throughout the book. I find this to be a somewhat common move in the growing body of work on queer temporality. Even Halberstam, when providing a literary example in the introduction to *In a Queer Time and Place*, cites *Mrs. Dalloway* as an instance of queer time.

Since I am arguing that modernist experiments with time have played an important role in helping theorists conceive of and describe queer temporalities, it is necessary to examine some of the work of those critics who have made important contributions to the understanding of time in modernism. The exploration of time in modernist literature goes back to at least 1927 when Wyndham Lewis accused his contemporaries of being members of a "time-cult" in *Time and Western Man*, and the books exploring this topic since are too numerous to recount here. However, there are a few significant texts on modernist temporality whose insights will be important moving forward. Ronald Schleifer's *Modernism and Time* (2000) examines the transition from the late nineteenth to the early twentieth century to demonstrate the shift that took place across a variety of disciplines (history, science, philosophy, the arts) in their approaches to time. Enlightenment thought, which was dominant through much of the nineteenth century, imagined time as "homogenous," sequential, and progress driven (2000, p. 2). This configuration gave way to post-Enlightenment understandings of time "that called the self-evidence and universality of these assumptions into question" and began to recognized time as subjective, context-bound, and historically relative (2000, p. 3). Schleifer points out that "these classical conceptions of time are the central assumptions of Enlightenment 'modernity' that are called into question" in the work of many modernists (2000, p. 2). While Schleifer examines the changing notions of time in the disciplines and the arts, Stephen Kern examines the various technological innovations that affected people's perceptions of time between 1880 and 1918 in *The Culture of Time and Space* (1983). Kern's book discusses not only modes of transportation like the train and the motorcar, but also looks at the effects of the new machines of modern warfare. Through their different approaches, both texts help to explore and explain the temporal innovations we see in modernism through a historical framework.

While most work on modernist temporalities examine the transition between the nineteenth and twentieth century or the years surrounding WWI, Tyrus Miller's *Late Modernism* (1999) studies the often neglected late 1920s and 1930s. Miller demonstrates how the work on modernism often focuses on "on relatively unitary and 'vital' moments of its development" (1999, p. 5). The "grand narrative" of modernism has focused on beginnings, according to Miller, but his book turns "this historiographic telescope the other way around to focus on modernism from the perspective of its end" (1999, p. 5). Miller's angle of vision not only allows him to demonstrate the coexistence of what he calls "late modernism" (following architectural historian Charles Jenks) alongside the continued appearance of high modernist texts, but it also provides him the opportunity to theorize the temporality of this late modernist moment. Because critics most often regard it as "a peripheral issue," disconnected from the dominant narrative of twentieth-century fiction, late modernist fiction is marked by its "untimeliness," as the "cultural products of this period both are and are not 'of the moment" (1999, p. 13). As such Miller's work offers a way of thinking about modernist literary history that itself breaks the same narrative conventions that many fiction writers were subverting.

Like Miller, Bryony Randall also views modernism from alternative vantage point in *Modernism, Daily Time, and Everyday Life* (2007). Randall claims, correctly I believe, that critical accounts of modernism have privileged and valued the "exceptional moment, the transcendent or the epiphanic" (2007, p. 6). In critical accounts of these moments, they are often shown to be in opposition to the commonplace or to critique aspects of everyday life. Randall's work, however, shows how several modernist writers (including Woolf and Stein), "find new ways of imagining and representing the present, life now, ongoing daily time" (2007, p. 7). Randall's focus is thus not on the exceptional moment, but on "the temporality of dailiness," a modernist temporality that has been subjected to "relative critical neglect" (2007, p. 7). Randall's work directs much needed critical attention to this neglected modernist temporality.

Despite the fact that modernist temporalities have been studied for a long time and from a variety of perspectives, I believe that we are far from exhausting the possibilities for queer readings of these temporal configurations. In my own readings throughout this book, I have attempted to apply insights from recent work in queer theory in order to rethink the ways these modernist temporalities have often been analyzed. While I have followed the trend of modernist critics, one Bryony Randall has pointed out, of focusing on "the exceptional moments," I have attempted to place such moments within a new framework, one that allows me to point out their oddity and strangeness and consider their effects on narrative structures. These moments I focus on are all queer in this old-fashioned way (for us), which was current for modernist writers. But in their strangeness or peculiarity, these moments open up possibilities that are queer in a more present-day way. As such, I analyze these moments as "queer moments" of the type that Eve Sedgwick specifically theorizes. According to Sedgwick, the "queer moment" not only represents a present that is haunted by the past, but also a present that stretches into the future, making a "counterclaim against [its own] obsolescence" (1993, p. xii). These types of moments not only function to help us rethink the boundaries of narrative, but they also serve as a metonym for how modernism literary techniques persist in the present. In the individual texts I analyze in the following chapters, such moments operate in a variety of ways. They can complicate the narrative temporalities of the texts in which they appear, or they can act as an interruption to developmental narratives, genealogical time formations, and predictable plot development.

While my own work on queer moments draws from Eve Sedgwick's theories, she is not the only one to use this term. Indeed, Alan Sinfield's 1994 book *The Wilde Century* is subtitled "Effeminacy, Oscar Wilde, and the Queer Moment." However, in Sinfield's text the "queer moment" is framed as a historical moment. Sinfield characterizes the Oscar Wilde trial as a "queer moment" because it helped to produce a legible form of queerness in the cultural imagination (even if this could only be recognized retrospectively). Likewise, following Sinfield, Laura Doan refers to the obscenity trial for Radclyffe Hall's *The Well of Loneliness* as a "queer moment" because it was "*the* crystallizing moment in the construction of a visible modern English lesbian subculture" (2001, pp. xii–xiii). Sinfield and Doan's use of the queer moment in their scholarship is thus quite different than my own. They each locate a historical moment that helped to produce lesbian, gay, or queer identities, whereas I seek to analyze the textual moments that disrupt narrative in ways that open it up to queer possibilities.

Because my own work lingers on these types of moments, I have subtitled this book "Eddies in Time," which is itself a particular type of queer moment. The phrase plays on Eve Sedgwick's description of the queer moment as "recurrent, eddying" (1993, p. xii). This title not only shows the central role that Sedgwick has played in my own thinking about queer temporality but also serves as an apt metaphor for the specific moments that I explore. The word eddy literally describes water that "runs contrary to the direction of the tide or current," especially a "circular motion in water" or "small whirlpool" (def. 1).[3] As a temporal metaphor, the eddy represents a moment in which time does not flow steadily forward but moves in strange ways. It is important to note that both of the words that Sedgwick uses to describe the queer moment (recurrent, eddying) are associated with flowing water. Rivers and streams have served as some of the dominant metaphors for the movement of time. The image of flowing water is especially apparent in a term like "stream-of-consciousness." Like a stream, the style of writing that mimics its flow is also subject to snags and eddies.

The figure of the eddy is operative in those instances where, apart from the main flow of narrative, we have another narrative, almost hidden, and certainly moving differently from the more dominant one. Here I am reminded of Joseph Allen Boone's analysis of the "libidinal currents" that helped to shape modernism (1998, p. 18). Or, perhaps, Kathryn Bond Stockton's phrase for queer children who do not "grow up" but instead grow "sideways" (2004, p. 279). The movement of these queer children is contrary to the dominant narrative of childhood growth—and thus their movement through time might be described as eddying. The whirlpool is one specific variation of the eddy, but one that pops up a few times across the writers that this book explores.

The whirlpool is an especially important metaphor for Sedgwick in her memoir, a metaphor that allows her to talk about the connection across time between the child and the adult. This is perhaps what I like about the eddy as a figure, that it helps us to make sense of seemingly contradictory understandings of time. When Sedgwick claims that "queer is a continuing moment," her claim seems contradictory, impossible. As a figure, the eddy not only shows us that Sedgwick's claim is possible, but it also offers up alternative modes of temporality.

QUEER TIMELINES, QUEER TEXTS

To conceive of a project that theorizes queer forms of temporality and then stick to a very traditional timeline would seem to prevent any attempt to think outside of conventional temporal frameworks. This book thus takes an unorthodox approach and explores sets of texts from two different periods. The texts in the first set are all modernist proper. They were written by canonical high modernist authors (Woolf, Eliot, Faulkner, and Stein) and were published between about 1925 and 1942. These particular authors were chosen because of the centrality of issues of time to their literary projects as well as the surprising ways in which sexuality and temporality intersect in their writing. These are four of the most time-obsessed modernists, to use Wyndham Lewis's phrase. And yet, their projects, ideologies, political leanings were quite different, and they offer divergent temporal configurations in their works. The texts in the second set are all from contemporary writers, authors who have come to be known in the last forty years or so.[4] The texts that I focus on from these authors all date from the late 1980s to the late 1990s—a period that encompasses the publication Eve Sedgwick's 1993 collection of essays *Tendencies*, written during a time she describes in her preface as "the moment of Queer" (xii). These are the years that saw not only the increasing deaths of the AIDS epidemic but also the rise of queer activism in the U.S. and Great Britain and the coining of the term "queer theory" in the academy. These contemporary author's texts are each paired with the modernist whose temporality their work most closely echoes. In pairing texts in this way, I am able to show the continuities between the modernist aesthetic experiments occurring earlier in the century and the reemergence of these concerns (in both literature and theory) as the twentieth century was coming to a close.

In my second chapter, for example, I trace particular temporalities that emerge in Virginia Woolf's 1925 novel *Mrs. Dalloway* into Michael Cunningham's 1998 novel *The Hours*. *The Hours* is often referred to as a rewriting of *Mrs. Dalloway*. The title of Cunningham's text is actually taken from Woolf's original title for her novel when it was in manuscript form. In naming his novel *The Hours*, Cunningham highlights the temporal aspect of Woolf's original text and explores it further in his own work. Woolf's text is a layering of multiple temporalities, from the clock-time that is constantly clanged out by Big Ben to the idiosyncratic temporalities experienced by the characters whose stream of consciousness the novel records. In my own reading, I focus on the "exquisite moment" of the kiss between Clarissa Dalloway and Sally Seton, a moment that returns to interrupt Clarissa's present throughout the novel.

In Michael Cunningham's novel, this kiss becomes an even more central trope. In *Mrs. Dalloway*, there is only one kiss; it occurred more than thirty years before the events of the novel, but it has remained ever-present in the title character's mind. In *The Hours*, however, Cunningham presents us with three different kisses, each of which helps to unpack the complex temporalities of these moments. His own style mimics that of Virginia Woolf, but his explorations of the kiss go beyond what was presented in *Mrs. Dalloway*. For instance, Cunningham's novel follows three central characters from three different time periods through one day in their lives (as opposed to Woolf's focus on a single day in June 1923). One of Cunningham's central characters is Clarissa Vaughn, a late twentieth-century version of Clarissa Dalloway. Like Clarissa Dalloway, Clarissa Vaughn remembers a kiss from her youth, a kiss she shared with her gay friend Richard. On the day in which the novel takes place, Richard is in the advanced stages of AIDS. Cunningham's consideration of the temporality of this kiss is addressed against the backdrop of the AIDS epidemic, a phenomenon that itself was producing new temporalities.[5] In imagining these kisses as particular types of moments, this chapter attempts to theorize the role of "the queer moment" in so-called narratives of development. These moments have effects on narrative that go well beyond the momentary interruptions of a plot moving towards its inevitable conclusion.

In the connection between Woolf and Cunningham, we can see the way in which a modernist temporality reemerges in the recent past to tackle new concerns. There is something in Woolf's style, in its ability to break with the conventions of plot development, that remains a useful strategy for writers today. It is for this reason that Cunningham can repurpose Woolf's kiss for a new context, that the kiss as Woolf imagines it can return to explode normative temporalities even now.

A similar relationship is at work in my third chapter between the seemingly odd couple of T. S. Eliot and Jeanette Winterson. While the connection between Woolf and Cunningham makes itself quite apparent in Cunningham's choice of subject matter, the relation between Eliot and Winterson requires a bit more unearthing. In 1996, Winterson published a collection of essays on art and literature entitled *Art Objects*. The collection is a praise song of modernist writing and establishes Winterson as an inheritor of the modernist tradition. Imagining Winterson as a modernist not only disrupts common notions of chronology (modernism is most often said to have ended in the 1940s) but also positions her quite differently than most critics have. Over the past twenty years, Winterson's writing has been constructed as a prime example of a particular brand of lesbian-feminist postmodernism. In tracing her genealogy through authors like Eliot and Woolf, Winterson makes her investment in modernist aesthetic experiments explicit. In this way, Winterson is constructing herself as something of an anachronism, as someone who is writing in this manner long after modernism is said to have lost its hold.

Winterson's specific reverence for T. S. Eliot also seems to be a bit of a contradiction. Eliot's conservative politics, his religious affiliations, and his elitism position him quite differently than Winterson's critics have imagined her. And yet, Winterson continually returns to Eliot as a literary precursor, going so far as to say "There is at present no twentieth century poem that means more to me than *Four Quartets*" (129). The relation between T.S. Eliot and Winterson is thus an interesting one to theorize.

I have approached the connection between these two authors specifically through Winterson's 1989 novel *Sexing the Cherry*. This text, as Winterson explicitly makes clear in *Art Objects*, was meant to be a reading of Eliot's *Four Quartets*, a poem sequence published between 1936 and 1942. The relation between these two texts is all the more interesting for my purposes because each text is invested in an extended exploration of time. Indeed, it is in Winterson's exploration of time (an aspect of her work that has often been overlooked) that she sounds most like Eliot. When we read Winterson for her evocative temporalities, we catch a glimpse of Eliot's poetics in her novel. As Lyn Pykett elegantly puts it, Eliot is a ghost of "high Modernism who haunt[s] Winterson's fiction" (55). In reading these two authors alongside one another, I focus on the image of the dance, as this specifically temporal image is the one in which Eliot's ghost becomes most visible in Winterson's work. As it turns out, the dance is more than just a recurring trope for these authors. Instead, it represents the imagining of a temporality that complicates the press toward particular narrative endings, one that deconstructs the workings of narrative itself.

In conjunction, my second and third chapters set up the framework and methodology for my project. In each case, I was trying to make visible the queer relation of authors across time. In doing so, I am drawing on Carolyn Dinshaw's notion of "touching across time" (1999, p. 36). Both Cunningham and Winterson use their novels as vehicles to reach out across a temporal divide and touch upon an earlier time. These contemporary authors do not merely stop at inhabiting a past moment; they each work to bring those moments into the present. They make available in the present moment these modernist configurations of time and use them to respond to normative temporalities particularly dominant in the late twentieth century, temporalities like that of "reproductive futurism." The temporality of the dance that I explore in Eliot and Winterson, for example, is placed in direct opposition to the temporality of marriage and reproduction. And Cunningham's kisses emerge within his stories as moments that interrupt the seemingly inevitable scripts of the characters' lives.

My temporal framework also draws from a particular account of the history of modernism. While many accounts of twentieth-century literature trace the linear trajectory of fiction from realism to modernism to postmodernism, Brian Richardson makes the case that this history can "more accurately and effectively be viewed as the site of continuous contestation between at least four principle competing narrative poetics— realism, postmodernism, expressionism, and high modernism—each on stretching in fact from the beginning to the end of the century" (1997, p. 293). Richardson's description of the ways in which these forms of narrative, which are often imagined to occupy static positions in time, can be seen to overlap and coexist is helpful in supporting my claims about the presence of modernist temporalities in contemporary texts. However, instead of thinking of modernism as in "continuous contestation" with later forms, I imagine it as cohabitating or harmonizing.

The language of contestation implies opposition and battle, whereas the examples I explore repurpose modernist tropes to perform a different type of work in a different historical moment.

These two chapters also help to contextualize the way in which I am using the term "queer" throughout the book. Although some of the authors I examine could be identified as gay, lesbian, or queer, I do not see sexual identity as the primary way in which queer is functioning within this text. Instead, I have imagined queerness as a peculiar relation to normativity. Here I am following an established tradition in queer theory. As David Halperin has said, "queer is by definition *whatever* is at odds with the normal, the legitimate, the dominant. *There is nothing in particular to which it necessarily refers.* It is an identity without an essence" (emphasis in original, 1997, p. 62). At the same time, however, I reject the idea that "all forms of temporal disruption of as necessarily 'queer,'" a tendency that Ben Davies has criticized in queer theory (2016, p. 16). I see as queer those particular moments of temporal disruption where the opposition to what is "normal" or "legitimate" produces strange effects, often in the form of nonnormative desires. Most often, I deal with textual moments in which the movement of linear time comes undone and the queer moment becomes legible, visible as something to read. For example, in my readings of Eliot and Winterson, there is not much in either text that deals with sexual identity specifically. However, the temporalities that both authors produce and explore are in direct opposition with the discourses of linear history and of "reproductive futurism." It is for this reason that I come to read them as queer. In Cunningham we even have an example of a lesbian life that is specifically not queer. Clarissa Vaughn, a present-day lesbian, remembers throughout her life her kiss with Richard, her gay friend. This kiss is placed in direct opposition to her conventional life with her partner Sally (a rather homonormative life). As Heather Love has said, "the specificity of same-sex identities has not been an absolute criterion in the tracing the queerness of a particular textual object, author, or set of relations" (744). In my own work, the attention paid to same-sex sexual identities has been minimal, partly because I am drawn to the moments in texts where strange things happen, when queer desires pop up where you would least expect them. It was just such a moment, in fact, that produced my fourth chapter.

William Faulkner may at first seem an odd choice for a project on queer temporality. While the connection between Faulkner and temporality has been explored for many years, it is less common to address his temporalities as queer. My own reading of Faulkner begins with an attempt to understand his relation to genealogical time, one of those normative temporalities that so often presuppose the shape of a life or a narrative. In the process of reading genealogical time in Faulkner's *Absalom, Absalom!*, I kept discovering strange moments in the text, moments that yearned for a space outside the linear chains of genealogy, moments rich with homoerotic desires. These moments convinced me that Faulkner's literature has something to tell us about the working of queer temporality in relation to genealogical time.

My fourth chapter thus considers the strange temporalities that emerge in the gaps opened up within genealogical storytelling. Genealogical time seems to permit only one outcome. It depends on sexual reproduction and traces time forwards and backwards along this linear trajectory. As Lee Edelman has said, genealogical succession is used toward the end "of perpetuating sameness, of turning back time to assure repetition" (60). In this way, genealogical time is often figured as a burden that does not allow for change. To analyze these concepts, this chapter employs novels invested in the exploration of genealogical time, specifically Faulkner's *Absalom, Absalom!* (1936) and Angela Carter's *Wise Children* (1991). Despite their differences, Faulkner and Carter actually share a number of common interests. Across a number of their novels, Faulkner and Carter explore issues like genealogy, family history, and paternal authority. They are also both authors who are hyperaware of storytelling itself, authors who attempt a meta-commentary on the nature of storytelling.

In reading Faulkner's *Absalom, Absalom!* alongside Carter's *Wise Children*, I have focused on the way in which certain forms of storytelling are able to produce queer moments in these texts. As the narrators of these novels seek to narrate their stories, they search for modes of storytelling that allow them to keep what genealogical storytelling might erase—specifically those incestuous and homoerotic desires that occupy a problematic position in genealogy. Interestingly, for both Faulkner and Carter, it is these nonnormative, nonreproductive desires that emerge in the spaces outside genealogical time. It is for this reason that I think it is important to read Faulkner and Carter together; both authors approach genealogy seeking to pull the hidden string that will allow it to unravel.

Despite its title, Carter's novel does not explicitly explore the concept of "wise children." The title comes instead from the old saying that "it's

a wise child that knows its own father," placing the child squarely within
the logic of genealogy. The title of the novel itself, though, becomes
quite interesting when read alongside Kathryn Bond Stockton's work on
queer children. The phrase "wise children" is almost a contradiction in
terms when we take children to be those who do not know and thus cannot be wise. The world "wise" is also most commonly connected with
age. A wise child is thus a queer child, a strange child, one that does not
fit common definitions of the term.

In my fifth chapter, we encounter these types of queer children in
the work of Wyndham Lewis, Gertrude Stein, and Eve Sedgwick. In his
book *Time and Western Man*, Lewis critiques Gertrude Stein's writing
for being "pure 'child'" (55). His text provides a detailed description of
the rather strange child he sees responsible for Stein's work. Lewis sets
out in his chapters on Stein to analyze her work on time but only succeeds in describing her over and over again as a child. My chapter takes
Lewis's analysis seriously and attempts to think through the connection
between the temporality of Stein's writing and this image that Lewis presents of the child. This path leads me to consider Stein's concept of "the
continuous present," a temporality that I claim is able to undo narratives
of succession.

The "continuous present" is a temporality that Stein places in direct
opposition to narratives that depend on linear movement through beginning, middle, and end. In Stein's description of this particular imagining
of the present, I am reminded of Eve Sedgwick's work on temporality.
Sedgwick speaks of a "continuing moment," a phrase that while not
exactly the same as "continuous present" is at least structurally equivalent. This chapter thus follows my discussion of Stein's "continuous
present" into Sedgwick's body of work. But here, in my last chapter, I
focus primarily on Sedgwick as a memoir-writer, as someone who theorizes through personal experience. Sedgwick's 1999 memoir *A Dialogue
on Love* recounts the therapy she underwent during the period following
her diagnosis with breast cancer. I focus on this text because I believe
that it is the space in which she most powerfully theorizes a queer form
of temporality that accounts for the connection between the child and
the adult. Sedgwick recounts her own experiences through prose, poetry,
and her therapist's notes in a manner that shows the complicated ties
between her child and adult selves. Across this text we see a temporality that, to use Barber and Clark's phrase, "dissolves the difference,

chronologically conceived, between the queer adult that one *is* and the queer child that one *was*" (5; emphasis in original). This connection between the child and adult that Sedgwick lays out here (and in her more properly theoretical texts) is an essential component to the "queer moment."

In tracing the continuities between the "continuous present" and the "continuing moment," I find in both Stein and Sedgwick a resistance to certain normalized forms of growth, to developmental narratives that see childhood only as a stage one progresses through on the way to mature adulthood. Beyond this, however, I see both of these terms ("continuous present" and "continuing moment") as major contributions to the rethinking of narrative temporality and as inextricably tied to the modifier queer. Perhaps more than the other authors I address in this book, these two thinkers have tackled issues of temporality across a wide range of texts (poetry, autobiography, essay)[6] and have produced temporal configurations specifically attributed to them. It is for this reason that I chose to end by exploring the connections between the temporalities of these two important authors.

In fact, the relation between the work of Sedgwick and that of Stein might constitute a microcosm for the work that this book is meant to do more generally. Sedgwick has been a central figure for my own project, the theorist whose work has influenced my own thinking about this topic more than any other (she figures centrally in three of my four body chapters). In examining Sedgwick's work in relation to the modernist literature and theory that I explore here, I see the opportunity for a productive rethinking of what constitutes queer temporality. It includes those important theoretical texts born out of queer theory and published in the last twenty years, but it also includes those modernist experiments with narrative that produced queer moments in literature. In order to understand what is at stake in the recent work on queer temporality, we must return to these modernist experiments and read them with a different set of questions, questions made possible only recently. In the foreword to *Tendencies*, when Sedgwick claims that "queer is a continuing moment," she means that the queer moment will anachronistically endure, that it makes "a counterclaim against [its] obsolescence" (xii). I would like to make a similar claim about modernism, that it too is a "continuing moment," a moment that has remained live and relevant well beyond its supposed expiration date.

NOTES

1. The term "Lesbian Modernism" was coined by Makiko Minow-Pinkney in 1989.
2. See Shari Benstock's *Women of the Left Bank* (1986), Laura Doan's *Fashioning Sapphism* (2001), Elizabeth English's *Lesbian Modernism* (2015), Robin Hackett's *Sapphic Primitivism* (2004), Erin G. Carlston's *Thinking Fascism: Sapphic Modernism and Fascist Modernity* (1998), and Joanne Winning's *The Pilgrimage of Dorothy Richardson* (2000).
3. All definitions in this book are taken from the *Oxford English Dictionary Online Edition* unless otherwise noted.
4. For want of a better term, I will refer to the second set of texts as contemporary. Some of these texts could also be referred to as postmodern (especially those I explore by Jeanette Winterson and Angela Carter), but I do not engage with them specifically as postmodern texts.
5. As a number of queer theorists have pointed out, the AIDS epidemic is responsible for much of the rethinking of temporality that has occurred in the last twenty years. Citing Lee Edelman and Leo Bersani, Halberstam notes "some gay men have responded to the threat of AIDS...by rethinking the conventional emphasis on longevity and futurity" (2).
6. Sedgwick has written a book of poetry, a memoir, as well as several books of criticism and theory. Stein has written two autobiographies and many poems, novels, essays, and lectures.

REFERENCES

Barber, Stephen M., and David L. Clark. 2002. Queer Moments: The Performative Temporalities of Eve Kosofsky Sedgwick. In *Regarding Sedgwick: Essays on Queer Culture and Critical Theory*, ed. Stephen M. Barber and David L. Clark, 1–56. New York: Routledge.

Bennett, Arnold. 1975. Article in *Evening Standard*. In *Virginia Woolf: The Critical Heritage*, ed. Robin Majumdar and Allen McLaurin, 189–190. London: Routledge.

Benstock, Shari. 1986. *Women of the Left Bank: Paris, 1900–1940*. Austin: University of Texas Press.

Boellstorff, Tom. 2007. When Marriage Falls. *GLQ: A Journal of Gay and Lesbian Studies* 13 (2–3): 227–248.

Boone, Joseph Allen. 1998. *Libidinal Currents: Sexuality and the Shaping of Modernism*. Chicago: The University of Chicago Press.

Bristow, Joseph. 1995. *Effeminate England: Homoerotic Writing After 1885*. New York: Columbia University Press.

Carlston, Erin G. 1998. *Thinking Fascism: Sapphic Modernism and Fascist Modernity*. Stanford: Stanford University Press.

Carter, Angela. 1991. *Wise Children*. London: Penguin.

Cunningham, Michael. 1998. *The Hours*. New York: Farrar.

Davies, Ben. 2016. *Sex, Time, and Space in Contemporary Fiction: Exceptional Intercourse*. London: Palgrave Macmillan.

Detloff, Madelyn. 2009. *The Persistence of Modernism: Loss and Mourning in the Twentieth Century*. Cambridge: Cambridge University Press.

Dinshaw, Carolyn. 1999. *Getting Medieval: Sexualities and Communities, Pre- and Postmodern*. Durham: Duke University Press.

――― et al. 2007. Theorizing Queer Temporalities: A Roundtable Discussion. *GLQ: A Journal of Gay and Lesbian Studies* 13 (2–3): 177–195.

Doan, Laura. 2001. *Fashioning Sapphism: The Origins of Modern English Lesbian Culture*. New York: Columbia University Press.

Edelman, Lee. 2004. *No Future: Queer Theory and the Death Drive*. Durham: Duke University Press.

Eliot, T. S. 1941. *Four Quartets*. New York: Harcourt.

English, Elizabeth. 2015. *Lesbian Modernism: Censorship, Sexuality and Genre Fiction*. Edinburgh: Edinburgh University Press.

Faulkner, William. 1936. *Absalom, Absalom!*. New York: Random House.

Freccero, Carla. 2006. *Queer/Early/Modern*. Durham: Duke University Press.

Freeman, Elizabeth, ed. 2007. Queer Temporality. Special issue of *GLQ: A Journal of Gay and Lesbian Studies* 13 (2–3): 159–421.

―――. 2010. *Time Binds: Queer Temporalities, Queer Histories*. Durham and London: Duke University Press.

Friedman, Susan Stanford. 1989. Lyric Subversion of Narrative in Women's Writing: Virginia Woolf and the Tyranny of Plot. In *Reading Narrative*, ed. James Phelan, 162–185. Columbus: Ohio State University Press.

Goldberg, Jonathan, and Madhavi Menon. 2005. Queering History. *PMLA* 20 (5): 1608–1617.

Hackett, Robin. 2004. *Sapphic Primitivism: Productions of Race, Class, and Sexuality in Key Works of Modern Fiction*. New Brunswick: Rutgers University Press.

Halberstam, J. 2005. *In a Queer Time and Place: Transgender Bodies, Subcultural Lives*. New York: New York University Press.

Halperin, David. 1997. *Saint Foucault: Towards a Gay Hagiography*. Oxford and New York: Oxford University Press.

Herrmann, Anne. 2000. *Queering the Moderns: Poses/Portraits/Performances*. New York: Palgrave Macmillan.

Kern, Stephen. 1983. *The Culture of Time and Space: 1880–1918*. Cambridge: Harvard University Press.

Lewis, Wyndham. 1927. *Time and Western Man*. New York: Harcourt.

Love, Heather. 2007. *Feeling Backward: Loss and the Politics of Queer History.* Cambridge, MA: Harvard University Press.

———. 2009. Introduction: Modernism at Night. *PMLA* 124 (3): 744–748.

Miller, Tyrus. 1999. *Late Modernism: Politics, Fiction, and the Arts Between the World Wars.* Berkeley: University of California Press.

Randall, Bryony. 2007. *Modernism, Daily Time, and Everyday Life.* Cambridge: Cambridge University Press.

Richardson, Brian. 1997. Remapping the Present: The Master Narrative of Modern Literary History and the Lost Forms of Twentieth-Century Fiction. *Twentieth Century Literature* 43 (3): 291–309.

Rohy, Valerie. 2009. *Anachronism and Its Others: Sexuality, Race, Temporality.* Albany: State University of New York Press.

Schleifer, Ronald. 2000. *Modernism and Time: The Logic of Abundance in Literature, Science, and Culture, 1880–1930.* Cambridge: Cambridge University Press.

Sedgwick, Eve Kosofsky. 1993. *Tendencies.* Durham: Duke University Press.

———. 1999. *A Dialogue on Love.* Boston: Beacon Press.

Sinfield, Alan. 1994. *The Wilde Century: Effeminacy, Oscar Wilde and the Queer Moment.* London: Cassell.

Stein, Gertrude. 1935. *Narration: Four Lectures by Gertrude Stein.* New York: Greenwood. Reprint 1969.

Stockton, Kathryn Bond. 2004. Growing Sideways, or Versions of the Queer Child: The Ghost, the Homosexual, the Freudian, the Innocent, and the Interval of Animal. In *Curiouser: On the Queerness of Children*, ed. Steven Bruhm and Natasha Hurley, 277–316. Minneapolis: University of Minnesota Press.

———. 2009. *The Queer Child: Or Growing Sideways in the Twentieth Century.* Durham: Duke University Press.

The Oxford English Dictionary. 1989. 2nd ed. Online.

Trask, Michael. 2003. *Cruising Modernism: Class and Sexuality in American Literature and Social Thought.* Ithaca: Cornell University Press.

Winning, Joanne. 2010. Lesbian Sexuality in the Story of Modernism. In *The Oxford Handbook of Modernisms*, eds. Peter Brooker, Andrzej Gasiorek, Deborah Longworth, and Andrew Thacker, 218–235. Oxford: Oxford University Press.

———. 2000. *The Pilgrimage of Dorothy Richardson.* Madison: University of Wisconsin Press.

Winterson, Jeanette. 1989. *Sexing the Cherry.* New York: Grove Press.

———. 1996. *Art Objects: Essays on Ecstasy and Effrontery.* New York: Knopf.

Woolf, Virginia. 1925a. Modern Fiction. In *The Common Reader*, 146–154. New York: Harcourt. Reprint 1984.

———. 1925b. *Mrs. Dalloway.* San Diego: Harcourt. Reprint 1981.

———. 1927. *To the Lighthouse*. Foreword by Eudora Welty. Orlando: Harcourt. Reprint 1981.

———. 1929. *A Room of One's Own*. London: Harcourt.

———. 2002. *Moments of Being*, ed. Jeanne Schulkin, intro. Hermione Lee. London: Pimlico.

CHAPTER 2

Exquisite Moments and the Temporality of the Kiss in *Mrs. Dalloway* and *The Hours*

More than thirty years after it occurred, Clarissa Dalloway still remembers the kiss between herself and Sally Seton as "the most exquisite moment of her whole life" (1925, p. 35). In scholarship on *Mrs. Dalloway*, this moment has most commonly been read as evidence of a repressed lesbian identity or dismissed as representing the innocence of childhood friendship. More recently, however, the kiss between Sally and Clarissa has sparked conversation among queer theorists regarding its relationship to temporality.

These theorists, specifically Kathryn Bond Stockton and Annamarie Jagose, tend to focus on the kiss between Clarissa and Sally as a moment that temporarily interrupts her inevitable movement toward marriage and reproduction. This is a moment that is out of sync with the dominant narratives about heterosexual development. And though some feminist critics attempt to see this kiss as representing a somewhat conventional phase in the development toward mature adulthood, these queer theorists have focused on the radical disjunction between this moment and the heterosexual future that follows it. This moment is thus an "erotic pause," part of the novel's tendency to create pockets where time functions in a different manner (Stockton 2004, p. 302). This moment may have little result on the plot of the novel, as we know from the beginning the shape that Clarissa's life has taken, but it is nonetheless insistent in its importance—"the most exquisite moment of her whole life." Another queer theorist, Jack Halberstam, follows this "exquisite moment" into a different novel: Michael Cunningham's rewriting of

© The Author(s) 2019
K. Haffey, *Literary Modernism, Queer Temporality*,
https://doi.org/10.1007/978-3-030-17301-2_2

Mrs. Dalloway: The Hours. Halberstam's brief reading of this text focuses on Cunningham's use of the kiss as the moment where multiple temporalities brush up against one another (2005, p. 3).

Perhaps this kiss has drawn the attention of queer theorists interested in temporality because it seems to upset or rupture the forward flow of time in narrative. It is a moment that recurs for Clarissa throughout the text, a moment that the text marks as significant, but one that seems to be outside the cause and effect logic of narrative. Such issues are of particular interest within the discourse of Queer Temporality.[1] Though Queer Temporality has only rarely directly considered the question of narrative temporality, theorists like Stockton, Jagose, and Halberstam investigate the way in which cultural narratives are based on a sense of time that directly correlates to heterosexuality. For example, within narrative, time often moves according to the progression through a set of normal life stages from childhood through adolescence to marriage and reproduction (Halberstam 2005, p. 4). In such a framework, a single kiss can hold little significance. And yet, *Mrs. Dalloway* repeatedly insists on the significance of this moment. For this reason, I think it is important to investigate the moment of the kiss specifically as a moment, a moment that is counter to the normal flow of time in narrative.

Though a number of Woolf critics have tried to assimilate Clarissa's and Sally's kiss to a conventional stage in Clarissa's development toward adulthood, the moment of the kiss ultimately deviates from the temporal movement toward marriage. Instead, the kiss, as constructed in Woolf's text, offers strange and unpredictable forms of temporality. In this chapter, I would like to read those forms of temporality that emerge from Woolf's representations of this kiss. Though many scholars interested in queer desire have used Woolf's novel as a basis for their arguments, my reading is unique in its invocation of Eve Sedgwick's concept of the "queer moment" to analyze the significance of the "exquisite" moments that *Mrs. Dalloway* depicts.[2] Thus, in building on the work of Sedgwick and other queer theorists, I would first like to reexamine the kiss and its significance for our understanding of Woolf's narrative project. I would then like to turn my discussion to what might be the most detailed analysis of the Clarissa–Sally kiss: Michael Cunningham's novel *The Hours*. Cunningham's novel offers three readings of this kiss, readings that represent three related insights about temporality based on Woolf's representation. My reading of Cunningham's novel will serve to further theorize these exquisite moments as well as to demonstrate their significance. Ultimately, it is in these moments that we can see a queer kind of temporality at work, a temporality that does not press on toward closure or conclusion, but that moves in strange and unpredictable ways.

* * *

In the passages that focus on Clarissa, *Mrs. Dalloway* oscillates between two distinct time periods: the present day of her party in 1923 and the summer she spent at her family's vacation home in Bourton when she was eighteen years old. Because of the large gap between these two periods, critics have often treated these distinct time frames as if they were snapshots representing adulthood and adolescence. In *Virginia Woolf and the Fictions of Psychoanalysis*, Elizabeth Abel, for example, refers to the Clarissa in the Bourton scenes as "adolescent Clarissa" (1996, p. 32) and speaks of the division between adolescent and adult Clarissa "as a binary opposition between past and present," emphasizing a clear distinction between these two times (1996, p. 31).

   This time at Bourton is also the period within which Clarissa met and fell in love with Sally Seton. Those who have written about Clarissa's relationship with Sally have thus placed it squarely within the developmental framework of her adolescence. The scholarship that deals with this relationship most often presents it in terms of childhood friendship or "adolescent love" (Jagose 2002, p. 97). Sally Seton is positioned as "the wildly charming and reckless friend of [Clarissa's] youth" (Transue 1986, p. 69). And the love between the two women is described as "girlhood fascination" (Showalter 1994, p. 144), as "romantic idealism" (Transue 1986, p. 69), as a "love that may leave virginity and ... purity intact" (Raphael 2001, p. 138), and as "unclouded by sexual masks and societal roles that often muddle adult heterosexual relationships" (Henke 1981, p. 135). Though there has been an important thread of modernist criticism that analyzes the eroticism of this kiss and focuses on the ways that lesbian sexuality more generally has shaped modernism itself, there is also often a tendency, despite the quite sexual nature of Clarissa's descriptions of her affections for women, for critics to construct Clarissa's feelings for Sally as representing a period of girlhood innocence that is sharply contrasted with the adult self who remembers this love.[3]

When this love is not described in terms of its "innocence," it is positioned as part of that "unruly" phase of adolescence, a period incompatible with female maturity. As Halberstam states, "in Western cultures, we chart the emergence of the adult from the dangerous and unruly period of adolescence as a desired process of maturation" (2005, p. 4). In figuring the romantic connection between women as an adolescent phase, Woolf critics are not alone, as this trope appears clearly in the more general discourses that deal with sexuality. Indeed, even Clarissa Dalloway repeats this idea in thinking about the relationship between her daughter Elizabeth and Miss Kilman, her daughter's tutor. She states: "But it might be only a phase, as Richard said, such as all girls go through" (1925, p. 11). Clarissa's statement, a statement that is merely a repetition of what her husband has said, positions desire between women in a specific temporal frame. It is a "phase" that all "girls" go through. Desire between women is thus framed as a conventional stage in the narrative of female development. It has a clear before and after, and it does not affect the woman that this "girl" will ultimately become. Following Clarissa's lead, critics have treated the relationship between Clarissa and Sally as a phase by focusing on her desire for women as being located solely in the past (Abraham 1996, p. 152). Its status as a phase is reinforced by the fact that the relationship is figured as an "interruption" in the march toward an inevitable heterosexual conclusion (Jagose 2002, p. 85).

Reading Clarissa's life in terms of the movement between different stages or phases has meant that many critics end up telling a story of female development wherein Clarissa becomes a mature heterosexual adult. Elizabeth Abel's reading of the novel is perhaps the most detailed of these. Clarissa's story, according to Abel in "Narrative Structure(s) and Female Development: The Case of *Mrs. Dalloway*," illustrates the "distinctive features of female experience and female plots" (1983, p. 162). Abel's work attempts to take another look at those plots that have been "relegated to the background of a dominant romantic or courtship plot" (1983, p. 163). While this is certainly an important goal and Abel is correct in stating that it is not the courtship plot that is central in *Mrs. Dalloway*, her reading of the novel normalizes Clarissa's experience into a universal (read: heterosexual) narrative of female experience. Because she sees Clarissa's life in terms of the development from one life stage to the next, Abel is unable to read the intricacies of the plot as anything more than the progression from girlhood to mature adulthood.

Abel's tendency to normalize the effects of Clarissa's experiences can be seen through her treatment of Sally. In Abel's reading, Sally becomes an integral part of a coherent narrative of female development toward "maturity." Abel focuses on the fact that Clarissa's childhood "suggests a tableau of female loss" (1983, p. 167). It is "within this barren atmosphere" that Sally is able to "immediately spark love in the eighteen-year-old Clarissa." In this way, Sally "replaces Clarissa's dead mother and sister" and inspires a love "equivalent in absoluteness to a daughter's earliest bond with her mother, a bond too early ruptured for Clarissa" (1983, p. 167). Clarissa's love for Sally is read primarily as the recapturing of the lost mother–daughter bond.[4] In Abel's reading, Sally seems to have little significance as a character in her own right. Rather, she serves as a stand-in for Clarissa's mother. Because the kiss between Clarissa and Sally is read as a recapturing of the lost mother–daughter bond, Sally becomes the vehicle by which that story of "female development" is told. Abel's reading thus makes central the "mother-daughter" bond at the expense of close attention to the bond between these two young women.[5]

For Abel, Clarissa's memories of her love for Sally are clearly a problem in the text. When writing about Clarissa's relation to her past, a past that seems to consist solely of Clarissa's "love for Sally and Bourton," Abel describes it as "a conflict more suppressed than resolved," an "unresolved relation to her past," and a "recurrent preoccupation with the past" (1983, p. 177). In order for Clarissa to become a mature adult, she needs to resolve this relation to the past and to stop being preoccupied with her adolescent love of Sally. Abel's reading positions the novel's climax at the moment in which Septimus's suicide "enables Clarissa to acknowledge and renounce" the past's hold on her and allows her "to embrace the imperfect pleasures of adulthood more completely" (1983, p. 179). Clarissa's development is thus complete when she is able to let go of the past (a time when women are bonded with women) and become a mature adult (a time when women "embrace the imperfect pleasures of adulthood more completely," pleasures which consist primarily of heterosexual coupling with men).

In her book *Are Girls Necessary?*, Julie Abraham provides an interesting critique of Abel's reading of *Mrs. Dalloway*. According to Abraham, the way that Abel has set up the past as female and the present as male results in a situation where "the passage of time itself requires and naturalizes Clarissa's 'development' towards a heterosexuality identified with adulthood" (1996, p. 147). The problem with Abel's essay and others who read the novel in terms of the progression toward adulthood is that Woolf's narrative cannot be "easily assimilated to a story of personal and/or gendered development" (Abraham 1996, p. 142). Not only do such stories rest on a type of narrative structure that this novel vehemently rejects, but also the past and present are not as easily separated as readings like Abel's would have us assume. Readings that attempt to plot the development within Clarissa's character must work to create divisions in the texts (like those between adulthood and adolescence) that the novel's narrative structure is constantly working to undermine. Take for example the novel's opening pages where Clarissa first plunges into her past: "What a lark! What a plunge! For so it had always seemed to her, when, with a little squeak of the hinges, which she could hear now, she had burst open the French windows and plunged at Bourton into the open air" (1925, p. 3). This often cited passage is quite clear in what it accomplishes: the rendering of past and present simultaneously in a single moment. The temporal location of this "little squeak" that Clarissa hears is quite ambiguous. Clarissa could "hear now" in the present of the story this sound, but the sound's origin seems to be located in the past as she "burst[s] open the French windows at Bourton" (1925, p. 3). The "squeak" could be her own door as she sets out that morning, it could be the sound of "Rumpelmayer's men" taking the doors "off their hinges" to prepare for the party, or it could be the sound of the French doors opening at Bourton, a sound heard across time (1925, p. 3). As this scene continues, the division between the present Clarissa walking down Bond Street and the memories of herself at eighteen is never entirely clear. As Richard Pearce states, Woolf's writing presents "a new kind of sentencing" in which "past and present interpenetrate" (1991, p. 146). Such a style seems to eschew attempts to read the past and present as clearly separate because they are continually represented side by side within the text. This interpenetration of past and present could be part of what Joseph Allen Boone calls "Woolf's most radical contribution to modernity's breakdown of logocentric conceptions of sexuality, identity, and narrative" (1998, p. 192). According to Boone, Woolf's contribution consists of her "continual slippage back and forth across boundaries assumed to divide subject and object, self and other, interior and exterior, body and text" (1998, p. 192). As such, her continual slippage between past and present operates not only to connect two disparate

moments, but also to throw a wrench in the gears of narrative (and conventional narratives of sexual identity).

The interpenetration of past and present especially occurs when
Clarissa calls forth her memories of Sally. Thus to focus on Clarissa's feelings for Sally as located only in the past, in the unruly period of Clarissa's
adolescence, is to ignore the ways in which this moment returns again
and again to affect Clarissa's present. Indeed, we only know of the past
in this novel through the present, so the past is not gone, not past. In
describing Sally, Clarissa states:

> But the charm was overpowering, to her at least, so that she could remem-
> ber standing in her bedroom at the top of the house holding the hot-wa-
> ter can in her hands and saying aloud, 'She is beneath this roof. ... She is
> beneath this roof!' No, the words meant absolutely nothing to her now.
> She could not even get an echo of her old emotion. But she could remem-
> ber going cold with excitement, and doing her hair in a kind of ecstasy
> (now the old feeling began to come back to her, as she took out her hair-
> pins, laid them on the dressing-table, began to do her hair). (1925, p. 34)

While initially Clarissa is unable to get "an echo of her old emotion,"
she then is able to experience the "old feeling," which includes "a kind
of ecstasy." In the process of recollecting this memory of Sally, Clarissa
is able to actually experience again the feelings that she had when she
was eighteen years old. The feeling attached to this memory seems to
rupture the divisions between Clarissa's past and her present, as she feels
the effects, "a kind of ecstasy," of an incident that occurred over thirty
years before. The passage continues: "She could remember ... dressing,
and going downstairs, and feeling as she crossed the hall 'if it were now
to die 'twere now to be most happy.' That was her feeling ... all because
she was coming down to dinner in a white frock to meet Sally Seton!"
(1925, p. 35). This moment is the "most happy" one of Clarissa's entire
life, one that leaves her with the feeling that she is ready to die because
she has experienced such a moment. These moments that Clarissa
describes are ones in which Clarissa is able to break through the temporal divides between past and present in order to experience pleasure and
desire across them. When we examine such moments it is hard to create
stiff divisions between the adolescent Clarissa who fell in love with and
desired Sally Seton and the adult for whom that "phase" has passed.

To talk of moments in this way, to consider the relation of their temporality to the narrative as a whole, is perhaps to call up distinctions between narrative and lyric time. Lyric and narrative time are often described in opposition to one another. While narrative time is said to represent "a sequence of events that move dynamically in time and space," lyric time is commonly described as "a simultaneity" (Friedman 1989, p. 164). Narrative time is figured as change or as a progressive moment; lyric time is figured as stasis or a pause. As Monique Morgan states, "lyric creates a timeless present, an indefinitely suspended moment, which contrasts with narrative's past progression of events" (2008, p. 301). Likewise, we might call narrative time diachronic and lyric time synchronic.

Scholars who study narrative and lyric, however, have shown that such distinctions are often over-simplifications. Narrative and lyric are not always necessarily separate from each other; nor is their temporality so clear-cut. As Heather Dubrow demonstrates, definitions of lyric and narrative are complicated by the fact that those doing the defining are often invested in proving that the genre they study is superior (2006, p. 257). Still, there has been some excellent work that attempts to understand the complex relationships between lyric and narrative. For example, in her reading of Wordsworth's *Prelude*, Monique Morgan shows how narrative can be used "to promote lyric effects" (2008, p. 299). And Heather Dubrow focuses on the interplay of narrative and lyric, offering the "anticipatory amalgam" as a strategy that texts use to "blend modes and temporalities" (2006, p. 264). Both of these readings reconfigure the relationship between lyric and narrative and attend to the ways in which these reconfigurations can lead to new analyses of literary texts.[6] In a similar vein, I would like to suggest another way of describing the relation between these modes that exists in the moments I have been discussing in *Mrs. Dalloway*—a relation that points to a queer form of temporality.

A look at Susan Stanford Friedman's brief reading of the kiss between Sally and Clarissa can perhaps show how rethinking the relationship between lyric and narrative can allow us to see a different type of temporality at work in *Mrs. Dalloway*. Friedman's essay is useful in that it relies on lyric and narrative as key terms to discuss what she calls "the tyranny of the plot." Though Friedman's essay is primarily an analysis of three other texts, her brief mention of *Mrs. Dalloway* can perhaps demonstrate the difference between her reading and my own.

"The young Clarissa," she states, "had moved past the lyric moment with Sally to follow the narrative pattern of Oedipal wedlock in her marriage to Richard. Similarly, Clarissa at fifty cannot remain in her attic womb bathed in her lyric memories of Sally. ... Restored by the lyric moment, the interrupted narrative can continue to unfold" (1989, pp. 167–168). In Friedman's reading, the lyric moment is in opposition to narrative. The lyric moment is something that Clarissa "had moved past." It is a moment that interrupts the narrative, but after which the "narrative can continue to unfold."[7] Conversely, I would suggest a different relationship between lyric and narrative. The lyric moment in *Mrs. Dalloway* is not something that characters can move past; it is not a moment that begins then ends or that momentarily interrupts narrative. Here I would second Dubrow's claim that "interplay is a more apt description than interruption" (2006, p. 256). Instead of a figuring as just a momentary interruption, these moments endure. They exist alongside and within narrative. The moment is a presence that continues to make itself known throughout the course of the narrative.

My reading here also acknowledges Bryony Randall's claims concerning the "different daily temporalities" in *Mrs. Dalloway* (2007, p. 156). Her reading of the novel shows how "the everyday and ongoing act of remembrance explores the resonance of one day, any one day, far beyond its temporal boundaries" (2007, p. 164). Randall's reading shows how a day can exceed the temporal boundaries of a day in Woolf's writing in order to make a larger point about the "various temporalities of everyday life" (2007, p. 155). The way in which a day, any day, can exist beyond "its temporal boundaries" is parallel to my claim about how the moment operates temporally in *Mrs. Dalloway*. However, it is not only that these moments are able to endure beyond their usual limits that make them significant. Such moments have lasting effects that work to undermine particular normative narratives of development, effects that are best explored through the tools of queer temporality. It is in moments like these that we can see the connection between the work in queer temporality and modernist literary experiments that I sketched out in the introduction.

Indeed, the moment as it is constructed in Woolf's text closely resembles a form of time theorized by Eve Sedgwick: the "queer moment." In her 1993 collection of essays *Tendencies*, Sedgwick refers to queer as "a continuing moment" (p. xii). Sedgwick's word-choice here seems to place two contradictory terms next to each other. A moment is generally understood to be an instant; it is that which, by definition, does not continue. If we consider this in relation to lyric and narrative time, this description of a "queer moment" seems to encompass the temporality of both narrative (continuing) and lyric (moment). A queer moment is thus a moment that has lyric properties and yet continues beyond its proper placement in time. Despite its seeming contradiction, a queer moment continues, not linearly forward, but instead in ways that Sedgwick describes as "recurrent, eddying" (1993, p. xii). The word "recurrent" is defined as "occurring or appearing again or repeatedly." A "queer moment" is a moment that repeats, that comes again. Sedgwick's use of the word "eddying," is even more telling. In the American Heritage dictionary, the word "eddy" is given two definitions. The first defines it as "a current ... moving contrary to the direction of the main current, especially in a circular motion." Queer moments, then, might represent whirlpools within the flow of time. They move "contrary to the direction of the main current" or linear progression of time and have a tendency to recur or repeat. The second definition describes an eddy as "a drift or tendency that is counter to or separate from the main current, as of opinion, tradition or history." This definition also seems useful in thinking about queer moments in relation to Clarissa and Sally. Clarissa's memories of Sally not only represent a glitch in a forward-moving temporality, but also a moment that is "counter to or separate from" the normative narratives or histories of female development. Sedgwick's references to "queer moments," then, seem to position them as moments in the present where time might seem to run opposite to an expected or dominant course.

Sedgwick develops this notion of "queer moments" in the foreword and introduction to *Tendencies*, pieces that are somewhat haunted by the presence of adolescents who no longer exist. To get a better sense of what Sedgwick means by "queer moments," I would like to turn briefly to this introduction to sketch out a more nuanced reading of this term before returning to my discussion of *Mrs. Dalloway*. The introduction begins: "I think everyone who does gay and lesbian studies is haunted by the suicides of adolescents" (1993, p. 1). She goes on to say: "I look at my adult friends and colleagues doing lesbian and gay work, and I feel that the survival of each one is a miracle" (1993, p. 1). This statement rests on an imagining of each of Sedgwick's "adult friends and colleagues" as a queer adolescent who was once under the threat of erasure. The very act of surviving constructs a link between these two identities.

It is because the adults have survived this threat that there is such an intense connection across their adolescent and adult selves: the adult who has survived works to keep alive the adolescent who was almost lost. In bringing together these two identities, Sedgwick seems to create a temporality that eschews the easy division between adulthood and adolescence. Likewise, the child, who is supposedly temporally located in the past, is able to have an effect on the adult. For Sedgwick and her colleagues, the child often dictates the work that the adult chooses to do: "I think that many adults (and I am among them) are trying, in our work, to keep faith with the vividly remembered promises made to ourselves in childhood" (1993, p. 3). This is a promise made across time, an instance in which the adult's work is directed by the child across a temporal divide.

Sedgwick's text itself enacts a certain queer temporality, one that breaks down the division between different developmental stages (childhood, adolescence, adulthood) and that enacts journeys across what is normally constructed as a divide. We might then call this temporality one type of "queer moment." These are moments, to borrow language from Stephen Barber and David Clark's work on Sedgwick, that "dissolve ... the difference, chronologically conceived, between the queer adult that one is and the queer child that one was" (2002, p. 5). Sedgwick's writing also calls up some of Kathryn Bond Stockton's statements about the connection between queer adults and children. "Queers," Stockton observes, "trail children behind them or alongside them, as if they are wedded, one to another, in unforeseen ways" (2004, p. 278). The queer moment, as constructed by Sedgwick, is thus able to disrupt the progressive temporality that insists individuals move linearly through a set of life stages. In Sedgwick's construction, the adolescent does not develop into the adult. Instead, the adult answers to the desires and demands of the adolescent. This is a temporality that folds backwards or, as Sedgwick might say, "eddies."

Like Sedgwick's text, *Mrs. Dalloway* also enacts a temporality in which Clarissa is able to transcend the divide between her adolescent and adult selves. Because of this, I am suggesting that we read the moments between Clarissa and Sally as "queer moments," as moments that disrupt the common distinctions between adolescence and adulthood, as moments that make nonsense of the developmental narratives that critics try to impose on them. It is quite easy to see in *Mrs. Dalloway* the way in which Clarissa seems to "trail" a child "alongside" her (Stockton 2004, p. 278). What might be harder to see, without close attention to the text, is the way in which this functions to "dissolve the difference," as Barber and Clark claim, between the adult that one is and the child or adolescent that one was (2002, p. 5). Ultimately, it is through this dissolution that Woolf is able to challenge normative narratives of female development.

Mrs. Dalloway is a text that itself insists on the power of moments. The words "moment," "moments," and "momentary" appear seventy times in the text (Dowling 1991, p. 128). Even from the beginning of the novel, Clarissa's attachment to the moment is clearly established. We learn that what she most loves is "life; London; this moment of June" (1925, p. 4). And for Clarissa, part of "this moment" is the other moments that it calls up across time.

When Clarissa "plunge[s] into the very heart of the moment" at different points in the text, it becomes apparent that the moment as described in Woolf's text is not an instant divided and separated from all other time (1925, p. 37). Indeed, Clarissa's own thoughts about the morning that the novel takes place help establish this point: "the moment of this June morning on which was the pressure of all other mornings" (1925, p. 37). The moment is thus acted upon or affected by the force applied by these other mornings. They have a presence that colors this specific morning. Clarissa's plunging "into the heart of the moment" does not divide her from her past, but allows her to see the presence of that past.

Clarissa's experience of the moment thus allows her to bring together her adult and adolescent selves. At a number of times throughout the text, there are instances of Clarissa describing herself as simultaneously young and old. In one such moment, when she says the word "lake," it instantaneously brings to her mind two connected images: "she was a child, throwing bread to the ducks, between her parents, and at the same time a grown woman coming to her parents who stood by the lake, holding her life in her arms" (1925, p. 43). This moment presents us with quite a strange temporality. Clarissa is "at the same time" a "child" and "grown woman." The difference between these two positions in time has momentarily dissolved, and the adult and child exist simultaneously.

Because the adult and the child exist side by side in Clarissa's psyche, it becomes quite difficult to think of *Mrs. Dalloway* as a story of female development. Within the Clarissa who remembers, there exists not a

continuous progression of selves, but a collection of seemingly contradictory parts. While examining herself in the mirror, Clarissa thinks: "That
was her self when some effort, some call on her to be her self, drew the
parts together, she alone knew how different, how incompatible and
composed for the world only into one centre, one diamond, one woman
who sat in her drawing-room and made a meeting point" (1925, p. 37).
Clarissa is not shown as a woman who has developed through stages to
mature adulthood. Rather, she is a "meeting point" of "incompatible"
parts, parts that are "composed so for the world only into one center"
(1925, p. 37). These "parts" represent the many different Clarissas that
have existed across time. Rather than being the end result of those identities, she seems to be the space in which all the previous identities are
preserved. It is in this way that she can be a "grown woman" (1925, p.
43), an adolescent, and a child simultaneously.

Thus, moments seem to do a few things in *Mrs. Dalloway*. Rather
than merely recalling the past, they make visible the very presence of that
past. Moments also function to dissolve the difference between Clarissa's
childhood, adolescence, and adulthood. Finally, they are the place in
which narratives of development break down because they do not show
progression but rather depict the simultaneous presence of multiple
identities. Though these aspects seem to be characteristic of many of the
moments that Clarissa experiences during the June day on which the
novel takes place, nothing cuts across time with quite the same intensity
as her memories of Sally Seton. Indeed, the most "exquisite moment" of
her life is the kiss she shares with Sally:

> She and Sally fell a little behind. Then came the most exquisite moment of
> her whole life passing a stone urn with flowers in it. Sally stopped; picked a
> flower; kissed her on the lips. The whole world might have turned upside
> down! The others disappeared; there she was alone with Sally. And she felt
> that she had been given a present, wrapped up, and told just to keep it,
> not to look at it—a diamond, something infinitely precious, wrapped up,
> which, as they walked (up and down, up and down), she uncovered, or the
> radiance burnt through, the revelation, the religious feeling! (1925, p. 35)

This kiss is figured as a "present," as "a diamond," as "something
infinitely precious" that Clarissa is "told just to keep, not to look at"
(1925, p. 35). Certainly, this figures the kiss as an expensive gift, both
desired and unexpected. But let's not ignore the other meaning of the

word "present." This is also a memory that becomes "present" as it is recollected. Christine Froula states that this is "a moment once present now past, yet preserved in memory and symbolically 'present' again" (2002, p. 135). In contrast to Froula, I would argue that this moment is not merely "symbolically" present but rather functions to momentarily collapse the distinction between past and present. In recalling her time with Sally Seton, Clarissa actually reexperiences, "the old emotion," "the religious feeling" (Woolf 1925, pp. 34, 35).

In her adult life, Clarissa carries with her the "present" that Sally has given her. The "religious feeling" associated with this relationship is sometimes able to burn through the layers of time ("the radiance burnt through") (1925, p. 35). At various points in the text, Clarissa seems to unwrap Sally's "present" to reexperience different moments of their relationship. The return of these moments shows the way in which Clarissa's desire and love for Sally is preserved and ever-present. Furthermore, this "present" seems to figure an aspect of herself that Clarissa feels needs to be preserved at all cost. When contemplating the meaning of Septimus's suicide, Clarissa thinks: "But this young man who killed himself—had he plunged holding his treasure? 'If it were now to die, 'twere now to be most happy,' she had said to herself once, coming down in white" (1925, p. 184). As many critics have noted, the use of the word "treasure" here is strikingly similar to the "present," that "something infinitely precious," which Clarissa receives from kissing Sally (1925, pp. 35, 184). Clarissa herself is clearly connecting this treasure to her memories of Sally as she repeats the words she said coming downstairs to meet her at Bourton. Clarissa feels "somehow very like him—the young man who had killed himself," and "she felt glad that he had done it" (1925, p. 186). Clarissa's gladness seems to be centered on the fact that Septimus would plunge to his death rather than give up his "treasure." She understands the desire to die in order to preserve something "exquisite." Clarissa's way of preserving this "treasure," however, is quite different from Septimus's.

Though a number of critics have read Septimus's suicide as the vehicle through which Clarissa is able to finally put her past behind her, I would suggest that the incident does not represent Clarissa closing the door to her past, but rather shows how the preservation of her feelings for Sally is essential to her life. Without the space to keep her memory of Sally alive, Clarissa too might have plunged to her death. Many critics argue that Septimus's suicide causes an epiphany for Clarissa, one that allows her to leave the internal world of her memory and return to the physical world of the party. If this scene is an epiphany, it is one of quite a different sort. It is a moment that allows Clarissa to see the presence of her past, to experience the pleasure of having her past return to her:

> She had schemed; she had pilfered. She was never wholly admirable. She had wanted success. Lady Bexborough and the rest of it. And once she had walked on the terrace at Bourton.
>
> It was due to Richard; she had never been so happy. Nothing could be slow enough; nothing last too long. No pleasure could equal, she thought, straightening the chairs, pushing in one book on the shelf, this having done with the triumphs of youth, lost herself in the process of living, to find it, with a shock of delight, as the sun rose, as the day sank. (1925, p. 185)

Critics like Abel who describe Clarissa as healing her relation to the past interpret this passage with an emphasis on the line: "It was due to Richard; she had never been so happy" (1925, p. 185). According to Abel, "the joy inspired by Clarissa's thought of Richard persists as she celebrates 'this having done with the triumphs of youth.' … By recalling to Clarissa the power of her past … he enables her to fully acknowledge and renounce its hold, to embrace the imperfect pleasures of adulthood more perfectly" (1983, p. 179). In Abel's reading, Richard represents the present, and thus Clarissa's statement that "it was due to Richard" means that she has embraced the present (her adulthood) over "the triumphs of youth." She attributes Clarissa's happiness to Richard and thus interprets the line as saying that it was due to Richard *that* she had never been so happy. The problem with this reading is that it ignores the semicolon that separates the two independent clauses and treats the clauses as dependent on each other. This sentence makes two direct statements that are related, but not necessarily in terms of cause and effect.

Because of the structure of this sentence, a quite different reading is also possible. The phrase "she had never been so happy" could also refer back to the last line of the previous paragraph: "And once she had walked on the terrace at Bourton" (1925, p. 185). This line recalls the "most exquisite moment of [Clarissa's] whole life," the kiss with Sally that occurred on the terrace at Bourton (1925, p. 35). The happiness might then be traced back not to Richard but to Sally. In my reading of this passage, it is not that Richard causes Clarissa's happiness, that her marriage to him has brought her the type of marital bliss meant to be the happy ending of the traditional marriage plot, but rather that Richard allows for the space for the moment of her most intense happiness to endure over time.

However, we must not ignore the clause "it was due to Richard" that separates the walk "on the terrace at Bourton" and Clarissa's happiness (1925, p. 185). Linda S. Raphael's work gets at the ambiguity of this sentence: "[W]as it that she had never been so happy as at Bourton, or she had never been so happy as she is now?" (2001, p. 165). Was it that "she had never been as happy as in youth, or that she now has the chance to remember her youth" (Raphael 2001, p. 165)? In order to make sense of Richard's appearance at this moment in the text, it is important to consider why Clarissa married Richard in the first place. Clarissa does not marry Richard because her love for him is more intense than her love for her other suitors. Her love for Peter is most certainly a more intense love. But Clarissa finds herself "still making out that she had been right—and she had too—not to marry [Peter]. For in a marriage a little license, a little independence there must be between people living together day in day out in the same house; which Richard gave her and she him. … But with Peter everything had to be shared; everything gone into" (1925, p. 8). Clarissa thus married Richard because he allows for space, both mental and physical. She does not marry him to join herself emotionally to someone else, but to preserve a space for herself. By Clarissa's fiftieth year, she is sleeping in a narrow bed in her own room in the attic. Her relationship with Richard is amiable and warm but far from passionate. It seems that Richard's primary character attribute is his ability to allow for Clarissa's emotional freedom. Clarissa may be restrained in a number of ways by her marriage and by the society she lives in, but she has seemingly managed to maintain a bit of emotional space in her choice of marriage partners. With Peter, "everything had to be shared; everything gone into" (1925, p. 8), and thus Clarissa could not have maintained this space had she married him. Indeed, it is Peter who interrupts the kiss between Clarissa and Sally on the terrace at Bourton. Peter's approach to a relationship with Clarissa thus would not have allowed her the space to preserve the Clarissa who once "had walked on the terrace at Bourton" (1925, p. 185).

But this leaves us with perhaps the most complex sentence of that passage, a sentence that seems to resist clear explication: "No pleasure could equal, she thought, straightening the chairs, pushing in one book on the shelf, this having done with the triumphs of youth, lost herself in the process of living, to find it, with a shock of delight, as the sun rose, as the day sank" (1925, p. 185). This sentence is often read as establishing that "no pleasure could equal … this having done with the triumphs of youth,"—that Clarissa takes the greatest pleasure in knowing that her youth is over with (1925, p. 185). While this reading seems to account for the first half of the sentence, it doesn't seem to deal with the second half. The second half of the sentence is perhaps more complex than the first. In particular, the phrase "to find it," seems difficult to connect to the rest of the sentence. What exactly does the "it" refer to? The "pleasure"? "The process"? A particular form of happiness? Does it repeat the "it" of "it was due to Richard"?[8] Or perhaps there is no clear antecedent to "it" in this passage. As Patricia Matson has shown, Woolf often writes sentences in which "it" seems to be an unknown (1996, p. 169).[9] None of these readings seems satisfactory, and yet understanding what exactly Clarissa finds "with a shock of delight" seems quite crucial to the meaning of this section.

I would like to suggest an alternate reading of this "it," one that poses a possible antecedent for that puzzling pronoun, and one that is compatible with the syntax of the sentence. What if "it" refers to "youth"? Clarissa's pleasure, then, stems from the process of living in which she goes from feeling at one moment that she is done with the triumphs of youth to suddenly and unexpectedly finding her youth in the next moment. This reading also helps us to recognize a connection between Clarissa's reflections here and her reflections about that thing "that mattered" to Septimus a few paragraphs earlier? The passage reads: "They (all day she had been thinking of Bourton, of Peter, of Sally), they would grow old. A thing there was that mattered; a thing, wreathed about with chatter, defaced, obscured in her own life, let drop every day in corruption, lies, chatter. This he had preserved" (1925, p. 184). This "thing ... that mattered," this thing that Septimus "had preserved," is "his treasure"—that thing without which life is not worth living (1925, p. 184). Could "it" also be what Clarissa finds "with a shock of delight, as the sun rose, as the day sank" (1925, p. 185), the treasure of her youth, her "present"–that exquisite kiss with Sally—that Clarissa has been holding onto for all these years?

While this reading is only one of several possible, the fact that there is no clear antecedent to the word "it" in the passage offers a space for speculation. While previous readings (including Abel's) seem to focus on this moment as representing Clarissa's movement beyond her past, these readings do not account for the multiple references to her moments with Sally in the passage nor do they account for Clarissa's very apparent gladness that Septimus had killed himself in order to preserve "his treasure."

What Septimus's suicide ultimately shows is that this is not a text about development. Clarissa does not finally recognize her past as past and thus does not complete what had before been an incomplete journey to adulthood, as Abel argues. This is not a text about moving from the past into the future, but rather one about the preservation of the past in the present. And the kiss between Clarissa and Sally is absolutely crucial to this understanding. The entire climax of the novel hangs on Clarissa's mulling over Septimus's suicide. Clarissa is happy that he has plunged to death with "his treasure." This treasure, as a number of critics have shown, calls up Clarissa's description of Sally's kiss. She had been given "a present" and told to hold it. Clarissa understands Septimus's suicide as a desire to hold onto that "treasure" because a life without it is a life not worth living. Clarissa's interpretation of this suicide shows her the importance of her "present" from Sally and the necessity of its preservation for a life worth living. For Clarissa, then, it is this "present," this kiss with Sally, that remains, that returns to disrupt linear narratives of development. It is a moment of queer temporality; it hangs between life and death, between youth and adulthood, and crashes through all the barriers meant to keep the past and the present separate. In this sense, my reading of *Mrs. Dalloway* deviates significantly from Annamarie Jagose's. Jagose claims that "lesbianism is enjoyed on borrowed time. It has no continuity of its own and [...] is always vulnerable to interruption," and the kiss "interrupts the smooth chronologies of Clarissa's everyday life" (2002, p. 85). While Jagose's reading is convincing in its focus on the lesbian as a figure, her understanding of temporality in the novel is quite different from my own. In my reading, the moment of the kiss between the two women is defined by its continuity, by its very ability to endure and to disorder and trouble "the smooth chronologies of Clarissa's everyday life."

The kiss between Clarissa and Sally ultimately is the way in which Woolf affirms the power of moments. If "ideology is coiled ... in narrative structure," as Rachel. DuPlessis claims (1998, p. 324), then it is quite difficult to escape the tyranny of traditional plots. The kiss between Clarissa and Sally has little effect on the plot of *Mrs. Dalloway* but significant effects on the character Mrs. Dalloway. By naming the kiss "the most exquisite moment of her whole life" and having this moment repeatedly return to affect Clarissa's present (1925, p. 35), Woolf is able to present a queer temporality that disrupts and questions traditional forms of narration and traditional plots.

Perhaps one of the most interesting studies of Woolf's representation of "the moment" in *Mrs. Dalloway* is Michael Cunningham's 1998 novel *The Hours*. For Cunningham, there is something about the moment that is crucial to the understanding of *Mrs. Dalloway*. *The Hours* itself spotlights the earlier novel's focus on moments and takes it in a new direction. Cunningham's interest in moments is clear from the epigraph. He quotes a passage from Virginia Woolf's diary concerning "The Hours," the title of her working manuscript for *Mrs. Dalloway*: "I have no time to describe my plans. I should say a good deal about The Hours & my discovery; how I dig out beautiful caves behind my characters; I think that gives exactly what I want; humanity, humour, depth. The idea is that the caves shall connect, & and each comes to daylight at the present moment." By establishing Woolf's methodology for connecting her characters to the present moment, Cunningham begins his book by making visible the stylistics of the novel that inspired his own. In other parts of her journal, Woolf refers to this method as her "tunneling process" (Hungerford 1957, p. 164). This tunneling process is the means by which the past ends up side by side with the present in *Mrs. Dalloway*. Cunningham's prose seems to enact this same process, but his text also attempts to understand the riddle of the "exquisite moment" as it exists in Woolf's text.

Cunningham uses the concept of "the hours" to sketch out his own conception of time. In Cunningham's text, the term "the hours" takes on complicated and ambiguous meanings. While at times "the hours" seem to represent the clock time that bears down on various characters (like Big Ben's recurrent clanging in *Mrs. Dalloway*), Cunningham also uses the term in ways that seem synonymous with moments. "The hours" themselves are a queer form of time, meaning neither solely the clock time made up of sixty minutes nor a single moment. The definition of "the hours" oscillates between these various meanings depending on its context in the novel. In this way, *The Hours* is very much a text about the experience of time, both about the duration of time passing and about the moments that seem to rupture the experience of duration. My reading of Cunningham, however, will focus primarily on his exploration of the moment.

Though Cunningham explores the moment in other contexts as well, his primary focus seems to be on the jubilant moment of the kiss. More specifically, Cunningham provides us with three variations on the

Clarissa–Sally kiss, each representing a reading that considers the temporality of that kiss. I would like to consider each kiss in detail as a way to sketch out the distinct manner in which Cunningham is employing the moment as well as to show the significance of queer moments in general. Like Woolf, Cunningham uses the kiss as a vehicle that is able to cut across time and connect two disparate moments. The kiss between Clarissa and Sally thus becomes a model for a type of queer moment that Cunningham himself further develops. In *Mrs. Dalloway*, these moments are able to disrupt development narratives that normalize perceptions of time in the novel. In *The Hours*, however, Cunningham examines the way in which these moments represent a particular and perhaps peculiar relation to futurity. They represent times in the characters' lives when the future was unknowable, when they stepped outside the normal narratives of their lives and into a space of the unknown. In this way, Cunningham's text is not merely a re-telling of *Mrs. Dalloway* or a rehashing of its themes; instead, the novel demonstrates exactly what these queer moments make possible—a different relation to the future. This is particularly significant given the very different cultural context in which *The Hours* was published—in the years that followed AIDS epidemic, a disease that forced many to rethink their own relation to the future. While modernist texts like Woolf's are often imagined as being oriented toward the past, Cunningham is able to reconfigure Woolf's temporalities to ask new questions about the future.

Cunningham's novel is divided into a number of sections that follow the lives of three different women. The sections titled "Mrs. Brown" follow Laura Brown, a housewife with a young son in 1949. Laura is almost a caricature of a depressed American housewife. She lives in a suburban home bought by her husband who has returned safely from the war. She has one son and another child on the way. Laura is described as having difficulty maintaining this identity as a housewife.[10] She feels as if she is never quite able to perform the duties that she knows are required of her. Indeed, the sections of the novel that depict her life often focus on her relation to a script that dictates the conventions she should follow. She is often "possessed (it seems to be getting worse) by a dreamlike feeling, as if she is standing in the wings, about to go onstage and perform in a play for which she is not appropriately dressed, and for which she has not adequately rehearsed" (Cunningham 1998, p. 43). Laura knows the script, understands the play, but has trouble adequately playing the part. She feels disconnected from the roles she is meant to play in her own life. When she is alone with her son, "she can't always remember how a mother would act" (1998, p. 47). She believes that "other mothers of small children must maintain a body of rules," but her own relation to her son is much more confusing. She feels that she is playing "a mother" to her son rather than actually being one (1998, p. 47).

When her neighbor Kitty stops by to visit her, Laura is faced with a woman whose domesticity seems to be effortless. When Kitty confesses to Laura that she has to go into the hospital because of a tumor on her uterus, Kitty's façade too seems to slip away. Laura embraces Kitty: "Kitty nods against Laura's breasts. The question has been silently asked and silently answered, it seems. They are both afflicted and blessed, full of shared secrets, striving every moment. They are each impersonating someone. They are weary and beleaguered; they have taken on such enormous work. Kitty lifts her face, and their lips touch. They both know what they are doing. They reset their mouths, each on the other. They touch their lips together, but do not quite kiss" (1998, p. 110). This "not quite kiss" is born out of a shared moment when the women realize that they are "each impersonating someone." The kiss, however, takes them outside of those roles. Neither woman is acting, or even attempting to act, within the roles that dictate their life's progression. This kiss seems to be a moment outside of the narratives that script their actions on a daily basis.

Ultimately, this kiss is only momentary, and it immediately needs to be explained through narrative. It is Kitty who "pulls away" from the kiss first: "Laura releases Kitty. She steps back. She has gone too far, they've both gone too far, but it is Kitty who's pulled away first. It is Kitty whose terrors have briefly propelled her, caused her to act strangely and desperately. Laura is the dark-eyed predator. Laura is the odd one, the foreigner, the one who can't be trusted. Laura and Kitty agree, silently, that this is true" (1998, p. 110). After the kiss has ended, the two women wordlessly agree on a story about the kiss. The kiss must be placed into a familiar narrative and explained away. The silent story that they agree upon is a conventional narrative of a "predator" taking advantage of a woman who is momentarily confused and in need. The story also relies on other narratives, narratives of "foreigners" who "can't be trusted," of "odd" women with strange desires. This story can be the one that Kitty tells herself, but it has nothing to do with the actual moment of the kiss, the moment of mutual agency without subject or object ("their lips touch"), the moment in which they "both know what they are doing" (1998, p. 110).

While not strictly a moment outside of narrative, this is a moment that cannot fit into any of the narratives that they know. As readers of this text, we experience both the moment itself and its violent distortion when forced into a predictable narrative.

For Laura, this kiss hovers around her for the rest of her day and begins to take on a specific meaning. When thinking about her day, Laura recalls "the child, the cake, the kiss. It got down, somehow to those three elements" (1998, p. 142). The child and the cake represent Laura's domestic responsibilities, her only sometimes successful attempts to "pos[e] as a wife" (1998, p. 205). The kiss, however, is another matter entirely. While both "the child" and "the cake" are related to the continuance of an identity over time, the kiss becomes a representation for the power of the moment. Part of its value seems to be that it doesn't have a future. When Laura dreams of "kissing Kitty again some-day," it is "in a kitchen or at the beach as children shriek in the surf, in a hallway with their arms full of folded towels, laughing softly, aroused, hopeless, in love with their own recklessness if not each other, saying SHHHH, parting quickly, going on" (1998, p. 143). The kiss is located in a moment in Laura's fantasy. She does not imagine an alternate future in which she and Kitty can be together, but instead desires a moment with Kitty.

This moment of the kiss and the other perfect moments that Laura experiences are consistently placed in opposition to the work of contin-uance. She sees the hours as something that she needs to get through, continuing and relentless: "She herself is trapped here forever, posing as a wife. She must get through this night, and then tomorrow morn-ing, and then another night here, in these rooms, with nowhere else to go. She must please; she must continue" (1998, p. 205). While continuing seems to be an arduous chore for Laura, she believes that her husband and son's deepest wishes "have mainly to do with con-tinuance" (1998, p. 206).[11] Laura repeatedly asks herself whether or not the moment is enough. This is a trope from *Mrs. Dalloway* (the book that Laura is herself reading this day), but the question seems to have everything to do with her own life. "What if," Laura asks, "that moment at dinner—the equipoise, that small perfection—were enough? What if you decided to want no more?" (1998, p. 214). For Laura, it is hard to tell what the answer to this question might be. The "what if" suggests that for her the moment is not enough, that despite the exquisite nature of her moments, she still feels the pressure of the hours bearing down on her. But the moment, for Laura, is a respite from those roles she finds so difficult to maintain, those conventional scripts that dictate a predetermined future, and a space in which she can forget about what will come next.

The sections titled "Mrs. Dalloway" follow Clarissa Vaughan, a woman living in New York City in the mid-1990s. Clarissa is the modern day Mrs. Dalloway and her life echoes the earlier Clarissa's in a multitude of ways. One major difference, however, is that this Clarissa has made a life with her Sally. Clarissa has been living with her partner, Sally, for eighteen years. The relationship is described as a marriage, and Clarissa refers to herself multiple times as a wife. Cunningham has created a situation in which the relationship that had no future in 1923, according to many critics, is able to develop into a somewhat conventional marriage.[12] Clarissa's and Sally's relationship has all the markings of a marriage. They live together, own property together, and have raised a child together. The relationship is only nontraditional in the fact that it contains two women. Though some critics maintain that Clarissa's marriage "undoubtedly challenged society" (Povalyaeva 2004, p. 273), most highlight how "ordinary" the marriage is (Chatman 2005, p. 272) or talk about it in terms of "uninspired lesbian domesticity" (Iannone 2003, p. 51). In *The Hours*, Clarissa's marriage with Sally is meant to parallel the marriage to Richard in *Mrs. Dalloway*. And like the Clarissa in Woolf's novel, Clarissa Vaughan also has a kiss in her past that often returns to disrupt her present. Her kiss, however, was with Richard, a gay man who is currently her best friend. For this Clarissa, it is this kiss that is transgressive and not her relationship with Sally. By switching the gender of these characters, Cunningham is able to more clearly delineate the significance of the kiss. These moments hold such power not because they are same-sex kisses (indeed, one is not) but because they exist outside an imaginable, scripted future. The queer moment disrupts not only hetero-normative time but also homo-normative time. It complicates those temporalities that naturalize the development through conventional life stages.

The kiss between herself and Richard returns to Clarissa many times over the course of her day. It is first mentioned by Richard when Clarissa goes to visit him in his shabby apartment where he is withering away from AIDS-related illnesses. He says to her:

"You kissed me beside a pond."
"Ten thousand years ago."
"It's still happening."
"In a sense, yes."
"In reality. It's happening in that present. This is happening in this present."
(1998, p. 66)

Richard's statement divides these two presents, but at the same time maintains that that other present is "still happening" elsewhere. However, a few sentences later he brings these two presents together:

He says, "Here we are. Don't you think?"
"Pardon me?"
"We're middle-aged and we're young lovers standing beside a pond. We're everything, all at once. Isn't it remarkable?"
"Yes." (1998, p. 67)

Echoing lines from *Mrs. Dalloway* in a different context, Richard's statement positions the kiss as the gateway through which these "middle-aged" individuals and these "young lovers" can exist simultaneously. In this way, he seems to echo Clarissa Dalloway's visions of herself as both young and old. Richard, however, has become somewhat disoriented both from the drugs that he is on and from his deteriorating health.[13] When Clarissa initially enters his apartment, Richard says, "I seem to have fallen out of time" (1998, p. 62). Despite Richard's mental state, there is a way in which he seems to function as a visionary, as one who is able to see time in a way that is the most pleasurable and the most "remarkable" (1998, p. 67). He posits a view of temporality wherein individuals can "in reality" connect back to earlier moments in their lives (1998, p. 66). For Richard, as for Clarissa Dalloway, the pleasure of this moment seems to come from the touching of the adult and adolescent across a temporal divide. For Clarissa Vaughan, however, the pleasure of this moment seems to be tied to something slightly different.

When Clarissa begins pondering her own memory of the kiss between herself and Richard, her thoughts give readers a bit of the backstory to this moment. When she was eighteen, Clarissa took part in a "little experiment" living with Richard and his lover Louis for a summer (1998, p. 52). The three lived together for only that summer, and their complicated relationship ended as soon as the summer did. But what Clarissa carries with her for the rest of her life is the memory of this one specific kiss with Richard. This is not the only kiss she and Richard shared, but it is the one that has stayed with her: "What lives undimmed in Clarissa's mind more than three decades later is a kiss at dusk on a patch of dead grass, and a walk around a pond as mosquitoes droned in the darkening air" (1998, p. 98). For Clarissa, this kiss is tied to a very specific feeling: the feeling that "anything could happen" (1998, p. 95). She states: "That summer when she was eighteen, it seemed anything could happen, anything at all. It seemed that she could kiss her grave, formidable best friend down by the pond, it seemed that they could sleep together in a strange combination of lust and innocence, and not worry about what, if anything, it meant" (1998, p. 95). Clarissa's memory of that kiss is linked to a feeling of overwhelming possibility. It takes her back to a moment when the future has not yet been decided, when it need not even be considered. The feeling that "anything could happen" is a feeling of not knowing the future. And not to know or anticipate the future is to be able to fully occupy the present. In this instant, Clarissa was able to slip out of the normal temporality of her life, of worrying about the future, of trying to make sense of the present, and fully occupy the moment.

Clarissa experiences a similar moment earlier in the novel when she enters her apartment and feels dislocated from her own home. In this moment, "Clarissa feels the presence of her own ghost, the part of her at once most indestructibly alive and least distinct" (1998, p. 92). With this line, she seems to enter into a different temporality in which she is hyper-conscious of the present, of the objects around her as objects rather than as the things that tell the story of her life. About her life, she thinks: "She could simply leave it and return to her other home, where neither Sally nor Richard exists; where there is only the essence of Clarissa, a girl grown into a woman, still full of hope, still capable of anything. ... She feels briefly, wonderfully alone, with everything ahead of her" (1998, p. 92). In this moment, Clarissa feels "still full of hope, still capable of anything," as if she has "everything ahead of her." She sees herself as a "girl grown into a woman," but the repetition of the word "still" shows that she still maintains those qualities she sees associated with childhood: "hope" and being "capable of anything." Clarissa's experience of the moment therefore returns her to the feeling that the future is still undecided. To fully occupy the present is to be cut off from knowing what the future holds. Though Clarissa seems to associate this feeling with being young, it is a feeling that resides in her still; it is the feeling that comes to the surface when she surfaces within this queer moment.

Clarissa Vaughan's experience of the moment is thus caught up in the moment's relationship to futurity. For Clarissa, it is the openness to the future that marks her experience of the present. Her experience of the moment is connected to chance, to possibility. According to Elizabeth Grosz, it is the concept of chance that signals an openness to the future (1999, p. 5). Because of chance, we cannot know what the future holds. If, in the moment, Clarissa feels that "anything could happen," then she gives up the need to know the future, to anticipate what will come next. As Grosz claims, "to know the future is to deny it as future, to place it as a given, as past" (1999, p. 6). According to Grosz, this is exactly what clock time does by imposing unity through notions of past, present, and future (1999, p. 18). Indeed, to be in the temporality of everyday life is to anticipate the future based on what one knows about the past. This is the type of temporality that Laura experiences when she talks about "continuance" (Cunningham 1998, p. 206). It is the belief that the future will be merely a repetition of the past. The moment, however, is able to disrupt this type of temporality, the temporality of cause and effect, of past projected into the future. For both Clarissa and Kitty, a kiss allows them to occupy the present momentarily and to feel the elation of a future that is on the horizon but is not yet decided.

Because the moment represents an instant in which the future is not yet decided, it is also in a strange relation to narrative. Narrative moves characters through different stages toward somewhat preexisting and predetermined endings; this movement is especially visible in something like the Bildungsroman or the marriage plot ending. This is certainly true of characters in stories, but as Halberstam has shown, individuals often feel the weight of these stories on their own lives. We often chart the development of individuals by their movement through different life stages (Halberstam 2005, p. 4). The moment, however, does not work to move narrative toward conclusion or closure. For this reason, the moment seems to be in a peculiar relation to narrative. This does not mean that the moment is outside of narrative, for certainly these moments I have described exist within frames of narrative, but moments disrupt the flow of time in the novel without any definitive teleological purpose. They simply are. For both Cunningham and Woolf, there seems to be an argument for the value of the moment in and of itself.

Clarissa Vaughan helps to make this point clear. Standing in her house with Louis, an old friend, "Clarissa, suddenly, wants to show her whole life to Louis. She wants to tumble it out onto the floor at Louis's feet, all the vivid, pointless moments that can't be told as stories" (1998, p. 132). For Clarissa, moments "can't be told as stories." They can be tumbled out into a scattered mess upon the floor, but they cannot be told as stories because they are not structured that way. It is perhaps because of their complicated relation to stories that Clarissa calls them "pointless." They do not have significance in the way that stories might. Clarissa cannot narrate these moments but can only offer them up at "Louis's feet." There seems to be a statement here about what narrative can and cannot do, about how the moment can do a type of work that narrative cannot.

I do not want my reading here to reinstate that old opposition between lyric time and narrative. As I established earlier, lyric is often described as a momentary "interruption" of narrative before narrative presses inevitably on. I would want to emphasize that the significance of the queer moment that I am describing—a moment that most definitely has qualities of lyricism—is not merely an interruption after which narrative continues indefinitely. Narrative does press on, but the queer moment remains. It is a remnant of a previous time that continues. And in this case, part of what continues on is a relation to an unpredictable future.

The relationship between narrative and the moment becomes even more complex when we consider what may perhaps be the most significant kiss in *The Hours*, the kiss between Virginia Woolf and her sister Vanessa, the kiss that is the inspiration for the kiss that Woolf creates between Clarissa and Sally in *Mrs. Dalloway*. If Laura's kiss takes her outside the script she feels she is following each day of her life, and if the memory of Clarissa's kiss returns her to a moment when "anything could happen," then the kiss between Virginia and Vanessa combines and extends these aspects. It is the queerest kiss of all. The kiss takes place in the presence of her servant Nelly when Virginia is sitting beside her sister in the kitchen: "Nelly turns away and, although it is not at all their custom, Virginia leans forward and kisses Vanessa on the mouth. It is an innocent kiss, innocent enough, but just now in this kitchen, behind Nelly's back, it feels like the most delicious and forbidden of pleasures. Vanessa returns the kiss" (1998, p. 154). The kiss is "innocent enough" or as Virginia will later call it "not quite innocent" (1998, p. 210). This slight deviation from innocence is something that remains as Virginia thinks of this kiss throughout the remainder of the novel. This focus on innocence does a few things. First, given that innocence is often associated with children, it sparks an association with childhood. At the same time, though, the emphasis on innocence actually highlights not the "innocent" nature of the kiss, but rather its illicitness. This modification of the kiss's initial descriptor from "innocent" to "innocent enough" to, finally, "not quite innocent" highlights the kiss as "the most delicious and forbidden of pleasures." Though the kiss may be seemingly connected to childhood, then, the modifiers seem to simultaneously separate it from childhood.

What the text ultimately shows, however, is that this kiss is part of a strange temporality that crosses the division between childhood and adulthood. Earlier in Virginia's day she is standing beside her sister when she thinks, "One moment there are two young sisters cleaving to each other, breast against breast, lips ready, and then the next moment, it seems, there are two middle aged married women standing together on a modest bit of the lawn before a body of children" (1998, p. 116). Virginia's observation here echoes the thoughts of many characters in both *Mrs. Dalloway* and *The Hours* who are able to see two disparate moments laid out next to each other. Clarissa Dalloway experiences herself simultaneously as a child and an adult standing beside the lake, and Richard experiences himself at once as a middle-aged man and a teenager beside a pond. But Virginia's thoughts here go beyond this. She recalls herself and her sister "cleaving to each other, breast against breast, lips ready." The image here calls up two young girls, sisters, in anticipation of a kiss. The kiss, however, does not occur in childhood, but between "two middle aged married women." This is a kiss that occurs across time. It is the children whose lips are ready but the adults who kiss, despite the fact that "it is not at all their custom" (1998, p. 154). This kiss, therefore, is a moment that is able to break through the barriers of time and collapse the distinction between the child and the adult.

But this kiss does something else as well: it highlights the difference between moments and narratives. This kiss is not about anything else but what it is like to experience a moment. After her sister has left:

[Virginia] thinks, suddenly, of Vanessa's kiss.

The kiss was innocent—innocent enough—but it was also full of something not unlike what Virginia wants from London, from life; it was full of a love complex and ravenous, ancient, neither this nor that. It will serve as this afternoon's manifestation of the central mystery itself, the elusive brightness that shines from the edges of certain dreams; the brightness which, when we awaken, is already fading from our minds, and which we rise in the hope of finding, perhaps today, this new day in which anything might happen, anything at all. She, Virginia, has kissed her sister, not quite innocently, behind Nelly's broad, moody back, and now she is in a room with a book on her lap. (1998, pp. 209–210)

The kiss between Virginia and Vanessa is ultimately a moment that can't be explained, that doesn't fit neatly into narrative. Its meaning can never become clear but is instead a "manifestation of the central mystery itself, the elusive brightness that shines from the edges of certain dreams." It is full of desire, "of something not unlike what Virginia wants from London, from life." And it is full of a love that resists description: "neither this nor that." Furthermore, this passage is full of those terms that have become associated with "the moment" in this text: "London," "life," (two words often followed in *The Hours* and *Mrs. Dalloway* by "this moment") and "anything might happen, anything at all."

This moment also resists narrative by virtue of its own subject matter. The kiss between the two sisters, if turned into a narrative, is a story of incestuous desire. Incest is often described as the most ingrained of taboos, and the elaboration of this story often seems to rely on the search for psychological explanations. Though there have only been a couple of dozen articles about Cunningham's novel, none of these deals with this kiss at length, despite the significance of this moment. In some ways, this omission seems to parallel early critics of *Mrs. Dalloway*, who often neglected to comment on the kiss between Clarissa and Sally. The film did not know what to do with this kiss either. Instead of displaying a "not quite innocent" kiss between Virginia and Vanessa, a moment of the "most delicious and forbidden" pleasure, audiences saw Virginia grabbing a terrified Vanessa and seemingly sucking the life out of her. Carol Iannone, one critic of the film, states that the kiss represents Virginia's effort "to draw vitality from another woman as well as to give expression of her own confused sexual identity" (2003, p. 52).

The kiss, in the film, became another mark of Virginia's insanity (Spengler 2004, p. 71), instead of a moment of elated pleasure in the experience of a moment. In order to present the moment in this way, the film had to convey Vanessa's shock at the kiss. This, however, is not the case in the novel where "Vanessa returns the kiss" (Cunningham 1998, p. 154). The novel does not allow this moment to be read as part of Virginia's confused mental state because it is a moment equally shared by Vanessa. Ultimately, this moment is one that eschews attempts to explain it. It is a moment of pleasure and elation, of possibility, of stepping outside daily routines and conventional narratives as well as a statement about the power of such moments despite their minimal effects on the plot.

Like the other kisses in *The Hours*, this kiss partakes in the feeling that "anything might happen" (1998, p. 210). It allows Virginia to experience a moment, to not know what the future holds, to step out of narrative and its conventions. It does not move the plot forward toward closure, climax, or conclusion but allows for the pleasure of a pause in action. The moment ultimately becomes an inspiration for Virginia who translates the feeling she had when kissing Vanessa into Clarissa's feeling at her kiss with Sally. Though the details are changed, the significance of this moment—"the soaring hope of it," as Virginia says—remains (1998, p. 210). Cunningham's representation of the kiss both follows from his reading of *Mrs. Dalloway* and allows us to reconceptualize Woolf's writing of the novel. Reading *The Hours*, in other words, allows us to entertain the possibility that, in placing the kiss within the book that will become *Mrs. Dalloway*, Virginia preserves this moment in a different kind of narrative, one that keeps alive the connection between past and present and allows this queer moment to continue.

*   *   *

In what is perhaps one of the most famous criticisms of *Mrs. Dalloway*, Arnold Bennett claims that he could not see "much trace of construction or ordered movement towards climax" in the novel (1975, p. 190). He states that "problems are neither clearly stated nor clearly solved" (1975, p. 190). These criticisms are part of a larger public conversation between Woolf and Bennett in which the two argue about techniques for creating character. In concluding his essay, Bennett states: "In the novels of Mrs. Woolf some brief passages are so exquisitely done that nothing could be done better. But to be fine for a few minutes is not enough. The chief proof of first-rateness is sustained power" (1975, p. 190).

Bennett's statement here gets to the absolute core of the disagreement between the two authors. Bennett concedes that Woolf does "some brief passages ... exquisitely" but claims that "to be fine for a few minutes is not enough" (1975, p. 190). Bennett's idea of a "first-rate" novel is one with "ordered movement towards climax," one in which "problems" are "clearly stated" and "clearly solved." He wants to see a narrative that moves through stages where characters develop and resolution occurs. No wonder he was disappointed with Woolf's novel.

What Bennett's criticisms show is the way in which "the moment" interferes with and disrupts traditional models of narrative. Bennett does not know how even to begin to comment on a novel that does away with what he calls "logical progression" (1975, p. 191). And Bennett is absolutely right here: the novel does do away with progression toward a solution or ultimate climax. In this respect, Bennett's criticisms are perhaps more astute than those later critics who try to force a story of female development onto Clarissa's character. The central disagreement between Woolf and Bennett, then, is whether or not "to be fine for a few minutes," as Bennett puts it, is enough. Throughout the course of their day, both Clarissa and Peter consider whether or not the moment is enough. It is perhaps Peter who puts it most eloquently. He states: "Life itself, every moment of it, every drop of it, here, this instant, now, in the sun, in Regent's Park, was enough" (Woolf 1925, p. 79). During those times where characters shake themselves out of the progression of their daily lives to experience "here, this instant, now," the moment is most definitely enough.

This point becomes even clearer in *The Hours*. At the end of her long day, a day in which her best friend has committed suicide, in which she has contemplated the meaning of her past and her present, Clarissa Vaughan thinks: "There's just this for consolation: an hour here or there when our lives seem, against all odds and expectations, to burst open and give us everything we've ever imagined, though everyone but children (and perhaps even they) knows these hours will inevitably be followed by others, far darker and more difficult. Still, we cherish the city, the morning; we hope, more than anything, for more" (Cunningham 1998, p. 225). The hours in which "our lives seem ... to burst open and give us everything we've ever imagined" are placed in opposition to the hours that continue relentlessly forward (1998, p. 225). But it is the pleasure of "an hour here or there" that we hope for "more than anything." These are the "vivid, pointless moments," as Clarissa Vaughan states earlier, "that can't be told as stories" (1998, p. 132).

But what makes these moments "enough"? To be in a moment is often constructed as being cut off from the past and the future. But as Woolf and Cunningham have shown, to occupy the moment can also mean recognizing the connection between disparate moments in time and enacting crossings across perceived divides. Moments can allow characters to fully occupy an instant in which the future is open and not yet decided. In these queer moments, the very functioning of time toward a necessary conclusion is questioned. We are allowed to celebrate the moment as a moment.

It is perhaps for this reason that the kiss became the central trope for the moment for both authors. In both texts, the kiss is explored as a kiss rather than as a stop along the way to sex, to a climax. The kiss itself partakes of an interesting and strange temporality. The moment of the kiss is the moment in which a relationship takes a sexual turn. It is a beginning of something that is yet unknown. Within the framework of presumptive heterosexuality, this future is often preimagined: courtship, marriage, reproduction, etc. But in these texts, the kiss is a moment in which we linger, celebrating not the possibility of a scripted future but the soaring hope of the moment itself, the moment in which our lives seem "to burst open and give us everything we've ever imagined." Perhaps it is only within the forward motion of reproductive time that the moment loses its significance and its power. For within queer temporality, the moment is not merely "enough"; it is the opening to a future that is not yet decided.

NOTES

1. See *GLQ: A Journal of Gay and Lesbian Studies*'s special issue on Queer Temporality.
2. The kiss between Clarissa and Sally is explored in far too many critical articles to innumerate here. Indeed, their relationship is invoked more and more as an example of the queerness that has always been a part of the modernist enterprise. Besides Halberstam, Jagose, and Stockton, mentioned above, Joseph Allen Boone also explores the relationship between the two as part of his larger argument about how representations of sexual desire shaped modernism in *Libidinal Currents* (1998).
3. For example, Joanne Winning begins her the introduction to her 2000 book, *The Pilgrimage of Dorothy Richardson*, with a discussion of the kiss between Clarissa and Sally. This introduction, titled "Reading for Difference: The Case for Lesbian Modernism," uses the kiss to show the ways that "lesbian desire [...] seems to weave its way through the modernist period with great tenacity" (2000, p. 4).

4. It is worth noting that Abel's text partakes of a particular moment in feminism. Written in 1983, the article was published in a collection of feminist literary criticism titled *The Voyage In: Fictions of Female Development*. Abel's article (and a similar one in her 1989 book on Virginia Woolf) is based on a Freudian conception of sexual development. Feminist critics at this time were often interested in exploring bonds between mother and daughter that had so often been sidelined in earlier psychoanalytic readings. Though such readings have their value, I fear that we miss something quite significant about *Mrs. Dalloway* when we read Clarissa's relationship with Sally through this narrative.

5. This is also true of Susan Stanford Friedman's article "Lyric Subversion of Narrative in Women's Writing: Virginia Woolf and the Tyranny of Plot." While Freidman convincingly sketches out a reading of the lyric and narrative temporality in relation to female plots, she, in a mode similar to Abel, reads homoerotic moments between women—across multiple texts—as consistently representative of a desire for the maternal body. In her conclusion, she uses the term homoerotic as a synonym for "centered in a desire for the female body" (1989, p. 179). Like Abel's text, this text is reminiscent of a particular moment in psychoanalytic feminism.

6. These are not the only texts that offer readings of the complex relations between narrative and lyric. For more on the cooperation between lyric and narrative, see James Phelan, "Rhetorical Ethics and Lyric Narrative: Robert Frost's 'Home Burial'" (2004a), "Toward a Rhetoric and Ethics of Lyric Narrative: The Case of 'A Clean, Well-Lighted Place'" (2004b), and Jay Clayton, *Romantic Vision and the Novel* (1987).

7. This is the type of configuration that Jagose is talking about when she claims that lesbianism is often figured as interruption to a narrative sequence (2002, p. 85).

8. Elsewhere in this passage, "it" also refers to both Septimus's suicide and his life ("she felt glad he had done it; thrown it away") as well as the sky ("Many a time had she gone...to look at the sky; or seen it between people's shoulders"). However, neither of these meanings of seems to offer much help in the sentence I am considering above.

9. As Matson states, "the proliferation of phrases [in Woolf's writing], one after the other in an often syntactically discordant manner, counteracts the possibility (and desirability) of linear progression" (1996, p. 169). Thus even the style of Woolf's sentence, with its ambiguous pronouns, its "proliferation of phrases" and of commas, seems to warn against reading it as part of a narrative of progressive development toward maturity.

10. In his depiction of Laura, Cunningham is clearly drawing on Doris Lessing's short story "To Room 19." Like Lessing's main character, Laura retires for a portion of her day to a hotel room to escape playing her domestic roles.

11. Laura's comments here recall Susan Stanford Friedman's claims about the "potentially gendered dimensions of this opposition between lyric and narrative" (1998, p. 165). However, I do not think that the association between lyric and female on the one hand and narrative and male on the other is bared out through the rest of Cunningham's text.

12. Pamela Transue, for example, asks "what future was there in [Clarissa's] relationship with Sally?" (1986, p. 70).

13. The fact that such statements about temporality come from a character who has AIDS is not insignificant. A number of scholars, including Eve Sedgwick, have considered the relationship between AIDS and new temporalities. What AIDS makes visible is perhaps our own precarious relationship with the future.

References

Abel, Elizabeth. 1983. Narrative Structure(s) and Female Development: The Case of *Mrs. Dalloway*. In *The Voyage In: Fictions of Female Development*, ed. Elizabeth Abel, Marianne Hirsch, and Elizabeth Langland, 161–185. Hanover: University Press of New England.

———. 1996. *Virginia Woolf and the Fictions of Psychoanalysis*. Chicago: University of Chicago Press.

Abraham, Julie. 1996. *Are Girls Necessary: Lesbian Writing and Modern Histories*. New York: Routledge.

Barber, Stephen M., and David L. Clark (eds.). 2002. Introduction: Queer Moments: The Performative Temporalities of Eve Kosofsky Sedgwick. In *Regarding Sedgwick: Essays on Queer Culture and Critical Theory*, 1–56. New York: Routledge.

Bennett, Arnold. 1975. Article in *Evening Standard*. In *Virginia Woolf: The Critical Heritage*, ed. Robin Majumdar and Allen McLaurin, 189–190. London: Routledge.

Boone, Joseph Allen. 1998. *Libidinal Currents: Sexuality and the Shaping of Modernism*. Chicago: The University of Chicago Press.

Chatman, Seymour. 2005. *Mrs. Dalloway* Progeny: *The Hours* as Second-Degree Narrative. In *A Companion to Narrative Theory*, ed. James Phelan and Peter J. Rabinowitz, 269–282. Malden: Blackwell.

Clayton, Jay. 1987. *Romantic Vision and the Novel*. Cambridge: Cambridge University Press.

Cunningham, Michael. 1998. *The Hours*. New York: Farrar.

Dowling, David. 1991. *Mrs. Dalloway: Mapping Streams of Consciousness*. Boston: Twayne.

Dubrow, Heather. 2006. The Interplay of Narrative and Lyric: Competition, Cooperation, and the Case of the Anticipatory Amalgam. *Narrative* 14 (3): 254–271.

DuPlessis, Rachel Blau. 1998. Feminist Narrative in Virginia Woolf. *Novel: A Forum on Fiction* 21 (2–3): 323–330.

Freeman, Elizabeth (ed.). 2007. Queer Temporality. Special Issue, *GLQ: A Journal of Gay and Lesbian Studies* 13 (2–3).

Friedman, Susan Stanford. 1989. Lyric Subversion of Narrative in Women's Writing: Virginia Woolf and the Tyranny of Plot. In *Reading Narrative*, ed. James Phelan, 162–185. Columbus: Ohio State University Press.

Froula, Christine. 2002. *Mrs. Dalloway*'s Postwar Elegy: Women, War, and the Art of Mourning. *Modernism/Modernity* 9 (1): 125–163.

Grosz, Elizabeth (ed.). 1999. *Becomings: Explorations in Time, Memory and Futures*. Ithaca: Cornell University Press.

Halberstam, J. 2005. *In a Queer Time and Place: Transgender Bodies, Subcultural Lives*. New York: New York University Press.

Henke, Suzette A. 1981. *Mrs. Dalloway*: The Communion of Saints. In *New Feminist Essays on Virginia Woolf*, ed. Jane Marcus, 125–147. Lincoln: University of Nebraska Press.

Hungerford, Edward A. 1957. My Tunneling Process: The Method of *Mrs. Dalloway*. *Modern Fiction Studies* 3: 164–167.

Iannone, Carol. 2003. Woolf, Women, and 'The Hours'. *Commentary* 115 (4): 50–53.

Jagose, Annamarie. 2002. *Inconsequence: Lesbian Representation and the Logic of Sexual Sequence*. Ithaca: Cornell University Press.

Matson, Patricia. 1996. The Terror and the Ecstasy: The Textual Politics of Virginia Woolf's *Mrs. Dalloway*. In *Ambiguous Discourse: Feminist Narratology and British Women Writers*, ed. Kathy Mezei, 162–186. Chapel Hill: The University of North Carolina Press.

Morgan, Monique. 2008. Narrative Means to Lyric Ends in Wordsworth's *Prelude*. *Narrative* 16 (3): 298–330.

Pearce, Richard. 1991. *The Politics of Narration: James Joyce, William Faulkner, and Virginia Woolf*. New Brunswick: Rutgers University Press.

Phelan, James. 2004a. Rhetorical Ethics and Lyric Narrative: Robert Frost's 'Home Burial'. *Poetics Today* 25: 627–652.

———. 2004b. Toward a Rhetoric and Ethics of Lyric Narrative: The Case of 'A Clean, Well-Lighted Place'. *Frame* 17: 27–43.

Povalyaeva, Natalia. 2004. The Issue of Self-Identification in Woolf's *Mrs. Dalloway* and Cunningham's *The Hours*. In *Woolf Across Cultures*, ed. Natalya Reinhold, 269–276. New York: Pace University Press.

Randall, Bryony. 2007. *Modernism, Daily Time, and Everyday Life*. Cambridge: Cambridge University Press.

Raphael, Linda S. 2001. *Narrative Skepticism, Moral Agency and Representations of Consciousness in Fiction*. Madison: Fairleigh Dickinson University Press.

Sedgwick, Eve Kosofsky. 1993. *Tendencies*. Durham: Duke University Press.

Showalter, Elaine. 1994. *Mrs. Dalloway*. In *Virginia Woolf: Introductions to the Major Works*, ed. Julia Briggs, 125–156. London: Virago.

Spengler, Birgit. 2004. Michael Cunningham Rewriting Virginia Woolf: Pragmatist vs. Modernist Aesthetics. *Woolf Studies Annual* 10: 51–79.

Stockton, Kathryn Bond. 2004. Growing Sideways, or Versions of the Queer Child: The Ghost, the Homosexual, the Freudian, the Innocent, and the Interval of Animal. In *Curiouser: On the Queerness of Children*, ed. Steven Bruhm and Natasha Hurley, 277–316. Minneapolis: University of Minnesota Press.

The Hours. 2002. Dir. Stephen Daldry. Perf. Nicole Kidman, Julianne Moore, and Meryl Streep. Paramount, Film.

Transue, Pamela J. 1986. *Virginia Woolf and the Politics of Style*. Albany: State University of New York Press.

Winning, Joanne. 2000. *The Pilgrimage of Dorothy Richardson*. Madison: University of Wisconsin Press.

Woolf, Virginia. 1925. *Mrs. Dalloway*. San Diego: Harcourt. Reprint 1981.

CHAPTER 3

"Still and Moving":
Winterson, Eliot, and the Dance in Time

Jeanette Winterson begins her essay "The Semiotics of Sex":

> I was in a bookshop recently when a young woman approached me.
> She told me she was writing an essay on my work and that of
> Radclyffe Hall. Could I help?
> "Yes," I said. "Our work has nothing in common."
> "I thought you were a lesbian," she said. (1996b, p. 103)

The essay, written in 1996, goes on to critique those who use sexual
identity as the primary way to understand a literary text. Here the reader
who connects Winterson to Radclyffe Hall because of a shared lesbian
identity is critiqued for, as Winterson states later, using lesbianism as "the
golden key to the single door of [her] work" (1996b, p. 103).

The significance of this story becomes clearer when we arrive at
the essay's conclusion and come upon another anecdote that begins
identically:

> I was in a bookshop recently and a young man came up to me and
> said
> "Is Sexing the Cherry a reading of Four Quartets?"
> "Yes," I said, and he kissed me. (1996b, p. 118)

© The Author(s) 2019
K. Haffey, *Literary Modernism, Queer Temporality*,
https://doi.org/10.1007/978-3-030-17301-2_3

These twin stories gain a deeper meaning in their juxtaposition. Unlike the reader who connects her to Radclyffe Hall, the reader who connects Winterson to T. S. Eliot despite the many differences between the two writers is honored with the essay's conclusion and is allowed to kiss her. This kiss between Winterson and the "young man" is born out of a moment of recognition. The young man recognizes Eliot's *Four Quartets* in Winterson's novel, and the affirmation of his own reading by the author results in an unexpected kiss. This kiss, this odd sexual turn of the text, is where the essay leaves us. I want to take this kiss as representative of Winterson's strange relationship with literary precursor T. S. Eliot.

As Marian Eide claims, "Winterson's second reader makes a queer connection between T.S. Eliot's poetry of spiritual faith" and the themes of *Sexing the Cherry* (2001, p. 280). Eide's reading of this connection as "queer" highlights the ways in which the first reader seems to essentialize identity categories, while the second reads with an eye for odd relations that the text itself makes visible. Winterson's anecdotes, thus, do two things: they critique reading practices that rest on the identity of the author, and they assert the text as the central locus of meaning.[1] Authors must be connected not through their lives but through their texts.

Winterson's stories are also a response to those scholars who have read her (and other gay and lesbian writers) primarily in terms of sexual identity. A significant number of her critics seem to line up with Winterson's description of the first reader. In the early 1990s especially, critics were particularly interested in Winterson's depictions of lesbians in print, asking whether her representations were positive or negative, realistic or unbelievable, subversive or conservative.[2] In 1996 when Winterson published "The Semiotics of Sex," much of Winterson criticism seemed to center on whether or not her work fit neatly into a lesbian, feminist, or lesbian-feminist political agenda.

What has become apparent in my reading of Winterson and her critics is the way in which Winterson does not easily fit into any theoretical paradigm, literary genealogy, or even genre. Her texts seem simultaneously to deconstruct history and uphold universal ideals about art, to tear down assumptions about gender and to testify to the healing power of romantic love. She has been called both a modernist and a postmodernist, with rather convincing arguments on either side. She has been aligned with the New Critics and been accused of having "a lesbian feminist agenda" (Müller 2001, p. 42).

Perhaps Winterson's relation to T. S. Eliot is the most striking example of her tendency to resist easy classifications. At first glance, it would be hard to find two authors who seem further apart than Winterson and Eliot. The two are writing in different genres during different historical periods and have quite different political leanings. But to understand a writer based on their period or political leaning is much like understanding them through their sexual identity—that method of the first reader in "The Semiotics of Sex." When we look to the text for evidence of a connection between Eliot and Winterson, the results are quite different. Winterson's novels are littered with references to various Eliot poems, and in many cases Eliot's words are spoken either directly or with slight variation by Winterson's narrators.

The relationship between the two authors has not gone unnoticed in Winterson criticism. Several critics have commented on Eliot's textual presence in Winterson's work.[3] These critics, however, cite the intertextual connection between the two authors briefly before moving on to other topics. Christine Reynier is the exception here. Reynier uses her article to think about the connection between Eliot's "Tradition and the Individual Talent," a work to which Winterson declares her allegiance in her book of essays, and Winterson's novels (specifically *Written on the Body*). Reynier seeks to discover "whether Winterson takes Eliot as a model, as she claims to do, and thus to evaluate her relation to tradition and her individual talent" (2005, p. 299). Reynier's article is compelling because it reads *Written on the Body* against Winterson's own reading of Eliot's "Tradition and the Individual Talent." While not merely taking Winterson's word for it, she is able to provide a reading of the connection between Winterson and the author whom she claims as an influence.

Winterson has been unequivocal in her statements about Eliot. She sees him as a great modernist and as an author who has heavily influenced her thinking about writing. Throughout *Art Objects*, the book of essays that includes "The Semiotics of Sex" and that references Eliot many times, Winterson only speaks negatively of his work once—saying that in Tennyson, Dickens, Joyce, and "even in T.S. Eliot" there are those "dreary passages...where the reader falls abruptly back to earth" (1996a, p. 72). Her use of the phrase "even in T.S. Eliot" gives Eliot a higher position than the other authors she mentions: even a writer as great as Eliot is capable in some instances of "dreary passages" (1996a, p. 72). In her praise of Eliot, however, Winterson even goes so far as to say: "There is at present no twentieth century poem that means more to me than *Four Quartets*" (1996a, p. 129).

Given Winterson's unambiguous statements about the importance of Eliot to her thinking about art, it is surprising that more critics have not dealt with this topic at length. However, I think there may be two things preventing such analyses. For one, some critics may see it as problematic to take the author's word as a starting point for encountering her texts. Secondly, her admiring relation to Eliot does not fit with her image as a postmodern lesbian writer, the position to which she is most often assigned by critics. It may be hard to read Winterson as the quintessential postmodern lesbian author if we take into account her admiration of T. S. Eliot.

Throughout Winterson's body of work, she incorporates many texts into her own novels. Besides Eliot's writings and poems, she alludes to fairytales, myths, fables, the Bible, the criticism of Northop Frye, and the list continues. In most cases, she engages these other texts in order to critique and to retell the stories in ways that change the meaning of the originals. However, the way she uses Eliot's poetry and prose does not fit this pattern. She is not placing Eliot into her text in order to mount a critique or to retell a story. Her work almost seems to be an attempt to extend Eliot's, to both preserve Eliot's concerns and to explore them in a new context. She seems to employ him in order that his work might touch her own.

This relationship can be seen in the story that opens my chapter. When Winterson tells the young man she meets that *Sexing the Cherry* is a reading of Eliot's *Four Quartets*, he kisses her. Though this kiss is initiated by the young man, this is clearly not an unwanted or forced kiss. Indeed, Winterson is the author of this anecdote, the agent who has turned this kiss into the ending of her own essay. In my previous chapter, the kiss was the opening into queer temporalities. In *The Hours* especially, I dealt with kisses that were transgressive because they represented nonnormative desire (the kiss, for example, between Clarissa and Richard, a lesbian and a gay man). Here we have a similar sort of kiss, a kiss between a self-declared lesbian and a man, a kiss made even more peculiar by the fact that it seems to be caused by T. S. Eliot.

Beyond the strangeness of this anecdote, Winterson's use of a kiss in this context is particularly significant given the fact that the kiss has been an important trope in a number of her novels. For example, in *The Passion*, Villanelle, one of the novel's narrators, twice discusses the types of kisses she prefers. For Villanelle, kissing should focus solely on the mouth; kisses should "fill the mouth and leave the body free" (1987, p. 59). She continues: "To kiss well one must kiss solely. No groping hands or stammering hearts. The lips and the lips alone are the pleasure" (1987, p. 59). Later when describing her first encounter with her lover, Villanelle explains how the two "lay at right angles... so that only [their] lips might meet" (1987, p. 67). In such kisses "the mouth becomes the focus of love and all things pass through it and are re-defined" (1987, p. 67).

Winterson's focus on the mouth here also calls up associations to speech, to words. This association is more clearly sketched out in *Art and Lies*, when Sappho, one of the novel's narrators, says: "She kisses me. The words that there are, fly from her lips, a flock of birds cawing at the sky.... The word and the kiss are one" (1994, p. 66). Sappho's description makes visible the connection, a connection that exists throughout Winterson's work, between sexual desire and the desire for words. It is for this reason that "The word and the kiss are one."

But what is even more significant about this line is that it is a trail leading directly back to T. S. Eliot. It echoes the last line of "Little Gidding," the final poem of *Four Quartets*, which states: "And the fire and the rose are one." Winterson's allusion to Eliot here places his words in a new context, within the language of sexual desire—rather unfamiliar territory for the poet.[4] And yet, this is continually how Eliot pops into Winterson's work—might that be why Eliot's mention at a bookstore results in a kiss between Winterson and a young man?

In the same essay that stages the kiss between Winterson and the young man, she critiques readers who will not put subjective concerns aside when choosing the authors they will read. Her examples of this are: "the man who won't read Virginia Woolf, the lesbian who won't touch T.S. Eliot" (1996b, p. 110). Winterson uses the word "touch" not in her first example of the "man who won't read Virginia Woolf" but in her example about the relation between "the lesbian" and T. S. Eliot. The lesbian should allow herself to "touch" T. S. Eliot despite the differences that may separate them. As Winterson says a few lines later, there is "artistic pleasure" to be had in this interaction (1996b, p. 110). When Winterson speaks of touching Eliot, she is speaking specifically about his writing. But her notion of touching goes beyond merely reading. It seems to imply a type of reading that includes "the ability to engage with a text as you would with another human being" (1996b, p. 111). She speaks of this relation between the reader and the text as a relation of love, a love "that offers an alternate paradigm" (1996b, p. 111). In this context, then, to "touch" T. S. Eliot is to enter into a textual love affair with his work.

Winterson's various allusions to Eliot across her novels and essays make clear her desire to "touch" T. S. Eliot. In contrast to the lesbian reader that she describes, Winterson is the lesbian who not only will, but loves to "touch T.S. Eliot" (1996b, p. 110). This is, of course, not a literal touch but a touch forged through language. If for Winterson "the word and the kiss are one," then the act of using Eliot's words is an act of desire, a desire to touch him across a temporal divide. This type of touch has been described by Carolyn Dinshaw as "a queer historical touch"—a term which she defines, with the help of Barthes, as "a desire for bodies to touch across time" (1999, p. 3). For Dinshaw, "queer histories are made...by making entities past and present touch" (1999, p. 12). Pleasure can come, she claims, from "a touching across time" (1999, p. 36).[5]

In this chapter, I am interested in examining the way in which Winterson's work might "touch" Eliot's. In this way, I am following the lead of the young man who made the "queer connection" between Eliot's poetry and Winterson's novels (Eide 2001, p. 280). Like the young man who kisses Winterson, I see the most compelling connections between the two authors in Winterson's 1989 novel *Sexing the Cherry*, a novel that, as the young man claims, can be seen as a reading of Eliot's *Four Quartets*.

But the connection between these two authors goes far deeper than the mere attempt by Winterson to produce a reading of Eliot's poem sequence. Across Winterson's novels, we can see strange temporalities emerging. As these temporalities come into focus, it becomes apparent that they are drawn directly from Eliot's work. These theories of time developed by Eliot (and critiqued by many as elitist and conservative) emerge in Winterson's work looking rather queer.

While temporality is certainly a dominant theme in Winterson's work, it is also an underexplored one. With all the attention that has been given to Winterson's role as a lesbian feminist author, her experimentations with time have often been overlooked. I would like to turn my own focus in that direction—to explore Winterson's particular (and peculiar) dealings with time. Oddly, Winterson presents us with a strikingly modernist time sense. The queer temporality that emerges in her texts is one that is underpinned by the writing of modernist authors, most visibly Eliot.[6] This is not because Winterson takes Eliot's view of time and queers it; quite the contrary, Winterson's texts show us how queer Eliot's temporalities always were. In my reading I concur with some of the recent scholarship on Eliot that highlights this "other" Eliot, to use Gabrielle McIntire's words, an Eliot who is sexier and more subversive in his purposes (2008, p. 7).

As I work to unpack the temporalities present in the work of Eliot and Winterson, there are two lines of inquiry I would like to pursue. The first concerns each author's use of the dance. In both Eliot and Winterson, the dance becomes a figure for certain temporal relations. Each author produces a form of the dance that stands in direct opposition to the temporality of reproductive futurism, to use Lee Edelman's phrase. My second line of inquiry addresses the narrative temporalities that unfold in each author's use of the journey plot. In reading the relation between the work of Eliot and that of Winterson, I hope to unpack the intricacies of this queer textual affair.

* * *

Eliot published the *Four Quartets* originally as separate poems in the years leading up to and during the Second World War. "Burnt Norton" (1936), the first of the sequence, is said to recount a trip that Eliot made to a house of the same name in North Gloucestershire in 1934. This poem begins Eliot's exploration of time with the famous lines: "Time present and time past / Are both perhaps present in time future / And time future contained in time past" (lines 1–3). The remaining poems— "East Coker" (1940), "The Dry Salvages" (1941), and "Little Gidding" (1942)—elaborate on and complicate this theme. At the center of these poems is a speaker who seeks redemption and communion with God, a speaker who must ponder the meaning of time and eternity in the course of this journey.

As I begin this section, I would like to focus specifically on the image of the dance in Eliot's poem sequence. Not only is the dance a specifically temporal image, but it is also one of the most visible ways in which Winterson's work takes up Eliot's specific brand of modernism and repurposes it to her own ends. I will therefore spend some time unpacking this image in Eliot's poems before turning to Winterson's novel.

Though mentioned in only three of the *Four Quartets*, the image of the dance is a central metaphor in the poems, one that has been analyzed often by critics. The dance, like many of Eliot's metaphors, does not have a singular meaning. Rather, there are two very distinct ways in which the dance appears throughout the poems. I will use the terms "figurative" and "literal" in order to distinguish between these two different uses. I will return to the literal, but I will first take an extended look at the more figurative uses of the dance.

The first portion of verse that deals extensively with the dance appears in part II of "Burnt Norton," the first poem of the sequence. Its appearance in this section is representative of what I will call his figurative use of this image. The portion reads:

> At the still point of the turning world. Neither flesh nor fleshless;
> Neither from nor towards; at the still point, there the dance is,
> But neither arrest nor movement. And do not call it fixity,
> Where past and future are gathered. Neither movement from nor towards,
> Neither ascent nor decline. Except for the point, the still point,
> There would be no dance, and there is only the dance. (lines 62–67)

At "the still point" is where "the dance is." This section functions to place the dance in space. Little is said to describe this dance except that it is located "at the still point." Additionally, the "still point" is the cause of the dance because "except for the point, the still point / There would be no dance" (lines 66–67). The poem thus establishes that the dance takes place *in* the stillness and *because* of the stillness.

The section relies on the pairing of various opposing elements. Besides the coupling of stillness and dancing, the neither/nor construction of the lines uses negative descriptions to show what the still point is not: "Neither flesh nor fleshless [...] Neither from nor towards [...] neither arrest nor movement [...] Neither movement from nor towards [...] Neither ascent nor decline." In contrast to these constructions, the dance is described in positive terms. It is the only term in the passage coupled with the word "is": "there the dance *is* [...] there *is* only the dance" (emphasis added). The word "is" not only places the dance in space ("there," "at the still point"), but also denotes existence, and in this case, existence in the present tense. The dance thus is perpetual and ongoing in the present. The dance "is."

Besides the movement that is inherent in the dance (for dance is, of course, a stylized form of movement), the only other definite movement we see in this section of the poem is "the turning world." The world's only descriptor is the word "turning," meaning that the world is defined solely by its movement, in contrast to the still point. And significantly, this movement is circular, a constant "turning." Thus, "the still point of the turning world" is where "the dance is." This image has often been described by critics through reference to a wheel (Bergsten 1960, p. 78).

The outside of the wheel turns, but the exact center remains motionless (Bay-Petersen 1985, p. 147). And it is here, in the stillness of the center, that Eliot's dance occurs.

But what is the dance exactly? Eliot is using the concept of the dance metaphorically in order to explore the relation between stillness and movement, but critics have often disagreed on exactly what the dance is meant to represent. For some, the dance represents the cosmic order. For Staffan Bergsten, the dance is "the unmoving motion of the time-less" (1960, p. 90). For Michael Spencer, the dance is "a manifestation of joy. It tells of a joy so intense from living with god that it is as if the soul is dancing" (Spencer 1999, p. 246). Despite the various interpretations of this metaphor, most critics agree that this image is tied to the poem's exploration of time.

The poem's figurative use of the dance metaphor works to demonstrate the coming together of two different temporalities. The still point, as a number of critics have pointed out, is representative of eternity. Only in eternity does all time exist simultaneously. Because of this, there is no movement through time but the stillness of simultaneous existence. Conversely, "the turning world" is representative of human time. Within this context, the image of the wheel becomes a temporal image. As Bergsten states, "The perpetually moving circumference of the wheel is the material world, which is subject to change and temporal flux; the center of the wheel, 'the still point,' is the world of the Absolute, of eternity" (1960, p. 79). Because it occurs at the still point, "time and eternity may be said to be reconciled in the dance" (Bergsten 1960, p. 178). The dance is the place at which seemingly contradictory elements are able to coexist, including time and timelessness.

This coexistence of stillness and movement, though introduced through the image of the dance, recurs through the poems. In "Burnt Norton" there are several references that describe something as "still and moving" (line 73), including "a Chinese jar" that "still / Moves perpetually in its stillness" (lines 142–143). In "East Coker," we are told: "We must be still and still moving / Into another intensity / For a further union" (lines 204–206). A variant on this trope also recurs in this poem in relation to the dance: "the stillness [shall be] the dancing" (line 128).

For Eliot, this union between movement and stillness, between time and timelessness, is significant because it represents the place in which humans can achieve momentary union with God. A few critics have talked about this aspect of the *Four Quartets* in terms of mysticism.[7]

Though I am not going to discuss whether Eliot's description of the "moment out of time" is synonymous with mystic experience, I think it is important to establish that this union of time and timelessness is something that the speaker of the poem seeks, that the dance at the still point seems to represent, in some ways, an object of desire for the speaker.[8]

This "figurative" use of the dance that we find in Eliot plays quite a central role in Winterson's *Sexing the Cherry*. Winterson's novel, published in 1989, presents us with four different speakers, two who are living during the seventeenth century in England and two who serve as their twentieth-century doubles. The two seventeenth-century characters, Jordan and Dog-woman, narrate the majority of the novel, with their counterparts only interjecting their voices in the final pages.[9] Because the novel's theories of time are best articulated though the character of Jordan, I have chosen to focus my discussion of the novel primarily on the sections narrated by this character. Jordan is a foundling who is raised by his adoptive mother Dog-woman, a mountain of a woman who lives with a few dozen dogs. As a child Jordan sails toy sailboats, and he grows up to be an explorer who brings back exotic fruits to England. But most of all Jordan is a dreamer and a narrator who gives precedence to his internal journeys over his "real" ones. Jordan spends the entire novel searching for Fortunata, a dancer who he sees in one of the journeys he takes in his "hidden life" (1989, p. 2). The narrative structure of the text makes it ultimately unclear as to whether Jordan ever finds her.

In Winterson's novel, the image of the dance is explored primarily through the character of Fortunata. Long before Jordan ever meets her, Fortunata has escaped a forced marriage and has instead chosen dancing as a way of life. She has opened up a dance school to teach others her particular manner of dance. Perhaps the most detailed sketch of Fortunata's dance can be found in the description of her school. Because of the richness of this description, I would like to quote from this passage at length:

> *At a dancing school in a remote place, Fortunata teaches her pupils to become points of light. ...She spins them, impaled with light, arms upraised, one leg at a triangle across the other thigh, one foot, on point, on a penny coin, and spins them, until all features are blurred, until the human being most resembles a freed spirit from a darkened jar...And at a single moment, when all are spinning in harmony down the long hall, she hears music escaping from*

their heads and backs and livers and spleens. Each has a tone like cut glass.
The noise is deafening. And it is then that the spinning seems to stop, that the
wild gyration of the dancers passes from movement into infinity…The polished
wooden floor glows with the heat of their bodies, and one by one they crumble
over and lie exhausted on the ground. Fortunata refreshes them and the dance
begins again. (1989, pp. 76–77; italics in original)

This section of the text is riddled with allusions to the *Four Quartets*.
The passage begins by stating: "*Fortunata teaches her pupils to become*
points of light" (1989, p. 76). This image of the "point of light" is drawn
from Eliot and is often connected to the paradoxical association of stillness and movement that he attributes to the dance throughout his poem
sequence. For example, the phrase "a white light, still and moving"
appears in "Burnt Norton," and the image is repeated later in the same
poem: "the light is still / At the still point of the turning world" (lines
135–136). This image connects Fortunata's dance to the dance that
occurs "at the still point," the dance that in Eliot is defined by the paradoxical association of stillness and movement.

But perhaps the most noticeable connection to the *Four Quartets* is
the moment in which "*the spinning seems to stop*" and "*the wild gyration*
of the dancers passes from movement to infinity." Like the reference to
light, this mention of the passing "*from movement to infinity*" is also an
image of something being both "still and moving." The dancers' "*wild*
gyration" becomes so fast, that that "*the spinning seems to stop*" and thus
stillness and movement appear to exist simultaneously.[10]

But beyond this, the "*single moment*" in which "*the spinning seems to*
stop" has an added significance. The appearance of the word "*infinity*"
in this context connects the image of the dance in Winterson to temporal concerns. Because dancing allows Fortunata's students to pass "*from*
movement to infinity," we can see how Winterson, like Eliot, is using the
image to denote the simultaneous existence of two modes of time. In
this dance, Fortunata and her students are able momentarily to transcend
human time in order to take part in eternal or infinite time.

The moment in which the dancers "*pass from movement to infinity*"
is also reminiscent of those moments of "sudden illumination," which,
for Eliot, often denote the experience of the eternal within the temporal. Though Eliot has multiple ways to refer to such moments—"the
moment in and out of time" ("The Dry Salvages," line 207), "the timeless moment" ("Little Gidding," lines 52, 235)—what defines these

moments is their ability to allow for a momentary connection to all time. For the speaker of the poem, these moments are only "hints and guesses" at what will ultimately be possible in an eventual union with God ("The Dry Salvages," line 212). Thus, in Eliot, as in Winterson, these "timeless moment[s]" seem to be transcendent moments. Winterson describes how Fortunata spins each dancer until "*the human being most resembles a freed spirit from a darkened jar*" (1989, p. 76). Such a description positions the dance as a conduit for transcendence, as an action that allows the "*spirit*" to be "*freed*" from its confines momentarily.

As Susana Onega claims, "what Fortunata is teaching Jordan—and her other pupils as well—is to spin himself into a point of light, to transcend time and reach what T.S. Eliot (1963) [sic] would call 'the still point,' that is, Jordan is taught to control the dance of life and to negotiate his leap into eternity or, in mythical terms, to transcend his human condition" (1996, pp. 310–311).[11] I agree with Onega that this dance is ultimately about the ability to "transcend time." However, I would assert that, like in Eliot, this transcendence is not necessarily about transcending time altogether, but about attaining a different relationship to time, a relation that allows for the experience of eternity in a single moment.

There is, however, one key difference between how Winterson and Eliot employ this image of the dance—a difference that can perhaps help to show how Winterson not only employs Eliot's modernist temporalities but also reinvigorates them to be more accountable to the materiality of bodies. While the text here seems to be referencing what I earlier called Eliot's figurative use of the image of the dance, I find it quite interesting that *Sexing the Cherry* places these elements of the "figurative" dance within a more literal, if not realistic, frame. Here we are not talking about the dance abstractly, as Eliot does, but about dancers and their specific dance. Winterson's use of this image brings the body into her exploration of time. For Eliot, the body seems to be outside this specific mode of time; it is a time that is capable of transcending the body. But in Winterson's descriptions of the dancers passing into infinity, it is hard not to notice the way in which the passage evokes the body in every sentence both in its effects (sweat, "the heat of their bodies") and in its parts (arms, leg, thigh, foot, heads, backs, livers, spleens).

While there are multiple ways to read this passage, the sheer presence of the body in the dance says much about Winterson's use of this image. Some Winterson critics have used this section to show how she is complicit in dualist understandings of the body/mind. In this, Winterson's work is said to line up with canonical readings of Eliot in believing that the body can be transcended. For example, Fortunata says to her dancers: "*Through the body, the body is conquered*" (1989, p. 76; italics in original). Fortunata's statement here echoes a line from *Four Quartets*: "Only through time time is conquered" ("Burnt Norton," line 90). In Eliot criticism, this line is often read (especially by those who focus on the Christian aspects of the poems) to mean that time is conquered by time because the return of the savior (an act that results in the end of time as we know it) unfolds within human time. Winterson's revision of this line, "Through the body, the body is conquered," can be read as a testament to the belief that transcending the body is both possible and desirable, that the body can be used as a conduit to attain that state most desired: release from the body. However, this line can also be read as doing something else, as reinserting the body back into philosophical understandings of time, like Eliot's in *Four Quartets*.[12] For ultimately, the bodies of the dancers are not "conquered"; they continue past the moment when "*the wild gyration of the dancers passes from movement into infinity*" (1989, p. 76; italics in original). Their bodies "*crumple over*" onto the floor before "*Fortunata refreshes them and the dance begins again*" (1989, p. 77; italics in original). It seems almost as though it is the body that allows for this momentary experience of a different temporality. It is the spinning of their bodies that allows them to pass into infinity and experience the intersection of movement and stillness.

The body's relation to time is quite complicated throughout Winterson's entire novel. As my reading of Fortunata's dance school shows, Winterson emphasizes the body in those same moments that seem to lean toward transcendence of the body. For Winterson, the body's existence in time is not defined by its movement through time. The body's ability to grow old and decay is not the aspect of the body on which Winterson focuses. Quite the opposite, in fact. She often shows how bodies that should have succumbed to time, have not. In discussing the dancers at Fortunata's school, the novel states: "*Bodies that could have bent double and grown numb [Fortunata] maintains as metal in a fiery furnace, tempering, stretching, forcing sinews into impossible shapes and calling her art nature*" (1989, p. 76; italics in original). Similarly, Fortunata too should be old, as her sisters say, but she is not. This is quite different from Eliot who often positions the body or the flesh as synonymous with decay and death, as the very thing that separates one from experiencing the eternal. For example, "Burnt Norton" states: "Yet the enchainment of past and future / Woven in the weakness of the changing body, / Protects mankind from heaven and damnation / Which flesh cannot endure" (lines 79–82). The body here is what separates individuals from eternal forms of time (the time of "heaven" or of "damnation"). By placing the body within these forms of time, Winterson thus shifts the grounds of this metaphor.

This is not to say that Winterson deviates very far from Eliot's depiction of the dance. Though Winterson does return the body to the image of the dance, the goal of the dance is ultimately the same in both texts: to achieve the union of stillness and movement, of time and timelessness. Winterson's description of the dance, like Eliot's, does seem to lean toward moments of transcendence. Significantly, however, for both authors, there is a moment after the moment of transcendence, a moment where, to use Winterson's words, our bodies "*crumble over and lie exhausted on the ground*" (1989, pp. 76–77; italics in original). For Winterson and Eliot, then, there is an ultimate recognition that these flashes of illumination are only momentary.

*   *   *

In contrast to this figurative usage of "the dance," a usage that is primarily philosophical, there are also a few times in the *Four Quartets* that Eliot uses dancing in a much more literal sense. In these instances, Eliot often presents images of actual dancers and explores the social functions and meanings related to dancing. The most significant instance of such a use occurs in the first section of "East Coker" and begins:

> In that open field
> If you do not come too close, if you do not come too close,
> On a summer midnight, you can hear the music
> Of the weak pipe and the little drum
> And see them dancing around the bonfire
> The association of man and woman
> In daunsinge, signifying matrimonie—
> A dignified and commodiois sacrament.
> Two and two, necessarye coniunction,
> Holding eche other by the hand or the arm
> Whiche betokeneth concorde. (lines 24–34)

Here Eliot refers to the dance within a passage that uses archaic language; dancing thus becomes "daunsinge." This "daunsinge" is the dance of man and woman around a bonfire, a dance that signifies the union of man and woman in "matrimonie." The language of the poem begins in modern English for the first six lines but then shifts to an older form of English, a move that places dancing as a ritual that connects multiple time periods. Dancing is thus part of the human life cycle across generations. It is worth noting also that the language used in the second part of this passage is drawn from Sir Thomas Elyot's "The Governour" (1531). This text, written by a distant relative of Eliot himself, is a book of manners designed to teach respectable young people how to conduct themselves. In drawing on the language of a text written by an ancestor, this section of Eliot's text enacts a genealogical time frame, a temporality which will be explored at length in my next chapter.

The dance not only links generations across time but also is directly connected to the institution of marriage. The "association of man and woman / In daunsinge," as the poem states, is what "signify[es] matrimonie." The dancers are "Holding eche other by the hand or the arm / Whiche betokeneth concorde." There is a focus in this part of the poem on the dance as a symbol for the coupling of men and women in marriage. Even the phrase "two and two" places individuals into coupled pairs. The phrase recalls the book of Genesis when the animals are loaded onto the ark: "There went in two and two unto Noah into the ark, the male and the female, as God had commanded Noah" (*King James Bible*, Gen. 7.9). The animals are loaded in the ark male and female, two by two, in order to ensure for reproduction. This "literal" dance, as I have called it, is thus inseparable from both the institution of marriage and from the coupling of male and female for the purpose of reproduction.

Because of this, the dance partakes of a particular temporality, the temporality of marriage and reproduction. Indeed, a few lines later the poem directly references this sort of temporality, referring to it as "The time of the coupling of man and woman / And that of beasts" (lines 44–45). In contrast to the time of eternity presented in the sections that deal with the figurative use of "the dance," here we have a temporality that is defined by coupling, by marriage, by reproduction.

Though the tone of the section that I quoted at length above might seem somewhat celebratory of the type of "daunsinge" that "signify[es] matrimonie," as the passage continues the tone seems to shift:

> Keeping time,
> Keeping the rhythm in their dancing
> As in their living in the living seasons
> ....
> ....
> The time of the coupling of man and woman
> And that of beasts. Feet rising and falling.
> Eating and drinking. Dung and death. (lines 39–46)

The passage highlights, in its echoing of Ecclesiastes, the rhythmic, repeating pattern of the seasons. Within this framework, all things fit into a larger cosmic order. But for the speaker of the poem, this form of time is ultimately unsatisfying as it leads inevitably to "Dung and death." The phrases "Feet rising and falling" and "Eating and drinking" seem to point to a cycle of endless, meaningless repetition. Likewise, the "coupling of man and woman" belongs to, and is representative of, a temporality defined by predictability and repetition. According to William H. Klein, this section "is an attempt to see the cycle of decay, death, and renewal as meaningful, for there is a purpose to every time under heaven," but this attempt is ultimately unsuccessful as the speaker is unable to see this form of time as anything more than meaningless recurrence (1994, p. 30).

What this section ultimately shows, then, is the way in which Eliot has positioned the dance of the couple in opposition to the dance that exists "at the still point." When used literally, the dance no longer represents the coexistence of various forms of time, but instead the repetitive (and, for Eliot's speaker, ultimately unfulfilling) temporality of marriage and reproduction. This is not the dance that ends in a "sudden illumination" but rather one whose ultimate result is "Dung and death."

Like the *Four Quartets*, Winterson's novel also shows considerable distaste for the temporality associated with the coupled dance. There is only one direct reference in *Sexing the Cherry* to a dancing couple, and this comes from Nicolas Jordan, Jordan's present-day doppelganger and one of the novel's four narrators. Nicolas speaks to his parents about his career in the navy:

> "What if there's a war?" said my mother.
> "You and I were both in the war," said my father. "We're all right."
> "It was nerve-racking," said my mother.
> "It wasn't too bad, we had good times – do you remember when we danced together and then made love in the dark?"

"Don't say that in front of Nicolas," said my mother. Then, after a
little pause, "It was nerve-racking."
Did she mean the war or making love to my father? (1989, p. 135)

In this passage, dancing is tied to "making love" for Nicolas's parents.
While it might be expected that the dancing and the making love would
be a positive memory for Nicolas's mother, her response that "it was
nerve-racking" raises doubt about her feelings regarding the experience.
As Nicolas notes, she could be referring to the war, but she could also be
referring to the lovemaking. The dancing that appears here is similar to
the type of dance that takes place around the bonfire in "East Coker,"
the courting dance of men and women. This is also the type of dance
this is connected inevitably to reproduction. Winterson perhaps makes
this association even more visible than Eliot by having the lovemaking
directly follow Nicolas's parents' dance. Winterson even goes so far as
to equate the dancing and lovemaking that occurs here with war. It is
thus significant that this type of dance is associated with feelings of stress
("it was nerve-racking") or at the very least remains uncelebrated by
Nicolas's mother.

   Though the above passage is somewhat ambiguous in its description of the coupled dance, elsewhere in the novel there is considerable
effort made to separate the type of dancing that the text valorizes (that
transcendent dance that Fortunata teaches at her dance school) from
the dance of the couple. Indeed, we might say that Fortunata's dance is
placed in direct opposition to the dance of the couple and to marriage
more generally. This can be seen most clearly through the fairytale of
"The Twelve Dancing Princesses."

   Early on in the novel, Jordan has occasion to meet the twelve dancing
princesses and hear their story. It is important to note, however, that the
story of "The Twelve Dancing Princesses," originally a fairytale written
by the Grimm Brothers, is radically rewritten within the novel.[13] Though
the story begins in a familiar fashion—the king will offer the hand of any
of his daughters in marriage to the man who is able to discover where
the women are disappearing to at night—the novel writes beyond the
ending of this particular fairytale. As the oldest sister tells Jordan, "we
were all given in marriage…and as it says lived happily ever after. We
did, but not with our husbands" (1989, p. 48). Eleven of the dancing
princesses then describe what happened to them after their wedding day.
After their marriages, all of the women eventually end up parting with

their husbands and live "scattered, according to [their] tastes," until they buy a house together to reside in (1989, p. 48). The *story* of "The Twelve Dancing Princesses" thus becomes the *stories* told by the twelve dancing princesses. Instead of being characters in their collective tale told by another, each princess becomes the narrator of her own story.

The role of dancing within the original tale about the princesses is that of the unknown. The king cannot figure out why their shoes are worn out each morning, as their doors are locked each night. The dancing takes place outside the princesses' conventional lives; they escape at night, without their father's permission. They are thus outside of the mandates of patriarchal law in two ways: they are disobeying their father as father and their father as king. They are also outside a normative sense of time. Their nights spent dancing do not seem to follow a "logical" temporality. How is it possible to wear out shoes by dancing a single night? Indeed, the city to which the princesses escape is described in temporal opposition to their own: "From this room, in the past, we had flown to a silver city that knew neither day nor night, and in that city we had danced for joy thinking nothing of the dawn where we lived" (1989, p. 105). The silver city knows "neither day nor night," and temporal markers, like "the dawn," belong not to this city but to the world of their father's house.[14]

Dancing thus places the princesses out of sync with conventional time, or more specifically, the temporality of marriage and reproduction. Since their father, in a plot device typical of fairytales, has offered them in marriage to whomever can discover where they escape to at night, the temporality of their dancing is in direct opposition to marriage.[15] The princesses' dancing is thus put to an end when a young prince discovers their secret by clinging to their skirts as they fly away for the night. For solving this mystery, he and his eleven brothers are each awarded one of the princesses in marriage. Marriage here puts the women back into a more conventional temporality. The strange temporality of the nightlong dance ends when the women take their places within the social order as wives. And this is where the traditional fairytale ends. The coupling of marriage has ended the princess's dancing and turns the fantastical time of the dance into normative time. Marriage has solved the problem posed at the narrative's opening and allows all the characters to proceed into the time of "happily ever after," which is, of course, synonymous with a long blissful married life complete with the reproduction of lots of little baby princes and princesses. The phrase "happily ever after" also suggests an eternity, a time that continues forever. In this sense, conventional marriage is presented within the fairytale as the norm for all time coming, as a timeless truth. There is no place for the princesses' form of dancing in the marriage plot and thus their dancing ends when marriage occurs to stop it. The temporality of dancing and that of marriage are diametrically opposed. In this way, Winterson follows Eliot in conceiving a form of dance that is separate from and opposed to the coupled dance.

Though Winterson writes beyond this fairytale ending such that the princesses all eventually part with their husbands and do not live "happily ever after" in the typical way, there is one princess who escapes the marriage plot ending entirely. The eldest of the dancing princesses recounts the story of how on their wedding day, one of her sisters "flew from the altar like a bird from a snare and walked a tightrope between the steeple of the church and the mast of a ship weighing anchor in the bay" (1989, p. 61). This is the youngest princess, Fortunata. And she, tellingly, is the one who still dances, the dancer whom Jordan seeks. "She was, of all of us," says the eldest sister, "the best dancer, the one who made her body into shapes we could not follow. She did it for pleasure, but there was something more for her; she did it because any other life would have been a lie" (1989, p. 61). Marriage does not end Fortunata's relationship with dancing. Because she, unlike her sisters, walks out (or rather flies out) of the fairytale before entering the temporality of "happily ever after," she occupies throughout the story a different temporality, one associated with the dance. Her sisters postulate that "she must be old now, she must be stiff. Her body can only be a memory. The body she has will not be the body she had" (1989, p. 61). And yet, we see that this is not true. Fortunata appears throughout the story as young and as "light" as her sisters describe her. Seemingly, her relationship to dance puts her out of sync with normative time. Because she does not move through marriage as her sisters do, she does not experience the passing of time in the same way. Similarly to how time behaved oddly for the sisters while dancing in the silver city, Fortunata's dancing keeps her perpetually in a strange relation to time.

It is important to note, also, that Fortunata's dance is a solitary dance. Fortunata is never described as dancing with someone else, but always dancing alone. Even at her dance school where she trains other dancers, their dances all seem to be solitary. At one point she even tells Jordan "that for years she had lived in hope of being rescued; of belonging to someone else, of dancing together. And then she had learned to dance alone, for its own sake and for hers" (1989, p. 112). Fortunata's dance is her own. She never couples, not with Jordan, not with the husband to whom she is promised, not to someone of her own choosing. Instead of desiring someone to dance with, she learns to desire the dance "for its own sake" (1989, p. 112).

I emphasize this point because it can help us to see how Winterson's use of the dance parallels Eliot's in its utter dismissal of the type of dancing that is associated with the couple, a dance that, as "East Coker" demonstrates, is inextricably tied up in the temporality of marriage and reproduction. Though it might seem predictable that Winterson would reject such temporality, Eliot's dismissal is a bit more surprising. While the two texts have different aims in their rejection of the coupled dance, what connects them is a similar figuration of "the time of the coupling of man and woman" as repetitive and predictably scripted. For Eliot, the coupled dance is associated with the endless repetition of "Eating and drinking. Dung and Death." For Winterson, it is associated with normative narrative endings, the "happily ever after." For both authors, then, the coupled dance represents a sense of time that leads invariably to predictable endings. Indeed—what is a more predictable narrative ending than marriage or death?

Both texts thus seem to reject the temporality of reproductive futurism that I have sketched out in both my introduction and second chapter. Winterson does this by refusing to allow stories to progress toward normative narrative endings. And Eliot shows how the temporality of marriage and reproduction is representative of oppressive, endlessly recurring cycles. Interestingly, both texts do this through reference to the couple. Both authors refuse to extend to the couple the privileged position that it so often occupies.

* * *

At this point, I would like to turn to consider the narrative temporalities of these two texts. Though I would not describe the *Four Quartets* as primarily narrative poems, I see two narrative strands that run through the complete sequence. These narrative strands are pivotal to sketching out how Winterson is taking up not only Eliot's image of the dance in her novel but also playing with his configurations of narrative time. Winterson's reconsideration of the journeys that occur in the *Four Quartets* show us that Eliot's narrative endings are perhaps more complex than they appear at first glance.

Because both narrative strands that I address are quite rich and stretch across all four poems, I will deal with each separately and at length. The first narrative thread of the *Quartets* concerns an experience that occurs in "the rose-garden" down a passage the speaker "did not take / Towards the door [he] never opened" ("Burnt Norton," lines 12–14). This is a journey that the speaker did not actually take, but one that he *might* have taken. Inside the garden, the speaker has what could be described as a visionary experience and hears in the leaves the laughter of children. This experience relates to what the poem calls "what might have been" or "a world of speculation" (lines 6, 8). The "rose-garden" image returns at the end of "Little Gidding," when we "arrive where we started / And know the place for the first time" (lines 241–242). It is here at the end of the poem that the speaker finally understands the meaning of the experience in the rose garden. Conversely, during the poem sequence, there was an emphasis on experience without understanding: "the sudden illumination— / We had the experience but missed the meaning" ("The Dry Salvages," lines 92–93). The reconsideration of the moment in the rose garden is important because it seems to give philosophical significance to "what might have been." Rather than discarding the experience that occurs only in the mind, the poem seems to affirm the ultimate presence of this "world of speculation" ("Burnt Norton," line 8).

A number of Eliot critics have attempted to examine the experience in the rose garden. Though these readings differ greatly, most critics focus on the significance of a moment that occurred in the rose garden, a moment often described as a vision. Fewer critics explore the fact this experience is a speculative one, a symbol for "what might have been." Winterson's novel, however, focuses heavily on this aspect of the poem. What was perhaps of lesser significance in Eliot's poem becomes a central concern in *Sexing the Cherry*. Winterson makes concrete this "world of speculation" and attempts to explore its implications.

From the beginning of the novel it is clear that Jordan, one of the text's four narrators, lives in two different worlds. Literally, he lives as a sailor who journeys to faraway lands and brings back fruits to England. Jordan has taken many literal journeys, but these are not the ones he narrates. We only hear about his sea voyages through his mother's narration. Instead, Jordan wishes to describe other journeys:

> Every journey conceals another within its lines: the path not taken and the forgotten angle. These are the journeys I wish to record. Not the ones I made, but the ones I might have made, or perhaps did make in some other place or time. I could tell you the truth as you will find it in diaries and maps and log-books. I could faithfully describe all that I saw and heard and give you a travel book. You could follow it then, tracing your finger, putting flags where I went. (1989, p. 2)

Jordan does not wish to tell the story of his travels in the manner of "diaries" and "log-books," but instead wishes to record "the path not taken," the journeys he "might have made." In this way, he seems to be interested in the type of experience signified by the "rose-garden" in *Four Quartets*, the journey "Down the passage which we did not take / Towards the door we never opened" ("Burnt Norton," lines 12–13). It is the "hidden life," as he states later, the "life flaring up undetected," that interests Jordan. And indeed, the stories that Jordan tells are the fantastical stories that belong to the temporality of "what might have been."

In this aspect, Jordan sounds a lot like Eliot's speaker who describes an experience in a rose garden that he never actually entered. According to Doris Wight in her reading of Eliot, the footfalls that echo in the memory is an instance of "remembering what hasn't yet happened" (1990, p. 65). This is made possible, Wight claims, by stepping "outside the 'real' world into the unreal one, the world of 'perpetual possibility' (line 7), a 'world of speculation' (line 8), '*in your mind*'" (1990, p. 65; emphasis in original). Throughout *Sexing the Cherry*, Jordan is continually stepping "outside the 'real' world into the unreal one." He explains: "To escape from the weight of the world, I leave my body where it is, in conversation or at dinner, and walk through a series of winding streets to a house standing back from the road" (1989, p. 11). In instances such as these, Jordan leaves the "real" world and enters into one that exists solely in his mind, much like Eliot's speaker, who, as Michael Spencer claims, "one minute...may be present in one world, but absent from it the next minute, gone into the other place" (2005, p. 41).

Jordan often talks about this experience of going to "the unreal world" as passing through a door. For example, early on in the novel, he describes how he "resolved to set watch on [himself] like a jealous father, trying to catch [himself] disappearing through a door just noticed in the wall" (1989, p. 2). Later he claims: "The self is not contained in any moment or any place, but it is only in the intersection of moment and place that the self might, for a moment, be seen vanishing through a door, which disappears at once" (1989, p. 87). This image of the door seems to be a direct reference to "the door we never opened" (line 8) in "Burnt Norton." Winterson's use of Eliot's door image seems to further connect those internal journeys that Jordan takes to the intense experience that the speaker has in the rose garden he never actually visited.

What becomes visible when we read the rose garden section in conjunction with *Sexing the Cherry* is the way in which a different temporality comes into focus. The experience in the rose garden thus seems to represent a type of temporality that is different from both human time and eternity. This is not the human time that measures past and future, nor is it the eternal time that is separate from life on earth. This is the time of "what might have been," to use Eliot's words. This is a temporality that runs parallel to human time—when Jordan leaves his body and travels internally, human time still passes normally, but Jordan is disconnected from it, born into a world of "perpetual possibility" ("Burnt Norton," line 7). Within this world, time is freed of many of its constraints.

Beyond this, both authors insist on the ultimate presence and significance of "what might have been." The experience that the speaker has in the rose garden is quite a significant one, one that is echoed throughout the poems and whose meaning becomes clear in the last poem of the sequence. In this way, this speculative experience is shown to have real effects on the speaker of the poem. The speaker repeats twice in "Burnt Norton" the lines: "What might have been and what has been / Point to one end, which is always present" (lines 9–10, 45–46). Though the speaker initially seems unsure how to characterize "what might have been," stating that it "is an abstraction" (line 6), the repetition of those two lines affirms the importance of "what might have been." Indeed, it places "what might have been" as parallel to "what has been." In this way, "what has been" and "what might have been" are equally and always "present." Like Jordan who believes his internal journeys are as significant as his more literal ones, the speaker does not prioritize "what has been" over "what might have been."

While critics who focus on the temporal aspects of the *Four Quartets* discuss a number of temporalities that exist in the poem, they often shortchange this speculative form of time. Reading Eliot through Winterson thus allows us to reexamine Eliot's use of the temporality of "what might have been." This form of time becomes particularly relevant in relation to the other narrative that runs through the poem sequence.

The second narrative strand in the *Four Quartets* is perhaps the more visible one, as it is a much more conventional quest narrative. In "Burnt Norton," readers are introduced to a speaker who seems to be on a quest. The purpose of this quest, according to most critics, is a perfect union with God. As Nancy Gish claims, this explorer is not on a quest for faith, for that is already assumed from the beginning, but searching for a type of understanding that will allow him to unite with the divine (1981, p. 92). This union with God is often described by critics in terms of Incarnation. While the term Incarnation is used most often to denote the doctrine that states that Jesus Christ assumed human form and was both completely God and man, here the term is used more loosely to mean the union possible between the divine and the human. Within this quest, then, the speaker's object of desire is this type of relation to God. When we come to the end of the poem, the speaker points to a future when such a union will be possible, "When the tongues of flame are in-folded / Into the crowned knot of fire / And the fire and the rose are one" ("Little Gidding," line 259).

This quest is paralleled in *Sexing the Cherry* by Jordan's quest to find the object of his desire, Fortunata. In Jordan's "hidden life," he first encounters Fortunata in a grand floating house, though he only sees her momentarily and from a distance. He initially describes her as "a woman whose face was a sea voyage [he] had not the courage to attempt" (1989, p. 15). Here Fortunata is figured as a voyage, and, indeed, Jordan will spend much of the novel attempting to find her. At first Fortunata is quite illusive, and Jordan's attempts to locate her lead only to dead ends. But in the process of this journey, Jordan begins to question its very nature. He asks himself: "Was I searching for a dancer whose name I did not know or was I searching for the dancing part of myself" (1989, p. 39). The literal journey to find a dancer is ultimately eclipsed by the more figurative journey to find and understand the nature of the dance itself and his own relation to it. As my readings of this novel have shown, dancing often represents a strange relation to time. Specifically, Fortunata's dance has been connected to the ability to be "still and moving" simultaneously. What Jordan is searching for, then, is a particular way of perceiving time, a time sense that does not lock him into one place and time but one that allows him to be both "still and moving."

Jordan's attempts to achieve this relation to time can be seen most clearly in his internal journeys. The novel recounts a number of instances where Jordan leaves his body and travels internally in his mind. In these instances, he leaves his "body where it is, in conversation or at dinner, and walk[s] through a series of winding streets" (1989, p. 11). When caught in one such moment by his mother, he is described as "standing stock still" (1989, p. 6). The stillness of his body is thus contrasted with the invisible movement of his internal journeys. This image of "still and moving" can also apply to the temporal mode associated with such experiences. For Jordan's body left "in conversation or at dinner," only a moment may pass, while internally time might be moving quite rapidly.

Jordan himself speaks of this desire to be both "still and moving" when he tells of a town he sometimes dreams about "whose inhabitants...knock down their houses in a single night and rebuild them elsewhere" (1989, p. 43). About this town, he states: "the inhabitants have reconciled two discordant desires: to remain in one place and to leave it behind for ever" (1989, p. 43). These "discordant desires," though he attributes them to the inhabitants of this town, are Jordan's own desires. They represent his incompatible desires that appear throughout the novel, most specifically the desire to be both "still and moving." The quest of the novel is thus the quest to achieve this particular relation to time.

Jordan's desire, then, is quite similar to that of the *Four Quartets'* speaker. While the speaker specifically seeks a particular relation to God, this relation is discussed primarily in terms of time. As Bodelsen states "The Quartets are about a certain kind of religious experience, but it would be equally true to say that they are about *time*" (1966, p. 33). The union with God that the speaker seeks is ultimately a desire to experience human time and eternity simultaneously. And Incarnation makes this possible. As Ole Bay-Petersen states: "Through the Incarnation time is redeemed, and the temporal (man) is forever united with the eternal (God)" (1985, p. 147). Indeed, in his reading of Eliot, William H. Klein describes Incarnation itself as "the point of intersection of the timeless with time" (1994, p. 29). In the only occurrence of the word "Incarnation" in the poem sequence, Eliot too positions it in relation to time:

> The hint half guessed, the gift half understood, is Incarnation.
> Here the impossible union
> Of spheres of existence is actual,
> Here the past and future
> Are conquered, and reconciled. ("The Dry Salvages," lines 215–219)

Incarnation is thus the "impossible union / Of spheres of existence." It is in Incarnation that multiple forms of time "Are conquered, and reconciled." This is the union with God that is "for most of us…the aim / never here to be realized" ("The Dry Salvages," lines 226–227). In this way, the union of God and human is also the union of two different forms of time. The speaker of the *Four Quartets* and Jordan thus seem to be on a similar journey. Both set out to seek a union with another (God or Fortunata), but each discovers in the course of their journey that they are predominantly searching for a certain relation to time.

And this returns us to the idea of a quest in and of itself. The quest is a quite familiar plot, and it partakes of a most conventional temporality. Quest narratives generally move forward linearly as the protagonist progresses toward his object of desire (and I use "his" deliberately because it conventionally is the journey of a male). At first glance, Eliot's poem seems to display this conventional temporality of the quest.

This form of temporality becomes visible as both of the poem's narrative strands approach resolution in the final stanza. The speaker gestures toward a time when "all shall be well and / All manner of thing shall be well" ("Little Gidding," lines 55–56). Though the desire to experience time and eternity simultaneously is not directly achieved at the end of the poem, the speaker implies that this will occur "When the tongues of flame are in-folded / Into the crowned knot of fire" (lines 57–58). If the speaker's quest in the poem is to achieve a certain relation to time, then the fulfillment of this goal is certainly figured as inevitable, if not in the present tense of the poem, then in a forthcoming future. Additionally, we are also pointed to a future in which that other narrative strand is resolved, in which the meaning of the experience in the rose garden will become intelligible. Though the speaker did not understand the significance of the rose garden experience when it was happening, he will eventually be able to return to this place with a new understanding. This way of figuring time is synonymous with the way time most often functions in narrative. Narratives are meant to move characters through time in a way that leads toward the fulfillment of desire (though it is not always fulfilled) and also toward better under-standing. The poem thus leaves the speaker in a moment where the future holds both the fulfillment of his desire and the understanding of his experiences.

And yet, reading Winterson alongside Eliot raises doubt as to the finality of the ending of his poem. Does this poem point to a future in which a union with God is inevitable, or do the very twistings of time that occur throughout the poem put this end perpetually in ques-tion? After all, throughout the poem sequence, Eliot often questions the very idea of endings. The question becomes: how do we read the complex and paradoxical temporalities that permeate Eliot's poem in relation to its quite conventional rendering of the quest narrative? To answer this question, I would like to turn to the ending of *Sexing the Cherry*.

Winterson's novel ends on quite a different note than Eliot's poem sequence. In Winterson, we have not the hope of a future in which desire will be fulfilled but the questioning of the notions of past, present, and future. Jordan states:

> The future lies ahead like a glittering city, but like the cities of the desert disappears when approached....We speak of it with longing and with love. *The future*. But the city is a fake. The future and the present and the past exist only in our minds, and from a distance the borders of each shrink and fade like the borders of hostile countries seen from a floating city in the sky. The river runs from one country to another without stopping. (1989, p. 167; emphasis in original)

The novel removes the future as that which we are oriented toward, as the object that can fulfill our desires. Perhaps this could be considered a rewriting of the *Four Quartet*'s ending, if it weren't for one thing. Winterson's understanding of time in this passage bears a striking resem-blance to lines from the poem sequence: "Time past and time future / What might have been and what has been / Point to one end, which is always present" ("Burnt Norton," lines 46–48). The central idea found in these lines, and a number of other times through the poem, is the coexistence of all time in the present. Winterson is thus using Eliot's idea in order to question past and future as separate from the present, since "the borders of each shrink and fade" and the "river runs from one ... to another without stopping" (1989, p. 167).

Winterson uses this idea to reconsider the temporality of narrative journeys. At one point in Jordan's quest to find Fortunata, he states: "The scene I have just described to you may lie in the future or the past. Either I have found Fortunata or I will find her. I cannot be sure. Either I am remembering her or I am still imagining her. But she is somewhere in the grid of time, a co-ordinate, as I am" (1989, p. 104). Winterson's description here complicates the temporality of the journey, the attainment of the object of desire, the idea that completion can ever be reached. Ultimately, it is her use of an Eliotian sense of time that allows her to rethink narrative journeys.

Eliot's sense of time, when applied to narrative, does not lead inevitably toward those predictable endings. Because of this, we might begin to wonder about the seeming convention and finality of the narrative journeys in the *Four Quartets*. Is it even possible to read the temporality of these journeys separate from the time sense the poem sets up in its more philosophical stanzas, a temporality in which "time past," "time future," "what might have been," and "what has been" are all "always present" ("Burnt Norton," lines 44–46)?

At one point in *Sexing the Cherry*, Jordan talks specifically about such narrative journeys. Speaking about his mentor, John Tradescant, Jordan states: "For Tradescant, voyages can be completed. They occupy time comfortably. With some leeway, they are predictable" (1989, p. 115). Jordan's mentor sees a voyage as something that progresses toward completion.[16] Such voyages, according to Jordan, "occupy time comfortably" (1989, p. 115). In narrative, time most often functions to progress us toward the end of a voyage. Because of this, most voyages are "predictable": they inevitably lead us to the same thing, "completion." But in a textual universe where "all time is eternally present" (Winterson 1989, p. 100; "Burnt Norton," line 4), the rules of narrative progression might fly out the window (like the dancing princesses who escape nightly to the silver city). In her use of Eliot's theories of time, Winterson's text thus makes us wonder if time can ever be occupied "comfortably."

* * *

In an essay that seeks to understand Winterson's connection to modernism—most specifically to the work of Eliot, Lyn Pykett examines the way in which the "ghosts of high Modernism...haunt Winterson's fiction" (1998, p. 55). Pykett's essay spends about six pages drawing out interesting and compelling connections between Winterson and these "high Modernists." She convincingly makes the claim that "Eliot's critical views... underpin Winterson's essays" (1998, p. 59). And yet, the essay ends on a strange note. Pykett critiques Winterson, saying: "by insisting so firmly on a particular version of Modernism from which she claims descent, Winterson erases a great deal of history of writing since the period of high Modernism....In particular Winterson's genealogy obscures the nature and extent of her indebtedness to her more immediate precursors and near-contemporaries, notably Angela Carter" (1998, p. 59). I find it surprising that after spending the greater part of the essay showing the way in which Winterson's work is illuminated by reading her alongside the modernists, Pykett would dismiss this connection in favor of a connection to Angela Carter, one which she spends only a paragraph or two describing.[17]

But this move is ultimately not so surprising or even so unique. Because of Eliot's reputation, any connection made between Eliot and Winterson risks problematizing Winterson's position as a lesbian feminist. It is for this reason, perhaps, that Pykett feels the need to back off her early assertions. In ending her essay, however, Pykett goes further than merely critiquing Winterson's own sense of her literary genealogy. She actually makes a suggestion for Winterson, telling her what she "needs" to do: "The criticism that has sometimes been leveled at Winterson is that she creates an alternative to reality and retreats from an engagement with political and material constraints. Perhaps she needs to close her Eliot and re-read her Woolf (*A Room of One's Own, Three Guineas* and the essays) and Carter" (1998, p. 60). Winterson, according to Pykett, needs to do some reading, but it must be the right kind of reading. Pykett's words here show that it is not modernism in general that is problematic for Winterson, but Eliot specifically. Winterson is told to "re-read her Woolf." Here Woolf here is figured as the good modernist because her relationship to feminism overshadows what needs to be discarded from modernism (notice which books Pykett specifically suggests). Likewise, Angela Carter's credentials as an experimental feminist writer are quite well established. What Pykett's essay makes clear is that T. S. Eliot is the baggage that we must get rid of if we want to read Winterson as a politically engaged lesbian feminist.

Pykett's essay is representative of the way that Winterson's connection to T. S. Eliot often is dealt with in Winterson criticism. Though perhaps other texts do not go to such ends to disassociate the two, there is often a reluctance to discuss this connection or its implications.[18] When the connection is discussed, as it is in Susan Onega's work, there seems to be an assumption that it is impossible for us to consider Winterson as subversive or politically engaged if we see her as close to Eliot. Onega, in connecting Jordan's quest to Eliot's form of modernism, argues:

> This transcendental component of Jordan's quest for identity is in keeping with the Modernist obsession for mythical closure and provides a neatly clenched alternative to the apparently open, heavily parodic and chaotic structure of *Sexing the Cherry*, thus undermining the liberating potential of Winterson's use of grotesque and carnivalesque imagery and of her subversive inversion of fairy tales and romance. (1996, p. 311)

Like other critics who deal with the Winterson-Eliot relation, Onega sees this connection, which includes a shared "Modernist obsession for mythic closure," as something that immediately undermines Winterson's "liberating potential" and her ability to be "subversive." Winterson cannot be connected to Eliot and subversive at the same time.

I would like to suggest the exact opposite, that perhaps reading Winterson's connection to Eliot is one of the most subversive things we can do with her work. The reading of Winterson solely alongside these familiar feminist writers (to whom she no doubt owes a debt) seems to have produced homonormative readings that often repeat the same findings and apply the same theories. This normative way of looking at her work has stripped us of certain possibilities for understanding her texts. In my opinion, the connection between Winterson and Eliot is the more "queer" one if we take queer to mean "strange, odd, peculiar, eccentric" (def. 1a). This is a connection that denies neat and simple identity in favor of more capacious understandings. Ultimately, we need to deal not with the Winterson some may wish existed, but with the one who *does* exist, the one replete with contradictions, the one who is both close to Eliot and still subversive, the one who is not singularly reducible to any ideology or political platform. And perhaps in doing so, we will realize that Eliot is not exactly who we thought he was either.

NOTES

1. Perhaps Winterson's essay is contradictory in its aims. It seems to assert the text and not the author as the locus of meaning. And yet, at the end of the essay, it is Winterson herself who affirms the meaning of *Sexing the Cherry* by giving the second reader the stamp of approval.

2. For example, there are arguments in Winterson criticism regarding whether her texts appropriately deal with homophobia (Palmer 1998, pp. 104–105). Winterson's relation to a particular political agenda is also the subject of debate among critics. Lynne Pearce, for instance, critiques Winterson for universalizing lesbian love and sees this as detrimental to "a serious political agenda" (Makinen 2005, p. 87).

3. For Winterson criticism that cites the intertextual connection between Winterson and Eliot, see Clingham (1998), Onega (1996), Seaboyer (1997), Pykett (1998), Eide (2001), Quadflieg (1997), and Heise (1997).

4. As Jaime Hovey has claimed, a particular version of modernism imagined through Eliot's theory of impersonality has often eclipsed the "queerer modernisms of the effete Oscar Wilde, the lesbian imagist Amy Lowell, the queer apologist Radclyffe Hall, and the sexually reticent Eliot himself" (2006, p. 6). Hovey's claim highlights the way in which Eliot has been read in competing ways in regards to his representations of desire and sexuality. While many see the impersonal Eliot, more recently there has been growing attention to the queerer aspects of his work, a trend in which my chapter participates. Gabrielle McIntire, for example, explores this in her book *Modernism, Memory, and Desire: T.S. Eliot and Virginia Woolf* in which she demonstrates how for Eliot "memory is always already invested and intertwined with writing sexuality, the body, and desire" (2008, p. 2).

5. Dinshaw's theory of the "queer historical touch" rests on a certain reconfiguration of the present. She sees the present not as "singular and fleeting" but as "a kind of expanded now in which past, present, and future coincide" (Dinshaw et al. 2007, p. 190). Dinshaw's words here sound quite similar to the view of the present espoused by Eliot (and Winterson). I find it interesting that Dinshaw's metaphor for the present should sound so much like modernist configurations of time.

6. In Winterson's exploration of time, we also get hints of other modernist authors including Virginia Woolf, W. B. Yeats, James Joyce, and Gertrude Stein.

7. For discussions of mysticism in the *Four Quartets*, see Michael Spencer's "Mysticism in T.S. Eliot's *Four Quartets*" (Spencer 1999) and Rajendra Verma's *Time and Poetry in Eliot's Four Quartets* (1979).

8. Eliot's use of the dance here also calls to mind whirling dervishes and the Sufi practice of meditative twirling in which the dervishes whirl ritually in order to reach a perfect state (Klein 1994, p. 28).

9. Winterson's tactic of having parallel narrators across large temporal divide allows her to present a variety of temporalities in *Sexing the Cherry*. At various times, the novel experiments with time in ways that correlate to Brian Richardson's "six kinds of temporal reconstruction" of postmodern narratives, especially "conflated" time in which "apparently different temporal zones fail to remain distinct, and slide and spill into one another" (2002, p. 50). While there is much to be said (and much has been said) about Winterson's temporalities in relation to postmodernism, I believe it is important to uncover how her temporalities, especially those that challenge various normative timelines, like reproductive futurism, are derived from modernist experiments like Eliot's.

10. In the description of Fortunata's dance school, we might hear echoes of another modernist writer, one perhaps less acknowledged by Winterson: W. B. Yeats. Yeats employs images of dancers in poems like "Byzantium" and "Among School Children." Indeed, it is hard not to hear the echo of Yeats's often used symbol of the gyre (a figure he used to describe the circular or spiral turns of history) in the "*gyration*" of the dancers. *Art Objects*, Winterson's book of essays that focuses predominantly on modernism, only mentions Yeats a few times, but when his name does appear, it is always within lists of writers she admires. In her last reference to Yeats, as she is discussing style, she says "I realise that I am coming close to Yeats and his planchette, but really, Yeats and his planchette has no quarrel with Eliot and his impersonal theory" (1996a, p. 187). In Winterson's description of the dance school, we might see another instance in which Yeats "has no quarrel with" Eliot. Winterson puts temporal theories of these two modernists to work simultaneously in her own prose. It is especially in moments like these that Winterson's time sense appears to be predominantly, and perhaps anachronistically, modernist.

11. Though I completely agree with Onega that Winterson's use of Eliot here leans towards transcendence, I am quite confounded by her next move in which she disqualifies the novel from having any "liberating potential" solely because of its connection to Eliot's modernism.

12. Winterson's focus on the body in *Sexing the Cherry* and other novels (*Written on the Body*, especially) places her within the tradition of "ecriture feminine," a style named by French feminists who sought to write more directly about the female body. Brian Richardson has argued that this style can be traced across a variety of twentieth-century authors including Woolf, Mansfield, Carter, and Winterson, among others (1997, pp. 303–304).

13. As she relates her own version of "The Twelve Dancing Princesses," Winterson not only rewrites the Grimm Brothers' tale but also borrows from and reimagines other texts, including Byron and Browning poems and the story of Rapunzel.

14. This might also recall the dance as representative of the paradoxical state of being both "still and moving." The princesses are dancing in this space that is untouched by the daily rhythms of sunrise and sunset. It is a still place where time does not pass, and at that "still point, there the dance is" ("Burnt Norton," line 63).

15. This use of time is quite common in fairytales. We enter into a fairytale "once upon a time" and exit it at "happily ever after." Since "happily ever after" is almost always the temporality entered into after a marriage, it seems to line up with the "reproductive futurism" that Lee Edelman describes. Beyond this, though, the temporality of the fairytale itself is often a strange one. Fairytales often take place during a period in which time is out of joint, in which something is wrong. Some event must happen to set things right and to progress the story toward its inevitable ending, "happily ever after."

16. John Tradescant is also a historical figure, a gardener who brought back many new fruits and vegetables to England in the late sixteenth and early seventeenth centuries. Winterson's use of an actual historical figure to represent a form of temporality that progresses toward an ultimate end perhaps can be seen as a critique of certain representations of history as linear.

17. This is not to say that there is no connection between Winterson and Carter (or Woolf, who Pykett will later reference). By including a chapter on Winterson between chapters on Woolf and on Carter, I too am connecting her to these authors. But the strongest connection, in my mind, the one that helps us to read Winterson's novels and understand the queer temporalities she employs, is the connection between Winterson and Eliot.

18. Not all Winterson critics dismiss this connection to Eliot. Those who talk about religion in Winterson's texts (Eide 2001, Morrison 2006) or history (Clingham 1998) take into account this connection. It is primarily those who wish to talk about Winterson as a lesbian, queer, and/or feminist writer that see her relation to Eliot as a problem that needs to be dealt with.

References

Bay-Petersen, Ole. 1985. T. S. Eliot and Einstein: The Fourth Dimension in the *Four Quartets. English Studies: A Journal of English Language and Literature* 66 (2): 143–155.

Bergsten, Staffan. 1960. *Time and Eternity: A Study in the Structure and Symbolism of T. S. Eliot's Four Quartets.* Stockholm: Svenska Bokförlaget.

Bodelsen, C.A. 1966. *T.S. Eliot's* Four Quartets: *A Commentary.* Copenhagen: Rosenkilde.

Clingham, Greg. 1998. Winterson's Fiction and Enlightenment Historiography. *Bucknell Review: A Scholarly Journal of Letters, Arts and Sciences* 41 (2): 57–85.

Dinshaw, Carolyn. 1999. *Getting Medieval: Sexualities and Communities, Pre- and Postmodern.* Durham: Duke University Press.

Dinshaw, Carolyn, et al. 2007. Theorizing Queer Temporalities: A Roundtable Discussion. Special issue of GLQ: *A Journal of Gay and Lesbian Studies* 13 (2–3): 178–195.

Eide, Marian. 2001. Passionate Gods and Desiring Women: Jeanette Winterson, Faith, and Sexuality. *International Journal of Sexuality and Gender Studies* 6 (4): 279–291.

Eliot, T.S. 1943. *Four Quartets.* New York: Harcourt.

Gish, Nancy K. 1981. *Time in the Poetry of T.S. Eliot: A Study in Structure and Theme.* Totowa: Barnes & Noble.

Heise, Ursula K. 1997. Jeanette Winterson (1959–). In *British Writers: Supplement IV*, ed. George Stade and Carol Howard, 541–559. New York: Scribner's.

Hovey, Jaime. 2006. *A Thousand Words: Portraiture, Style, and Queer Modernism.* Columbus: Ohio State University Press.

Klein, William H. 1994. Aspects of Time in Eliot's *Four Quartets. Yeats Eliot Review: A Journal of Criticism and Scholarship* 13 (1-2): 26–36.

Makinen, Merja. 2005. *The Novels of Jeanette Winterson.* New York: Palgrave Macmillan.

McIntire, Gabrielle. 2008. *Modernism, Memory, and Desire: T.S. Eliot and Virginia Woolf.* Cambridge: Cambridge University Press.

Morrison, Jago. 2006. 'Who Cares About Gender at a Time Like This?': Love, Sex and the Problem of Jeanette Winterson. *Journal of Gender Studies* 15 (2): 169–180.

Müller, Monika. 2001. Love and Other Dismemberments in Jeanette Winterson's Novels. In *Engendering Realism and Postmodernism: Contemporary Writers in Britain*, ed. Beate Neumeier, 41–51. Amsterdam: Rodopi.

Onega, Susana. 1996. Jeanette Winterson's Politics of Uncertainty in *Sexing the Cherry.* In *Gender, I-Deology: Essays on Theory, Fiction and Film*, ed. Chantal Cornut-Gentille D'Arcy and José Angel García Landa, 297–313. Amsterdam: Rodopi.

Palmer, Paulina. 1998. The Passion: Storytelling, Fantasy, Desire. In *'I'm Telling You Stories': Jeanette Winterson and the Politics of Reading*, ed. Helena Grice and Tim Woods, 103–117. Amsterdam: Rodopi.

Pykett, Lyn. 1998. A New Way with Words? Jeanette Winterson's Post-modernism. In *'I'm Telling You Stories': Jeanette Winterson and the Politics of Reading*, ed. Helena Grice and Tim Woods, 53–60. Amsterdam: Rodopi.

Quadflieg, Helga. 1997. Feminist Stories Told on Waste Waters: Jeanette Winterson's Novels. *Anglistik & Englischunterricht* 60: 97–111.

Reynier, Christine. 2005. Jeanette Winterson's Cogito-'Amo Ergo Sum'-or Impersonality and Emotion Redefined. In *Impersonality and Emotion in Twentieth-Century British Literature*, ed. Jean-Michel Ganteau and Christine Reynier, 299–308. Montpellier: Université Montpellier III.

Richardson, Brian. 1997. Remapping the Present: The Master Narrative of Modern Literary History and the Lost Forms of Twentieth-Century Fiction. *Twentieth Century Literature* 43 (3): 291–309.

———. 2002. Beyond Story and Discourse: Narrative Time in Postmodern and Nonmimetic Fiction. In *Narrative Dynamics: Essays on Time, Plot, Closure, and Frames*, ed. Brian Richardson, 47–63. Columbus: Ohio State University Press.

Seaboyer, Judith. 1997. Second Death in Venice: Romanticism and the Compulsion to Repeat in Jeanette Winterson's *The Passion*. *Contemporary Literature* 38 (3): 483–509.

Spencer, Michael D. 1999. Mysticism in T.S. Eliot's *Four Quartets*. *Studies in Spirituality* 9: 230–266.

———. 2005. The Garden in T. S. Eliot's *Four Quartets*. *Cithara: Essays in the Judaeo-Christian Tradition* 44 (2): 32–45.

Verma, Rajendra. 1979. *Time and Poetry in Eliot's* Four Quartets. Atlantic Highlands: Humanities.

Wight, Doris T. 1990. Metaphysics Through Paradox in Eliot's *Four Quartets*. *Philosophy and Rhetoric* 23 (1): 63–69.

Winterson, Jeanette. 1987. *The Passion*. New York: Grove.

———. 1989. *Sexing the Cherry*. New York: Grove.

———. 1992. *Written on the Body*. New York: Vintage, Print.

———. 1994. *Art and Lies*. London: Cape.

———. 1996a. *Art Objects: Essays on Ecstasy and Effrontery*. New York: Knopf.

———. 1996b. The Semiotics of Sex. *Art Objects: Essays on Ecstasy and Effrontery*, 103–118. New York: Knopf.

CHAPTER 4

Telling Queer Tales: Narration and Genealogical Time in William Faulkner and Angela Carter

About a fourth of the way through Angela Carter's last novel, *Wise Children*, Nora and Dora, two "song-and-dance" girls from the wrong side of the tracks, walk in on a comedian half-way through his act. The comedian, a man named Gorgeous George, is in the process of telling the following joke:

> "[A boy] says to his dad, 'I want to get married to the girl next door, Dad.' 'Ho, hum,' says his dad. 'I've got news for you, son. When I was your age, I used to get me leg over [...] the garden wall [...] and, cut a long story short, you can't marry the girl next door, son, on account of she's your sister.' [...] "So this boy buys a bike [...] and pedals off to Hove [...] He comes back, he says to his father: 'I've met this nayce girl from Hove, Dad.' [...] 'Sorry to say, son, I frequently hove to in Hove when I was your age and–' [...] "This poor boy, he buys himself a day return, he goes up to Victoria, he meets a girl under the clock [...] But his father says: 'We had trains in my day, son...' "The boy goes into the kitchen for a cup of tea [and sees his mother]" 'Looks like I'll never get married, Mum.' 'Why's that, son?' He told her all about it, she says: 'You go ahead and marry who you like, son [...] 'E's not your father!'" (1991, pp. 64–65)

"'E's not your father!" is not only the punch line of the joke, but it is also the punch line of the entire novel. *Wise Children* is a novel in which paternity is never definitively known, a text that raises doubt about all claims of kinship. But the issues raised in this joke are applicable beyond Carter's novel.

© The Author(s) 2019
K. Haffey, *Literary Modernism, Queer Temporality*,
https://doi.org/10.1007/978-3-030-17301-2_4

The joke plays on a whole plethora of recognizable familial anxieties. There's the male anxiety of being cuckolded, the anxiety on which the humor of the joke depends. There's the anxiety of the son who lives under the shadow of his father's sexual potency, a sexual potency that has already prevented the son from his own conquests. And there's the fear of accidentally committing incest that the son faces throughout most of the joke. While the punch line seems to alleviate the problem of the joke—the son's inability to marry any of the girls he has met because they are his sisters—it actually presents a bigger problem. After the mother's revelation, the son no longer knows who his father is, so the threat of incest, instead of lessening, has become all the more possible. Because his paternity is in question, every girl he meets is his possible sister. In a world where he does not know his father, he is always under the threat of incest.

This joke thus suggests, as cultural narratives often do, that a world in which paternal lines are unknown is a world thrown into chaos. In the absence of the father, the most universal of taboos—incest—becomes a perpetual possibility. If the institution of the incest taboo is, as Claude Levi-Strauss claims, the moment in which society is founded, then the appearance of incest represents a threat to the breakdown of society itself—a return to lawlessness.[1]

The joke also leaves the son in a less-than-comfortable position, at least within a narrative tradition that places extreme emphasis on the name of the Father and the tracing of origins. The son no longer stands in a genealogical chain of fathers and sons. He is now like the protagonist at the beginning of so many nineteenth-century novels who sets out to find his father and in so doing attempts to discover his own identity.[2] Because he is a man without a father, he is a man without a past and with an uncertain future.

Thus the moment in which the son discovers he does not know his own father is anxiety-ridden not only because of the perceived chaos it threatens to let loose, but also because the way we structure the past, present, and future—time as we know it—depends on the identification of fathers. This is a point that Patricia Drechsel Tobin makes quite convincingly in her book *Time and the Novel: The Genealogical Imperative*. According to Tobin, "Within the extended family the individual member is guaranteed both identity and legitimacy through the tracing of his lineage back to the founding father, the family's origin and first cause" (1978, p. 7). With the father as the point of origin, time proceeds in a linear fashion from him through his progeny. As an origin, the father gives meaning to those who come after him. Tobin refers to "this general social truth," as "the genealogical imperative" (1978, p. 9).

For Tobin, the genealogical imperative results from the "confusion of genetically linked descent, one of the oldest ideas of Western man, with mere chronological succession" (1978, p. 7). Descent has thus structured perceptions of time as a chain of events, with one event causing (or metaphorically giving birth to) the next. As Tobin puts it, "events in time come to be perceived as begetting other events within a line of causality similar to the line of generations" (1978, p. 7). Because this perception of time is seemingly so ingrained, it often remains an unexamined assumption. And yet, it is perhaps in the examination of these assumptions that we can begin to unearth the ways in which the family, with the father as the head, structures our notions of time.

This can be seen most clearly at the level of narrative. As Tobin shows, genealogical imperative extends to all narrative forms, whether they be historical, autobiographical, or fictional. Each of these forms, she states, "project[s] a direction for the transient and irreversible arrow of time" (1978, p. 8). In this way, narrative functions linearly. This is not to say that all narratives only move forward in time at the level of plot, but that a chain of events (events in a cause–effect relationship) will ultimately arrive at meaning—that "all possibly random events and gratuitous details are brought into an alignment of relevance, so that at the point of conclusion all possibility has been converted into necessity within a line of kinship—the subsequent having been referred to the prior, the end to the beginning, the progeny to the father" (1978, pp. 7–8). It is in this way that narratives come to "make sense," that they come into alignment with our sense of how meaning is made.

Tobin's comments are easily applicable to the novel, especially in its early manifestations. The tendency toward closure in many eighteenth and nineteenth-century novels demonstrates exactly this process of bringing "random events and gratuitous details...into an alignment of relevance" (1978, p. 7). The twentieth-century novel, on the other hand, often seems to question some of the assumptions of linearity and the connection of linearity to paternal descent. As Tobin claims, the "desire and repulsion for the world of the fathers informs in a major way those changes in narrative structure effected by the novelists of our own century, and their protagonists who, in their discontent within the family line, try to master their time outside of linearity" (1978, p. 12).

I heartily agree with Tobin's comments on the changing nature of "the world of the fathers" in twentieth-century novels. I would therefore like to take up, forty years after Tobin, similar concerns in two particularly rich twentieth-century texts: William Faulkner's *Absalom, Absalom!* and Angela Carter's *Wise Children*.[3] However, in reading these texts, my focus will be on the ways in which theories of queer temporality can help us to reframe our readings of these novels' portrayals of genealogy.

I have come to think of these two texts as tragic and comic versions of the same story. At their core, both are centrally concerned with questions of paternity and of genealogical succession. Faulkner's text focuses on the father's desire to produce a legitimate offspring and the son's inevitable position as shackled to the chains of linear succession. Carter's text looks at these issues from another position, through the lens of the daughter's relation to genealogy and with a satirical sense of humor. Her text stands in a position to deconstruct the idea of paternity and to poke fun at texts like Faulkner's that treat genealogy as a tragic affair. Far from dismissing genealogy as meaningless, however, Carter explores this concept with a complex understanding of the symbolic power associated with the capacity to trace a legitimate paternity.[4]

Beyond their connected subject matter, I find it interesting that both novels include a list of characters at the end of the text. These lists specifically delineate the parentage of the main characters. In Faulkner's novel, this section actually is titled "Genealogy"; in Carter's, it is called "Dramatis Personae" (1991, p. 233).[5] The inclusion of such lists bespeaks the central role that genealogy plays for both authors. Likewise, in both texts, the exploration of genealogy is examined through the child's relation to the father; the mother plays only a minimal role. Even the titles of these two novels point to an interest in the relation between fathers and their children. Faulkner's title refers to the Biblical story of Absalom who rebelled against his father King David and was killed by David's general.[6] And Carter's title comes from an old proverb that she cites as one of the epigraphs to the novel: "It's a wise child that knows its own father." Both novels explore not only the concrete aspects of fatherhood but also how fatherhood functions symbolically. In these texts, the capacity to trace a legitimate paternal line becomes both an object of desire and a symbol of authority.

The paternal line has another function in these novels—it represents a way of thinking about time. The time of the father represented in these texts is the genealogical time that Tobin describes. Since genealogical time generally reigns supreme in narratives that foreground fathers, as Tobin has shown, this connection is not all that surprising. What is perhaps more surprising is the way in which both novels attempt to turn away from a framework that privileges fathers and toward one that favors other members of the family. This turn toward other kinship relations also represents a turning toward different forms of temporality, temporalities outside the genealogical imperative.

Both novels thus foreground fatherhood in order to formulate narrative spaces outside or alongside the rule of the Father. In *Absalom, Absalom!*, there is an attempt to replace the father/child relationship with a relationship between siblings. And, in *Wise Children*, the father/child relationship is replaced with avuncular relations.[7] Such substitutions have significant effects on how the novels conceive of time. If the chain of genealogical succession from father to son imagines time as a forward-moving line, then positing a different familial relation as central breaks the chain of genealogical time—allows us to see time as moving in new and strange ways.

In this chapter, I will therefore ask the following question: what happens when we attempt to replace the paternal relation—and the temporality that it represents—with other familial relations? It is my belief that not only do we come up with different ways to conceive of time, but also that these new temporalities disrupt normative conceptions of gender, sexuality, and parenthood. So much of what we know (or think we know) about these concepts is based on a sense of progressive, linear time, a time born out of the genealogical imperative. Formulating ways of thinking about time outside of genealogy thus offers us a chance to understand what gender, sexuality, and parenthood might look like outside the Law of the Father.

To explore these questions, I first will consider *Absalom, Absalom!* at length. In Faulkner's text, the rebellion from genealogical succession takes an interesting form: sibling incest. In reading this novel, I will analyze sibling incest as a mechanism that jams linear genealogy. I will show how the imagining of sibling incest as a time outside of genealogy allows for new temporalities and new forms of desire. After I have sketched out my reading of *Absalom, Absalom!*, I will turn very briefly to Angela Carter's 1967 novel *The Magic Toyshop*. This novel deals with sibling incest in a way quite reminiscent of *Absalom, Absalom!* and will thus provide a transition between the work of Faulkner and that of Carter. When I turn to analyze my primary Carter text, *Wise Children*, my central focus will still be genealogy, but I will approach Carter's text with an eye toward avuncular relations. Like sibling incest, avuncular family relations allow us to see genealogy from another angle. Ultimately, my chapter seeks to find those gaps in genealogy where linear succession no longer seems inevitable, those queer moments in which we can believe that genealogical time could be evaded.

*   *   *

In *Absalom, Absalom!* a number of narrators attempt to tell the story of the Sutpen family from the scraps of knowledge each of them possess. The novel concerns itself with two connected narrative strands: the story of the Sutpen family and the attempt by other characters to recount and make sense of this family's story. As readers of the tale, we hear the voices of four different characters narrating, but this narration is filtered through a third-person omniscient narrator. Though many voices combine to tell the story of the Sutpen family, it is the young Quentin Compson, recently enrolled in Harvard, whose narrative voice dominates the story by its end.

Despite the fact that this is not the story of Quentin's own family, the telling of Thomas Sutpen's life has come to exemplify Quentin's relationship with his own father and grandfather. Throughout the first few chapters of the novel, Quentin serves as a listener to the stories from other characters. He hears bits of the story from Rosa, Thomas Sutpen's sister-in-law and one time fiancée. And he hears quite a bit from his father, who in turn heard much of the story from his own father. Quentin's grandfather was friends with Thomas Sutpen and served as his confidant on a number of occasions. For Quentin, the story of the Sutpen family is a story that has been passed down from grandfather to father to son. What Quentin hears in this narrative is thus not only the mysterious story of a family he barely knows but also vestiges of his own genealogy.

Quentin inherits this story and his family's obsession with it in the same way he inherits his own name. And like his father and his grandfather, Quentin too becomes a teller of this tale. Because Quentin's telling is part of a history of fathers narrating to sons, his story becomes a conversation with the ideology of paternal authority. His narrative is not only an attempt to tell the most complete story of the Sutpen family, but also an attempt to reconfigure his own relation to paternal authority.

This becomes quite apparent in Quentin's narration of Sutpen's life story, a story that is dominated by the struggle between fathers and sons. While the story of Sutpen's life is something we can never really know for certain (as we only get fragments of stories and elaborate conjectures about it from a variety of characters), I would like, nonetheless, to give a brief summary of Thomas Sutpen's life story as a way of demonstrating the importance that father/son relations play within it.

When Thomas Sutpen is a young boy, he is sent by his father to give a message to the latter's employer on a large plantation. When he arrives there, before he is able to deliver the message, he is sent to the back of the house and told never to come to the front door again. After ruminating upon this incident for a while, Thomas decides that he will one day achieve the success level of the man in the plantation house and the family name and dynasty to go along with it. As a young man, he sets out for the West Indies in an attempt to fulfill this desire. After achieving some wealth, he marries a local woman and has a son—Charles Bon—but he discovers that his wife is of mixed race and thus arranges a separation from her. Years later he arrives in Yoknapatawpha County and establishes a plantation called Sutpen's Hundred. He is then able to marry a respectable townswoman named Ellen Coldfield and has two children, Henry and Judith, with her.[8] His son, Henry, renounces his birthright. Sutpen is thus left without a legitimate (white) son. After Ellen's death, Sutpen tries later in life to father a son (once by attempting to convince his fiancée, Ellen's sister Rosa, to try to conceive a son before they are married and once by impregnating a poor white girl), but his attempts fail, and he dies without producing the family dynasty that he sought to create.

Though I have simplified Sutpen's life story quite a bit in order to highlight some key elements, what is undeniable in this story, no matter which way you tell it, is Sutpen's desire to propel his name and legacy forward in time by producing a son.[9] As Tobin claims, in her reading of *Absalom, Absalom!*, Sutpen attempts to erase the anonymity of his own past by making "a new proper beginning in time: he will make a name for himself" (1978, p. 109). For Joseph Allen Boone Sutpen's ultimate goal is "to create a male dynasty that will immortalize his name forever" (1998, p. 295). Sutpen wants to create a genealogy in which he will always figure as the patriarch, the founding father.

Paternal authority is thus what is at stake at both levels of this novel (in Sutpen's life story itself and in Quentin's narration of it). While Sutpen sets out to create his own paternal legacy, Quentin is constantly dealing with his father and grandfather's telling of the Sutpen story while attempting to construct his own. At first glance, we might read these father/son relations as part of the classic attempt of the son to usurp the father's authority and become the father himself. However, there seems to be a different dynamic at work here. Neither Quentin nor Henry, Sutpen's only "legitimate" son, seek to become fathers and uphold the idea of paternal authority. Instead, they attempt to subvert the law of the father in favor of different configurations.

John T. Irwin's now classic reading of *Absalom, Absalom!* is helpful in making this point. Irwin discusses the incident in Sutpen's childhood when he was turned away from the front door of the plantation. According to Irwin, Sutpen's decision that he will become as powerful as the man in the plantation shows that he accepts "the justice of that mastery which the powerful have over the powerless" (2003, p. 49). What he does not accept is his position within this system—that of the poor boy. Sutpen does not reject the injustice of the system, but seeks his revenge within the rules of patriarchal power (2003, p. 49). Sutpen thus attempts to "overcome the mastery of the personal father while maintaining the mastery of fatherhood" (2003, p. 50). The role of the father is the role through which Sutpen seeks to assert his own authority. Since he does not have a powerful name and legacy conferred upon him by his own father, he will seek to establish himself as a father who has authority by virtue of this position and who has the ability to pass on that authority to his son.

When we contrast Sutpen with the other ("legitimate") sons in the story, specifically Quentin and Henry, we can see that they, unlike Sutpen, do not seek to uphold the authority of the father so as to gain it for themselves. In the case of Henry, Sutpen's only acknowledged son, the son chooses to renounce his birthright and inheritance. He is described as having "repudiated the very roof under which he had been born" (1936, p. 15) and "repudiat[ed] his home and birthright" (1936, p. 18). The term "repudiate" is repeated often throughout the text with regard to Henry. Through the repetition of this term, the novel demonstrates quite clearly that it is Henry's choice to turn away from his father, that it is a break instituted by the son. Additionally, in giving up his birthright, he is giving up his place in a chain that stretches forward in time from father to son.

Quentin's break with his own father is not quite so concrete. Quentin never renounces his own father in the way that Henry does, but he does, in a way, reject his inheritance. If the story of the Sutpen family is what Quentin has inherited from his father and grandfather, then his rejection of his father's way of telling the story and the meaning that his father has made of it is a kind of rejection of his birthright. While it might be argued that Quentin's new way of telling the story is merely his way of usurping the father's authority so as to wield it for himself, this doesn't account for the character of Shreve, his college roommate, who by the end of the novel is narrating Sutpen's life alongside Quentin. In Quentin's hands, the telling of Sutpen's life story becomes a collaborative effort between two virtual brothers. Unlike the telling that had occurred between the Compson fathers and sons, in which a father spoke while a son passively received the story, Quentin and Shreve's method of telling the story involves conversation and questioning in which meaning is made out of the facts at hand. Quentin does not attempt to wield narratorial authority over Shreve, but instead seeks to create a different method of storytelling, a method at odds with genealogical succession and its reliance on the authority of the father figure.

The fraternal relationship between Quentin and Shreve is quite important because it is in the relation of siblings that we are given an alternative to the father–son relation. This is as true of Henry as it is of Quentin; in fact, Quentin and Shreve's relationship parallels in many ways that of Henry and Bon.[10] In order to demonstrate the way that sibling relationships function in this novel, I would like to focus at length on the tripartite relationship between Henry, Judith, and Bon. Not only does this relationship provide Henry an alternative role to that of son, but it also provides an alternate form of temporality, one at odds with genealogical time.

We hear the story of Henry, Judith, and Bon told a variety of ways through a number of different narrators. Despite these differences, a few facts remain the same. Henry and Bon meet at the University of Mississippi, where they become fast friends. Bon, a few years Henry's senior, acts as a kind of mentor to the younger, more puritanical boy. Henry brings Bon home for Christmas where he meets and becomes engaged to Henry's younger sister Judith. After the engagement, Henry has a conversation with his father that results in Henry renouncing his birthright. Henry and Bon then go off to fight together in the Civil War. Upon returning home, Henry murders Bon on the day he is meant to marry Judith.

Given these facts, a crucial question that all the narrators attempt to answer with their stories is why Henry murdered Bon. Both Quentin's father and Quentin/Shreve construct narratives that attempt to understand the motive behind this murder. While Mr. Compson believes that this murder came about because Bon was already married to an "octoroon" woman and wanted to make Judith his second wife, Quentin/Shreve paint an even more complex picture of the relation between these three characters. It is thus on the Quentin/Shreve version of the story that I would like to focus.[11]

According to Quentin/Shreve, Henry repudiates his birthright because Sutpen revealed that Bon was Sutpen's son from his first marriage (and thus Henry's half-brother). Not wanting to believe what Sutpen has told him, Henry renounces his father and returns to Bon. At this moment, Henry has chosen his brother over his father. He gives up his birthright and all of the rights and privileges that such a birthright includes in order to enter into a close relationship with his brother. This point is made quite clear in an exchange between Bon and Henry that occurs even before Henry learns Bon is his brother: Henry states "'If I had a brother, I wouldn't want him to be a younger brother' and [Bon]: 'Ah?' and [Henry]: 'No. I would want him to be older than me' and [Bon]: 'No son of a landed father wants an older brother' and [Henry]: 'Yes. I do'" (1936, p. 316). In this conversation, Henry makes it clear that he is willing to give up all that is afforded to him by patriarchal law in order to enter into a fraternal relationship.

But this relationship includes another party, Judith. If Bon is Sutpen's son, then Bon's engagement to Judith is an incestuous one. As Henry's own descriptions suggest, this is a form of incest that includes him as well, placing him in an incestuous triangle with his half-brother and sister. This is an aspect of the story that Quentin/Shreve dwell upon at length in the last few chapters of the novel. They attempt to understand how the puritanical Henry could be brought to accept, even temporarily, an incestuous union between his half-brother and sister.

It is my contention that this incestuous sibling union represents for both Henry and Quentin a space outside of the linear temporality of genealogical succession, an escape from the law of the Father they are attempting to evade. While Joseph Allen Boone's reading of this novel in his book *Libidinal Currents* makes a similar claim—that "the sexual perversion of sibling incest stances in direct opposition to the desire of the father" and is thus "a break in temporal and geneolgical progression" (1998, p. 310), I intend to use this idea as a starting point to analyze the queer moments that occur when genealogical time is subverted in narrative storytelling. However, in order to make this point, I will first need to consider the role of incest in Faulkner's work in more detail by drawing upon literary critics who discuss incest in the work of Faulkner and scholars who write about incest in a more anthropological sense. By referencing these texts, I would like to get at the specifics of sibling incest and attempt to uncouple it from parent–child incest. If, as I am suggesting, sibling incest functions as an alternative for these characters to a father–son relation, then these sibling relations need to be understood in their own right.

Incest in Faulkner is a topic that has been widely written about, though the meanings of incest are often underexplored. According to Karl Zender's convincing article on "Faulkner and the Politics of Incest," incest has always meant the same thing in Faulkner's work for critics—"something religious and something oedipal" (1998, p. 739). When writing about incest, rarely do critics make the distinction between parent–child incest and sibling incest. In this way, all incest can be conceived as connoting "something oedipal." As Zender points out, Otto Rank, a leading psychoanalytic explorer of incest, claims that brother–sister incest is a substitute for child–parent incest. Psychoanalysis tends to deal with incest within the framework of the oedipal complex and thus foregrounds the parent–child version of incest. This way of conceiving of incest is quite unhelpful in my project because it does not see sibling incest as in any way distinct. Under this rubric, sibling incest becomes a repetition of or a substitute for a more universal form.

According to Zender, the difference between parent–child incest and sibling incest is particularly important because of how these two tropes have functioned as political metaphors. If we go back to Romantic poetry, Zender claims, there are numerous images of sibling incest being idealized. These images were often connected to leftist politics in the name of a universal brotherhood and put in direct opposition to images of parent–child incest, which was couched in terms of force (1998, pp. 742–754). Faulkner's use of the sibling incest motif calls upon these meanings. Because Henry must deny his father in order to side with his brother, his own consideration of incest shows his desire to enter into what Zender calls a "fatherless egalitarian social order" (1998, p. 742).

This reading of sibling incest as a way to escape the rule of the father is echoed by a number of other Faulkner critics. According to Irwin, incest is a "primal affront to the authority of the father" (2003, pp. 59–60). It is by committing incest with one's sister, Irwin implies, that the son is able to usurp power from his father (2003, p. 60). Hironori Hayase sees the brother–sister incest as an attempt by Henry to undermine his father's design (1990, p. 103). As Hayase states, "Henry's choice of incest means the resistance against the society that has formed his loveless father's sense of morals" (1990, p. 103). The choice of incest is thus a resistance to the father himself and to a paternal society. And David Walter cites the novel to show how upon being introduced to Bon as the suitor of daughter, Sutpen "felt and heard [his] design—house, position, posterity and all—come down like it had been built out of smoke" (2007, p. 497).

But what is particularly interesting in these readings of sibling incest is the way in which temporality comes to play a key role. There seems to be a connection between these two concepts (sibling incest and time) that has not been satisfactorily articulated. All of the readings of Faulkner mentioned above, in fact, discuss the way in which the creation of this incestuous relationship allows the participants to take part in a different temporality. For example in Hayase's reading, Henry's desire to commit incest is based on a hope that incest can create a world of love uniting the three, a world in which their love can be "eternalized" (1990, p. 104). The incest thus "preserves the situation by lifting it out of time, just as Keats' urn preserves the lovers in a perpetual chase—the passion never to be completed yet never to fade" (qtd. in Hayase 1990, p. 104). Here love cannot wither and die because it is removed from the temporality of forward motion.

At the same time, these readings of incest also rely on the idea of returning to a pre-social moment in which incest is possible and permissible. This point is articulated perhaps more clearly by David Walter. In a reading that compares Faulkner's representation of sibling incest to Balzac's, David Walter claims that Henry "transforms [Judith's] Body into an Edenic American Womb" (2007, p. 495). This quote calls up two separate images of before-ness. The reference to Eden recalls a Judeo-Christian moment before original sin. In the tradition that treats incest as morally culpable, this might also be a moment before incest. The image of the womb also recalls a moment before birth, before entering into the realm of norms and laws. Incest is thus figured, by Walter, as a temporal return to a moment before, a moment before sin, a moment before laws.

While I find these readings extremely helpful in establishing a con-nection between sibling incest and the desire for alternate forms of temporality, I believe they both stop short of considering in detail the relation between incest and time. In order to sketch out my own read-ing of this, I would like to turn to the work of the scholar who has per-haps most famously theorized incest, Claude Levi-Strauss.[12] Though Levi-Strauss says precious little about incest in terms of its temporal-ity, he makes a quite striking statement in the closing sentences of *The Elementary Structures of Kinship*: "To this very day, mankind has always dreamed of seizing and fixing that fleeting moment when it was per-missible to believe that the law of exchange could be evaded, that one could gain without losing, enjoy without sharing" (1969, pp. 496–497). Levi-Strauss's statement here connects in many ways to the readings of Faulkner that I have been discussing. There is a desire to seize a past "moment" when incest "was" permissible, to return to an Eden where all things are possible, a pre-social moment before the institution of social law. But his quote also turns our attention to another compo-nent of the incest prohibition: "the law of exchange." It is the law of exchange that sets up the structure wherein men must give away their sisters and receive the sisters of other men in return. To commit incest, then, is to live in that "fleeting moment" of belief that one might not have to give away one's sister—"that one could gain without losing, enjoy without sharing" (1969, p. 497). As Levi-Strauss says in the very last sentence of this text, the dream of seizing that fleeting moment is the dream of "a world in which one might *keep to oneself*" (1969, p. 497; emphasis in original).

Levi-Strauss's statements about incest are key to understanding Henry's decision to give his consent to the marriage of his half-brother and his sister. In Quentin and Shreve's version of the story, when Henry first receives the information that Bon is his brother, he enters into a period of contemplation in which he must decide what to do: he holds "all three of them—himself, Judith and Bon—in that suspension while he wrested with his conscience to make it come to terms with what he wanted to do" (1936, p. 270). This period of "suspension," I would argue, represents that "fleeting moment," according to Levi-Strauss, "when it was permissible to believe that the law of exchange could be evaded" (1969, p. 497). What is noteworthy about Levi-Strauss's quote is the phrase "when it was permissible to believe." Levi-Strauss does *not* say, "when it was possible to evade the law of exchange," but instead focuses on the human belief in such a possibility. When Henry enters into contemplation about this incestuous relationship, he enters into that "fleeting moment" of *believing* that there is a way to evade that law of exchange. Additionally, because Henry thinks of himself as part of this incestuous union, he may in fact be in the perfect position. According to Levi-Strauss, part of what makes brother–sister incest undesirable for a man is that if he marries his sister, he gains no brother-in-law (1969, p. 485). However, if Henry enters into an incestuous triangle with his brother and his sister, he gains a brother-in-law and gets to keep his sister as his own.

Henry attempts to rationalize the incest, an act he has always seen in moral terms as a sin, through the invocation of others who have taken part in such acts. He states: "But kings have done it! Even Dukes! There was that Lorraine duke named John something that married his sister. The Pope excommunicated him but it didn't hurt! It didn't hurt! They were still husband and wife. They were still alive. They still loved!" (1936, p. 342). In calling upon aristocracy who have taken part in acts of incest, Henry seems to attempt to comfort himself with not only the fact that others have committed incest but also that the love of the couple endured despite that fact that the law condemned them. The repetition of the word "still" in these sentences seems to focus his attention on the enduring quality of the love on which these acts of incest are based. This is no surprise given the fact that it is an enduring world of love that Henry hoped to build between himself, his sister, and Bon before he found out that the latter is his brother. He had previously told Bon: "*From now on mine and my sister's house will be your house and mine and my sister's lives your life*" (1936, p. 318; italics in original). And later, "Henry talked about her to him, saying every time he breathed: *Hers and my lives are to exist within and upon yours*" (1936, p. 325; italics in original).[13] Even Bon begins to take Henry's lead and think of this relationship in terms of an alternative world: Bon "translated (the three of them: himself and Henry and the sister whom he had never seen and perhaps did not even have any curiosity to see) into a world like a fairy tale in which nothing else save them existed" (1936, p. 318). Thus, Henry shows his desire for an ideal social space to be created between himself, his sister, and Bon.

After he finds out that Bon is his brother, this desire to create a world of love between the three of them, as Hayase claims, does not dissolve. The incest might in fact make this desire even stronger because it has the ability to lift the three of them more completely out of time. Henry discusses how those who have committed incest are now eternally in hell: "There must have been lots in the world who have done it that people dont [sic] know about, that maybe they suffered for it and died for it and are in hell for it now" (1936, p. 343). If those who died for it are "in hell for it now," then their love has been eternalized, they live together even "now" in hell. If the three of them were damned to hell because of their sin, then they too might live eternally together. He states: "And so at least we will all be together where we belong...And we will all be together in torment" (1936, p. 348).

Even Shreve's thoughts about incest confirm this when he says: "who's to say if it wasn't the possibility of incest, because who...has been in love and not discovered the vain evanescence of the fleshy encounter; who has not had to realize that when the brief all is done you must retreat from both love and pleasure,...but maybe if there were sin too maybe you would not be permitted to escape, uncouple, return" (1936, pp. 323–324). Shreve's statement very specifically sets the temporality of incest apart from the evanescent temporality of "the fleshy encounter." Incest is different specifically because its status as a sin, in his mind, prevents one from ever moving beyond that moment. With incest, according to Shreve, there can be no uncoupling, no escape.

These are the thoughts that are said to occupy Henry's mind as he attempts to decide what to do. During this period when he is trying to decide whether or not to give Bon his permission to marry his sister, he keeps telling Bon (on four separate occasions within the space of only a few pages) to "wait": "Wait. Wait. Let me get used to it" (1936, p. 340); "Wait. Wait. I must have time to get used to it. You will have to give me time" (1936, p. 340); "But you will have to give me time to get used to it" (1936, p. 341); "But you will have to wait! You will have to give me time! (1936, p. 342). These pleas by Henry to make Bon wait are not attempts to gain time, but attempts to make time stop moving, to slow the progression of events. They are attempts to live in that "fleeting moment," as Levi-Strauss states, "when it was permissible to believe that the law of exchange could be evaded" (1969, p. 497). Since Henry spends this period of time trying to find a precedent for committing incest, he is attempting to find a way out of the law of exchange. Ultimately, he does not agree to the marriage until he is able to find another way to stop time from moving—a feat he accomplishes by constructing incest as that which can eternalize the love between him and his siblings. And so his acceptance is described as "the irrevocable repudiation of the old heredity and training and the acceptance of eternal damnation" (1936, p. 347). This line might bring us back to the idea of genealogical time. Henry's choice to allow incest represents the repudiation of the "old heredity," a term that seems quite close to the idea of genealogy. Choosing eternal damnation is a further attempt for Henry to escape the genealogical time that he seeks to evade in separating himself from his father. In seeking eternity with his siblings, he searches for a place outside the reach of his father.

At this point, I would like to shift my focus to consider Quentin and Shreve, the narrators of the story I just described. Before the two narrate the segment of the story analyzed above, we learn from Quentin in a previous chapter that "nobody ever did know if Bon ever knew Sutpen was his father or not" (1936, p. 269). And yet, when Quentin and Shreve tell the story of Bon, they construct an elaborate narrative about how he discovered that Sutpen was his father and how he handled this information. As Tobin states, Quentin and Shreve's narrations are sometimes so "plausible and powerful" that we forget they are often "wholesale fictions" (1936, p. 116). This story of Bon, Henry, and Judith thus says more about Quentin and Shreve than it does about the three siblings. Indeed, at one point during the storytelling, we are told that "the two of them creat[ed] between them...people who perhaps never existed anywhere at all" (1936, p. 303). Because the two young men are creating people "who perhaps never existed," their characters are injected, undoubtedly, with their own thoughts, values, and desires.[14]

This idea of incest as a way to eternalize love and escape from the law of the father might thus be read as a desire of Quentin and Shreve that manifests itself at the level of narrative. When Quentin first begins narrating the story to Shreve, he seems to see the story as inherited from his father, as a piece of his father's legacy that he carries with him. Thus, when Shreve first interrupts him to take his part in telling the story, he hears Shreve's voice as the voice of his father. He thinks: "I am going to have to hear it all over again I am already hearing it all over again I am listening to it all over again I shall have to never listen to anything else but this again forever so apparently not only a man never outlives his father but not even his friends and acquaintances do" (1936, p. 277). In Quentin's thoughts, his father's story becomes a symbol for the anxiety of the father's priority in time. Not only does the father come first temporally, he can never be outlived. In this quote, then, genealogy becomes storytelling (and vice versa). The father cannot be outlived because his stories remain even after he is gone. Even the primary definition of the term genealogy makes this point clear. A genealogy is a record or an "account of one's descent"; it is thus a story, a narrative (def. 1).

Though this might describe Quentin's initial take on his narrative situation, as he and Shreve continue to tell this story, the dynamics shift. Quentin no longer views Shreve's interruptions as disruptive to *his* story but instead sees them as contributions to a story they are telling together. After Shreve has interjected himself into the storytelling, the text reads: "There was no harm intended by Shreve and no harm taken, since Quentin did not even stop. He did not even falter, taking Shreve up in stride without comma or colon or paragraph" (1936, p. 280). Here the storytelling begins to become a collaborative effort with the two almost speaking as one. Indeed, at times it is unimportant which man is narrating: "it did not matter (and possibly neither of them conscious of the distinction) which one had been doing the talking" (1936, p. 334). This is quite different from earlier on when Quentin responds: "I tell you!" and "I am telling" to Shreve's interruptions (1936, p. 277). The process of storytelling for the young men becomes an intimate situation: "They stared—glared—at one another. It was Shreve speaking...it might have been either of them and was in a sense both: both thinking as one" (1936, p. 303). This method of storytelling is quite at odds with the passing of stories from one generation to the next. It does not partake in a linear chain of forward moving time, but instead creates a narrative space in which fraternal relationships can dominate.

This form of storytelling also cuts across time in a slightly different way; it becomes a way for Quentin and Shreve to connect to two earlier virtual brothers. As Quentin and Shreve's story progresses (and only after the two have begun to narrate as one), an increasing number of references are made to the merging of Quentin and Shreve with Henry and Bon. This is most often accomplished through the image of four men riding two horses: "not two of them there and then either but four of them riding two horses through the iron darkness" (1936, p. 295). Later the text states: "now it was not two but four of them riding the two horses through the dark over the frozen ruts of that Christmas Eve: four of them and then just two—Charles-Shreve and Quentin-Henry" (1936, p. 334). The merging identities of these four men becomes quite visible in such statements. The process of storytelling as practiced by Shreve and Quentin thus becomes a vehicle to cut across time in strange ways.

This story allows for the union of brothers across time and attempts to downplay the role of fathers. This can be seen even in the names that are used in the above. This is one of the few times in the text when Bon is referred to by his Christian name (Charles) rather than his last name. This change seems significant as it refers to him outside of the genealogical imperative, the matrix in which he is caught throughout the entire novel.[15]

Quentin and Shreve's method of storytelling is thus able to create a space in which identities become more complex. While this story is being told, a man no longer stands chronologically in the space between his father and his son. He might instead stand alongside a virtual brother or, and perhaps more significantly, his identity might merge with that brother. In describing the period in which Henry must figure out his feelings regarding the incestuous coupling between Bon and Judith, the novel reads "the two of them (the four of them) held in that probation, that suspension" (1936, p. 335). This little fragment is significant for a few reasons. First, it positions "the two of them" (Henry and Bon) as a stand-in for "the four of them" (Henry, Bon, Quentin, Shreve). Second, it positions Shreve and Quentin as also "held in that probation, that suspension" of Henry's long moment of indecision regarding incest. In my mind, this helps us to make an important connection between the period of Henry's indecision and the period of Quentin and Shreve's storytelling. While Henry constructs an ideal space between himself and his siblings through the imagining of an incestuous relationship that would eternalize their love, Quentin and Shreve's story is an attempt at a similar type of temporality. This can be seen especially through the similarities in language that are used by the two pairs of men. In much the same way that Henry repeatedly tells Bon to "wait" while he figures out what to do about the possibility of incest, Quentin and Shreve also repeat the refrain of "wait" to slow down the flow of time in their narrative.

It is in these moments of "waiting," I would argue, that genealogical time is derailed. For example, at one point during their narration, Shreve says to Quentin: "you wait. Let me play a while now" (1936, p. 280). Shreve sees the slowing down of the story as a space for "play," as a space for his own attempt at meaning-making. Though Quentin is surely the one with more of the "facts" about the Sutpen family, Shreve's contributions to the story are taken as significant. The act of storytelling becomes not the transmission of knowledge from one person or generation to the next, but a space of play, a space that allows for the breakdown of boundaries between narrator, narratee, and character. In this sense, genealogical time cannot be upheld because it depends on quite static identities and the ability to place events in a chain of cause and effect. Quentin and Shreve's story shows that nothing can be completely known, that all the stories they tell are at least partially fictions, that to tell a story is not to transmit old information but to create something new.

In his reading of Quentin and Shreve's storytelling, Joseph Allen Boone describes their retellings as "a fight to master a story that threatens to master them" (1998, p. 301). However, at the same time, according to Boone, "their narration reveal a paradoxical investment in *not* mastering this story, in letting it continue without end" (emphasis in original; 1998, p. 301). While I agree with Boone that the men are invested in "*not* mastering the story" and in delaying its end, I am less convinced that this story functions as a way "of putting their lives on hold, of postponing a confrontation with present day reality" (1998, p. 301). Instead, I see their form of storytelling as a rejection of the very logic of "mastering," invested as this logic is in a framework of patriarchal authority. Their method of shared storytelling and deliberate delay has a more specific purpose than escape. Indeed, hidden within the pauses of their story are the places where we can identity the queer moments of the text and consider what happens in these moments—what a non-genealogical time sense might allow for. Specifically, when genealogical time has been destabilized within the suspended moments of their storytelling, the expression of gender and sexuality becomes quite different.

During Quentin and Shreve's narrating, there are times when the omniscient narrator describes them from an outside perspective. At one particular pause, the text reads:

> There was something curious in the way they looked at one another, curious and quiet and profoundly intent, not at all as two young men might look at each other but almost as a youth and a very young girl might out of virginity itself—a sort of hushed and naked searching, each look burdened with youth's immemorial obsession not with time's dragging weight which the old live but with its fluidity: the bright heels of all the lost moments of fifteen and sixteen. (1936, p. 299)

The passage highlights "the way they looked at one another," an aspect that is dwelled upon in a number of other moments in which the story-telling pauses. In this particular moment, the look is differentiated from how "two young men might look at each other" and compared to the look between a "youth and a very young girl." This description works to complicate the gender identities of the two young men. In this scenario, one of the men is positioned as "a very young girl." And the comparison of the two men to a young man and woman seems to function to inject a form of sexual tension into the act of storytelling. In addition, the inti-macy of this act becomes quite clear as their look is described as "a sort of hushed and naked searching." In analyzing this part of the quote, we can see that this form of storytelling is quite different from those acts of sto-rytelling at the beginning of the text where Quentin's father narrates to his son, an act that solidifies the identities of father and son and attempts to establish a genealogical chronology. Here we have a situation in which the storytelling between two men acts as a destabilizing process, a space of play where gender and sexuality become more ambiguous outside the law of the Father. We might think of these pauses in the storytelling as connected to those "queer moments" that I described in Chapter 2. The act of telling the story together removes Quentin and Shreve from their place in a genealogical chain and opens up a moment in which all those things upon which genealogy depends (assumed heterosexuality, a distinct separation between male and female) dissolve. This is certainly a moment in which time eddies or moves counter to an expected path.

The second part of this quote deals with the conception of time that plays out in Quentin and Shreve's storytelling. "Each look," we are told, is "burdened with youth's immemorial obsession not with time's drag-ging weight which the old live but with its fluidity: the bright heels of all the lost moments of fifteen and sixteen" (1936, p. 299). The two young men are "burdened" with the "immemorial obsession" with time's "flu-idity." If immemorial means, as the *American Heritage Dictionary* states, "reaching beyond the limits of memory, tradition, or recorded history" (def. 1), then we have an interesting parallel to the temporality desired by Henry. Like Henry's desire to return to a pre-social moment, a moment before the incest taboo, the two young narrators are obsessed with the idea of a fluid concept of time, a time that would connect them to those seemingly "lost moments of fifteen and sixteen" (1936, p. 299). This is a longing for, or a desire to inhabit, a past that doesn't quite seem accessible. It is also a desire to resist the forward flow of time.

Though the novel seems to construct these intimate relationships between brothers (or virtual brothers) that allow for alternate, perhaps utopian, conceptions of time, these fraternal enclaves are ultimately unable to endure. In Henry's case, racial otherness crashes his idea of this utopia down. Though he initially gives his permission for Bon to marry his sister, the news that Bon is of mixed race leads him to kill his half-brother before the marriage can take place. The dream of an escape from the time that is instituted with the law of exchange is no match for the racist discourses of the American South during the Civil War. This dream of a utopian world of love between him and his siblings, as Henry imagines it, has no place for racial otherness—it destroys the very grounds through which the dream was deemed attractive or desirable.

At the level of narrative, we can see Quentin's ultimate fear that he is nothing more than a link in the chain of genealogy. In the novel's final chapter, Quentin and Shreve seem to uncouple as a singular narrating entity. Shreve begins to question Quentin about living amid stories from the past; he says, "what is it? Something you live and breathe in like the air?... a kind of entailed birthright father and son and father and son of never forgetting General Sherman, so that forevermore as long as your children's children produce children you won't be anything but a descendant of a long line of colonels killed in Pickett's charge at Manasses?" (1936, p. 361). This is Quentin's greatest fear, the fear of a time eternally ruled by genealogy—that there is no escape, no way to outline one's father's legacy. While the communal narrating of the story with Shreve allowed a long moment of escape from the genealogical imperative, the two must eventually uncouple and take their places as inheritors of their fathers' legacies.

In *Absalom, Absalom!*, then, this attempt at occupying a temporality outside the law of the Father, is possible, but fleeting. Characters are able to occupy that "fleeting moment" of belief that "that the law of exchange could be evaded" (Levi-Strauss 1969, p. 497). Although within these moments identities are destabilized and taboos are explored, the characters eventually discover that they are still subject to genealogical time.

*   *   *

There is a very strong parallel between Faulkner's use of sibling incest in *Absalom, Absalom!* and Carter's use of this same trope in *The Magic Toyshop*. Carter's 1967 novel tells the story of Melanie, a fifteen-year-old girl forced to move in with her tyrannical Uncle Philip after the death of her parents. She finds solace in the arms of her kindly aunt and her aunt's two brothers, who all live in fear of her uncle. Melanie's aunt is involved in an incestuous relationship with one of her own brothers, and, when Uncle Philip discovers this, his house literally goes up in flames. Sibling incest here functions as a resistance to the patriarchal authority of Uncle Philip. Carter even frames the temporality of incest in a similar manner to Faulkner, calling it "the most primeval of passion," and "an ancient passion" (1967, p. 195). Indeed, she even places the moment of revelation just as the characters have smashed the cuckoo clock that Uncle Philip had built, a clock that seems to tick out the normative temporality of paternal authority.

Carter, like Faulkner, positions sibling incest in opposition to patriarchal authority, as the mechanism that can perhaps halt the movement of time and return characters to a prehistoric Eden. Incest, here, has the power to cause destruction of the patriarchal house. And as the house burns, Melanie seems caught in a moment not unlike those I explored in Faulkner—a moment in which she seems to believe in the possibility of evading the law of the Father. In the last line of the novel, she is described as turning to her love interest in a Keatsian "wild surmise" (1967, p. 200). The novel thus leaves her frozen in that moment of conjectured possibility.

Interestingly, *The Magic Toyshop* uses not a literal father, but rather an uncle as the center of the tale. In this novel, the uncle seems to be a stand-in for the father, a symbol of patriarchal power. But as we move into Carter's later novels, the position of the uncle seems to change drastically, figuring not as a parallel form of paternal authority but as the very space of resistance to that authority. In her 1991 novel *Wise Children*, aunts and uncles come to figure in an alternative relationship to both genealogy and temporality. I would thus like to examine the formation and undoing of genealogical time in this novel with respect to avuncular relations. Along the way, I will turn to Eve Sedgwick's concept of the "avunculate" to sketch out a framework for my analysis before performing my own reading of Carter's novel. By examining genealogy from the vantage point of avuncular relations, I hope to trace the queer tales that become possible when storytelling (and with it, genealogy) is derailed.

Unlike *Absalom, Absalom!*, *Wise Children* examines genealogy from the vantage point of the daughter. In Faulkner's novel, genealogy is explored almost exclusively through a male point of view. Though Judith would play a major role in the happy incestuous community Henry has constructed in his mind, Judith's permission is never sought, nor is it ever clear whether she knows Bon is her half-brother. While this incestuous triangle might allow for the evasion of the law of the Father, this union is still rather male-centered. Faulkner's text thus leaves the question of the daughter's relation to genealogy relatively untouched. But Carter's interest in daughters is evident. One of *Wise Children*'s epigraphs comments: "How many times Shakespeare draws fathers and daughters, never mothers and daughters."

Wise Children draws all types of family relationships between the legitimate and illegitimate sides of the Hazard family. The novel is narrated by Dora Chance, one half of a pair of twins from, as she descriptively says, "the bastard side of Old Father Thames" (1991, p. 1). From the beginning of the novel, the twins are positioned in relation to a whole host of fathers. There's "Old Father Thames"; there's the man they assume to be their biological father, Melchoir Hazard; and there's the man who publicly acts as their father, Perry Hazard, Melchoir's twin brother. Early on in the novel, Dora gives an explanation for the story she relates to readers: "But the urge has come upon me before I drop to seek out an answer to the question that always has teased me, as if the answer were hidden, somewhere, behind a curtain: Whence came we? Whither goeth we?" (1991, p. 11). Dora's telling of her life story, at the ripe age of seventy-five, is thus in many ways an attempt to understand her origins and her future.[16] This goal leads her to consider many times throughout the story the role that fathers have played in her and her sister's lives.

What is perhaps most striking about the novel's portrayal of fathers is the eternal question mark that accompanies issues of paternity. There are very few characters in the novel, if any, whose paternity is known for certain. Indeed, most of the critics writing about Carter's novel mention this uncertainty regarding fathers. Anne Hegerfeldt talks about it as the "gigantic question mark over the question of [the twins'] paternity" (2003, p. 300). Michael Hardin discusses it as "the lack of definitive paternity" (1994, p. 78). And Celestino Deleyto claims that "to the end [Dora] entertains serious doubts as to who her father was" (1995, p. 163). In the absence of known fathers, other kinship relations become confused as well, as demonstrated by Dora's reference to a certain relative as her "half-brother/nephew" (1991, p. 119) and by Melchoir's reference to the twins as "my own daughters...my nieces" (ellipsis in text, 1991, p. 134). Given such ever-present doubt, the novel's epigraph "It's a wise child that knows its own father," takes on a quite ironic tone.

Because Nora and Dora inhabit this world of never-certain paternity, they see fatherhood as distinct from biological fact. Dora explains: "a mother is always a mother, since a mother is a biological fact, whilst a father is a moveable feast" (1991, p. 216). Though the novel also seems to deconstruct the idea of mother as "biological fact," Dora's statement here shows the way in which a father is an ever-changing construct—a fantasy, "a moveable feast." As Hegerfeldt claims, "the novel suggests that one does well to remember that [the idea of father] is a construct" (2003, pp. 358–359). Because fatherhood is usually not known for certain, its sole function is symbolic—but it is a symbol with very real consequences. For instance, the authenticity of biological paternity hardly matters in terms of social power. What matters is that a child is given the name of his or her father and is accepted by a community as the father's child. In the case of Nora and Dora, though they are the children of one of the Hazard brothers, they do not retain their father's name but instead retain the name "Chance," the name of the woman who raised them, a woman they call "grandma" though she is not. They may be the biological children of a quite important man, but they are not acknowledged as such and thus do not reap the social benefits of this relation. Conversely, a child born into a family as the result of the mother's unknown extramarital affair would likely receive the name of its mother's husband and the rights and privileges bestowed on a legitimate child. It is in this way that the father is a construct: it is based on a tacit agreement that a child will function as the offspring of its father that is completed when the child is given the father's last name.

However, just because "father" is a social construct and predominantly unknowable doesn't mean that patriarchal structures come crashing down. In her reading of *Wise Children*, Sarah Gamble asks, "how can the authority of the father be sustained in a world in which he cannot even be identified?" (2001, p. 170). Similarly, Michael Hardin claims that "lack of definitive paternity" leads to the dissolution of patriarchal privilege. He asks: "How can patriarchy exist if the very patriarchs/fathers themselves are not known? Without a clear patriarchal lineage, there can be no patriarchal privilege" (1994, p. 78). If what Hardin claims here were true, there would be no such thing as "patriarchal privilege" to begin with. It is always the case, not just in Carter's novel, that "patriarchs/fathers themselves are not known," at least not for certain. Ultimately, patriarchy doesn't function because of bloodlines; it functions because of symbolic power. The signifier of "father" is what matters, not the biological "truth" of fatherhood. Carter's novel does not, therefore, create a space where patriarchal privilege cannot function (for certainly even within this novel there are numerous places where we see it functioning quite well) but instead makes visible the way in which the idea of "father" is based on creating a coherent genealogical narrative out of fragments of information.

The idea of fatherhood not as fact but as narrative appears a number of times throughout *Wise Children*. The twins are first told that Melchoir, a famous Shakespearean actor, is their father by their "grandmother" who takes them to one of their father's productions and points at the man saying: "That man is ... your father!" (ellipsis in original, 1991, p. 56). Because the twins have not been given their father's name or raised near him, the news must come in the form of a story from their grandmother. The children's request later that day—"Tell us some more about fathers"—seems to position fathers clearly in the realm of stories, as their command is a request for a story. Even their father's family profession, stage acting, specifically Shakespearean acting, is indicative of a connection to narrative. As Hegerfeldt rightly points out, the Hazards are "confused about where the script ends and life begins" (2003, p. 363). However, it is important to note that the twins, as illegitimate children, lie far outside the official script or story of their father's family. As far as family genealogies go, they do not exist.

For Carter, the fantasy of fatherhood is put in direct opposition to the materiality of a variety of other kinship relations. This is demonstrated quite clearly when the twins ask their grandmother to explain to them about fathers. After hearing a description of how procreation occurs, Dora states that she and her sister "thought [Grandma] made it up to tease us. To think that we girls were in the world because a man we'd never met did that to a girl we didn't remember, once upon a time! What we knew for certain was, our grandma loved us and we had the best uncle in the world" (1991, p. 57). This quote sets up a distinction between the twins' parents, specifically biological parents, on the one hand, and their grandma and uncle, on the other hand. Their parents belong to the world of stories; they associate the act that resulted in their birth with the phrase "once upon a time" (1991, p. 54). They think their grandma "made it up" (1991, p. 54). Because their parents have no real involvement in or perceivable effect on their lives, the girls are unable to see them as anything other than a fantastical story that happened "once upon a time." Their grandmother and uncle, conversely, belong to the realm of "what we knew for certain." They represent the twins' material lives. Though their grandmother is not biologically related to them, her love is a felt reality for the girls.

Likewise, their Uncle Perry falls into the category of what is known "for certain." Though Perry is their biological father's twin brother, the twins cannot know this until they find out who their father is. Since they have no idea what a father is, as the above exchange seems to indicate, they cannot understand the concept of uncle as a kinship relation. Before they learn what a father is, for them the word "uncle" must function in its more symbolic meaning, the name for an older man with whom one is close. The novel thus places these relationships (those born out of emotional closeness) as more important for the twins. Though the fantasy of a reunion with their "real" father is an articulated desire that accompanies much of Dora's storytelling, it is these more material relationships between Dora/Nora and their grandmother and uncle that affect and influence their development.[17]

In fact, throughout the entire text, avuncular relations form more significant ties between individuals than parent/child relationships. This is certainly true of Perry who, though he disappears for long periods of time from their lives, serves as a loving and supportive relative to the twins. But this is also true of the twins themselves, who function as aunts to a number of characters in the text. In some cases the relation is biological, and in some cases the relationship is invented. The twins continue the tradition started by their grandma of creating their own family. Dora says of her grandma that she "invented this family. She put it together out of whatever came to hand—a stray pair of orphaned babes, a ragamuffin in a flat cap" (1991, p. 35). Thus, these are families born not out of biology or marriage but actively created. Families constructed in such a way move quite far away from models of genealogical succession that trace family lines from father to son.

In order to examine the way that alternative family arrangements affect the idea of genealogy, I would like to consider at length Eve Sedgwick's essay "Tales of the Avunculate: Queer Tutelage in *The Importance of Being Earnest.*" Sedgwick's essay claims that Wilde's play suggests: "Forget the name of the Father. Think about your uncles and your aunts" (1993, pp. 58–59). Her reading shows exactly what might "be at stake in the making visible of aunts and uncles" (1993, p. 61). Sedgwick's article provides a framework for my consideration of the nature of avuncular relations in *Wise Children* and their specific relation to temporality.

According to Sedgwick, an uncle-centered society, unlike a parent-centered society, incorporates homosexual impulses (1993, p. 61). For example, the uncle is especially important in groups that practice institutional or ritual forms of homosexuality (Owens 1994, p. 227). Beyond this, aunts and uncles often "hold the office of representing nonconforming or nonreproductive sexualities to children," because their access to children doesn't depend on "pairing or procreation" (1993, p. 63). A parent, conversely, has access to children precisely because of his or her relation to the heterosexual institution of marriage and reproduction. It is often through our aunts and our uncles, Sedgwick claims, that we come to have a sense of "the possibility of alternate life trajectories" (1993, p. 63).

Sedgwick's text begins to sketch out a vague relationship between the avunculate and alternate conceptions of time:

> if having grandparents means perceiving your parents as somebody's children, then having aunts and uncles, even the most conventional of aunts and uncles, means perceiving your parents as somebody's sibs—not, that is, as alternatively abject and omnipotent links in a chain of compulsion and replication that leads inevitably to you; but rather as elements in a varied, contingent, recalcitrant but reforming seriality, as people who demonstrably could have turned out very differently—indeed as people who, in the differing, refractive relations among their own generation, can be seen already to have done so. (1993, p. 63)

We can read Sedgwick's statement here as drawing out the distinction between a temporality based on the relation between grandparents, parents and children and one based on the relation between aunts, uncles, and nieces or nephews. A temporality based on parental relationships, on "perceiving your parents as somebody's children," means seeing one's relations as "links in a chain of compulsion and replication that leads inevitably to you" (1993, p. 63). Her use of the word "chain" here draws up an image of linearity. A link in a chain is connected only to the link that directly precedes it and the one that directly follows it. The image is also connected to the idea of cause and effect, as it is a common metaphor for cause/effect relationships.[18] This is supported by Sedgwick's use of the term "inevitably." If we see ourselves as one link in the chain that proceeds from our grandparents through us and perhaps to our children, then we are the "inevitable" result of that progression, the ultimate effect in a chain of cause and effect. Thinking about time through our parents, quite surely, is thinking about time genealogically.

Aunts and uncles, conversely, offer us an alternate way of thinking about time. Having aunts and uncles, as Sedgwick states, means seeing our "parents as somebody's sibs," a perception that doesn't inevitably result in imagining temporality as a linear chain that connects progressive generations. Indeed, acknowledging aunts and uncles means perceiving our parents "as elements in a varied, contingent, recalcitrant but reforming seriality, as people who demonstrably could have turned out very differently" (1993, p. 63). Aunts and uncles, therefore, allow for contingencies; they offer difference. They break the chain of cause and effect and show just how differently it all could have ended up.

The form of time offered by avuncular relations seems to bear a striking resemblance to the temporality of the kiss that I sketched out in my second chapter. In much the same way that the kiss can be representative of an "open future," a future that is not always-already decided, this form of avuncular time also seems to play on the idea of a future that is not predetermined. As Sedgwick states, it is most often aunts and uncles who offer 'the possibility of alternate life trajectories" (1993, p. 63). Our aunts and uncles remove the assumption that a certain future is inevitable. They are the space through which difference or chance can enter the equation.

This is in stark contrast with the temporality that Lee Edelman calls "reproductive futurism." For Edelman, part of the problem with linear histories or genealogies is the way in which the future does not represent a change from the present but rather results in the endless reproduction of the same. The notion of "reproductive futurism" is the key example of this. While reproduction may seem to bring about change, the new generation invariably produces "the past, through displacement, in the form of the future" (2004, p. 31). Edelman's terms here sound a lot like the idea of genealogy as a linear chain, a chain "that leads *inevitably* to you" (emphasis added; Sedgwick 1993, p. 63). If something is "inevitable" then there is no possibility for change. The future was already decided long in the past, and cause and effect have produced and continue to produce what will happen next.

Avuncular time moves away from "reproductive futurism," then, because it doesn't figure the future as always-already decided; it imagines life narratives as spinning off in, to use Sedgwick's terms, "varied, contingent, recalcitrant" directions. This point is quite visible when we examine the life trajectory of Uncle Perry in *Wise Children*. About their uncle, Dora states: "[Perry] gave us a Chinese banquet of options as to what happened to him next. He gave us all his histories, we could choose which we wanted" (1991, p. 31). Dora's statement about her uncle focuses on his lack of fixity. He does not have a history, but rather "histories." There is no definite way of knowing "what happened to him next"; his nieces are instead given a "banquet of options." And unlike their father, who marries three times, their uncle never marries. He, like his nieces, stands outside of legitimizing institutions. If the story offered by the biological father is one of linearity, then the story offered by aunts and uncles are quite different. Here Uncle Perry's story offers choice, a model for a different type of future.

Like their Uncle Perry, Dora and Nora's life narratives also seem to spin off in unpredictable directions. It is significant, I believe, that the women's last name is not that of their biological father, but instead is "Chance." It is precisely in deviating from the name of the Father that we have the possibility for chance to enter the equation.[19] For this reason, I would like to consider the women not as daughters, but instead as nieces and as aunts. The twins see their uncle and their (nonbiological) grandmother as the most significant of their relatives. In positioning themselves as nieces rather than as daughters, the twins seem to critique the symbolic grand narrative of fatherhood. In their role as aunts, likewise, they carve out a space for women within the family that is not purely biological.

Let's look for a second at the facts of the two women's lives. Though each comes close on occasions, neither woman marries. And though both are sexually active with men throughout their entire adult lives, neither woman gives birth to a child. On the day the narration of the story takes place, the twins are seventy-five years old. They are spinsters (though their sexual adventures may remove them from the most conventional image of spinsterhood). Spinsterhood, in fact, may be one of those "nonconforming or nonreproductive sexualities" that aunts and uncles represent to children (Sedgwick 1993, p. 63). Because they are beyond menopause and have neither reproduced nor married, they are outside, as are all spinsters, that normative life-narrative.

When spinsters make appearances in literature, it is quite commonly through the role of aunt.[20] As adults, the descriptor of aunt is the one that names Dora and Nora most accurately. Even their half-brother Tristram refers to them as "aunties." Dora asks: "Why does he call us 'aunties' when we are, in fact, his half-sisters?" (1991, p. 8). Though we find out later that neither aunt nor sister accurately describes the relation between Tristram and the twins, the descriptor of "aunt" is accurate in its more metaphorical meaning, as a term of endearment for an older woman.

Because I see "aunt" as perhaps the most significant role that the twins play, I would like to think of this novel as the narration of an aunt, as told specifically from the perspective of a certain type of aunt, an over-the-hill, nonreproductive spinster. If I were to follow Carter's trend of incorporating Shakespearean allusions, I might say that it is a tale told by an aunt, full of twists and turns, signifying a deviant form of narration. The histories of the words "aunt" and "spinster" are connected to the telling of stories. In Shakespeare, "aunt" can mean "an old woman" or "old gossip" (def. 2). To gossip is to tell stories, stories that are often in opposition to official histories. The most literal definition of the word "spinster" is someone who spins or twists fibers into threads (def. 1a). The word "spin" is very often used in connection to the telling of stories, as in "to spin a yarn" (def. 3b). Dora is indeed a gossip, a spinner of yarns, a teller who deviates from the official, legitimate narrative.

Dora's narrative, however, is most interesting in its pacing and in the value system that it constructs. These aspects of her story, I would argue, represent a specifically avuncular way of perceiving temporality. This form of avuncular time can be seen in a particular moment that Dora describes:

> The lights went down, the bottom of the curtain glowed, I loved it and have always loved it best of all, the moment when the lights go down, the curtain glows, you know that something wonderful is about to happen. It doesn't matter if what happens next spoils everything; the anticipation itself is always pure.
>
> To travel hopefully is better than to arrive, as Uncle Perry used to say. I always preferred foreplay, too. (1991, p. 54)

Dora values most of all "the moment when...you know that something wonderful is about to happen." She loves the moment not when something happens, but the moment before it happens. She values the anticipation over the arrival, the "foreplay" over the climax. Interestingly, she connects this value system with her Uncle Perry. It is from Uncle Perry that she learns "To travel hopefully is better than to arrive," a statement that she herself turns sexual. Through her Uncle Perry, she is able to see a "nonconforming or nonreproductive" sexuality, as Sedgwick states, a sexuality that favors foreplay over consummation.

But Dora's statements here are even more telling with regard to the pacing of her narrative. In her storytelling, Dora attempts to create these types of moments, moments that linger in the anticipation before something happens. Her narrative is a self-conscious one, and she often comments on this aspect of her storytelling: "But, truthfully, these glorious pauses do, sometimes, occur in the discordant and complementary narratives of our lives and if you choose to stop the story there, at such a pause, and refuse to take it any further, then you can call it a happy ending" (1991, p. 227). Dora knows that narratives are constructs, that she has to stop the story in a particular way in order to call it a happy ending; she knows that when the curtain does rise what happens next might spoil everything. And yet she attempts to draw out those moments because they are full of anticipation of what will happen next.

Though I have constructed my description of avuncular time specifically in relation to *Wise Children*, I believe that it is a form of time that also serves to describe certain moments of Quentin and Shreve's narration in *Absalom, Absalom!*. In those heavy pauses in their narrative, pauses in which a sexual tension between the young men becomes apparent, we are presented with a form of storytelling that allows for the existence of nonreproductive desires and sexualities. Additionally, what makes possible the telling of their tale is the information that Quentin has received from "Aunt Rosa," a woman who, though she is not Quentin's aunt, occupies fully the identity of "aunt." Indeed, Shreve continues to refer to her as "Aunt Rosa," even after Quentin tells him multiple times that she is not his aunt. It is ultimately Aunt Rosa who makes possible Quentin's ability to tell a different story about the Sutpen family than his father did. In this way, she allows Quentin to move away from a genealogical way of telling family narratives.

In the moments of pause I have described, characters teeter on the edge of an "open future," to use a term I elaborated on in my second chapter. Here we might think of the "open future" as specifically related to a form of avuncular time. If aunts and uncles offer a way of thinking about time in which the future is not predetermined, then this form of narration attempts to position characters (and readers) in moments where "anything might happen" (1991, p. 112). This phrase, that "anything might happen," was one that I spent a great deal of time discussing in my second chapter. Appearing in Michael Cunningham's

The Hours, the phrase describes the intense feeling of possibility that accompanied various kisses. This exact same phrase appears in *Wise Children* when Nora and Dora arrive on the movie set for the film version of *A Midsummer Night's Dream* in which they will star. Dora states: "We thought anything might happen" (1991, p. 112). This is the same feeling of anticipation that Dora is referencing when she describes "the moment when the lights go down, the curtain glows, you know that something wonderful is about to happen" (1991, p. 54). Even if this is ruined by what happens next, it doesn't matter, she states, because the "anticipation itself is always pure" (1991, p. 54). This value-system seems to be in direct opposition to the way time is conceived in genealogies. Genealogy is about movement to the next (the next generation, the next event), about charting the links between one generation and the next, between one moment and the one that follows or precedes it. Genealogical time doesn't really allow for the consideration of an isolated generation or an isolated moment. All time, and all people, are connected through a chain, specifically a chain structured through the logic of cause and effect.

The interruption of these forms of genealogical time is made possible in Carter's novel by symbolically equating acts of sex with acts of storytelling. If genealogy is the result of reproductive sex, then nonreproductive sex might function to allow for different modes of storytelling, for different stories or different narrative trajectories. This connection becomes quite clear in a passage where Dora describes having sex with her Uncle Perry. This act occurs when Dora is seventy-five and her uncle is one hundred. The sex is therefore not only incestuous but also stands no chance of producing offspring since Dora is well beyond her childbearing years. Their lovemaking is so vigorous that there is a moment when Nora believes her sister and uncle might "bring the house down, fuck the house down" (1991, p. 220). The house, symbolically, is their father's house. Incest, as I stated in my reading of Faulkner, often functions as the "primal affront to the authority of the father" (Irwin 2003, pp. 59–60). Dora and Perry's sex for a moment seems to have the possibility to bring the genealogical house down, to break the law of the father.[21]

Dora's own description of the lovemaking dwells on this idea but moves from it to the consideration of narrative. She states:

What would have happened if we *had* brought the house down? Wrecked the whole lot, roof blown off, floor caved in, all the people blown out of the blown-out windows…sent it all sky high, destroyed all the terms of every contract, set all the old books on fire, wiped the slate clean. As if, when the young king meets up again with Jack Falstaff in *Henry IV, Part Two*, he doesn't send him packing but digs him in the ribs, says: "Have I got a job for you!" (1991, pp. 221–222)

If the house were brought down by Dora and Perry's lovemaking, it would have "destroyed all the terms of every contract, set all the old books on fire, wiped the slate clean" (1991, p. 221). Each of these images is one of writing; contracts, books, and slates are all written documents. The mention of "contracts" seems to imply that bringing down the father's house would change the law. The destruction of the "old books" suggests that these stories would no longer serve as master narratives. And to wipe "the slate clean" implies the possibility of beginning again without established rules. But the most specific example of what would be possible if the father's house came crashing down comes from literature. *Henry IV, Part 2* could end quite differently, not with Henry sending Falstaff off packing, but with the offer of a job. This act, then, in bringing down the house of the father, would allow for different endings to stories. For *Henry IV, Part 2* to end in this fashion would mean quite a different story; it would turn the play from a tragedy into a comedy, as Carter critics have pointed out. Kate Webb explains in "Seriously Funny," her essay on *Wise Children*, "Near the close of her story, Dora tries to reimagine one of Shakespeare's cruelest moments: What if Hal, on becoming king, had not rejected Falstaff, but dug him on the ribs and offered him a job instead? What if order was permanently rejected, and we lived life as a perpetual carnival?" (2000, p. 281). The rejection of Falstaff in this play signals a triumph for paternal order and, consequently, for genealogical time. Prince Hal steps out of the matrix of relations that includes Falstaff and steps back into the successive line of kings to take his place as his father's son.

While I agree with Webb that this alternate ending to Shakespeares's play offers a rejection of a certain type of order, I am not as convinced that this is a rejection of order in and of itself and a vision of life as a "perpetual carnival" (Webb 2000, p. 281). In my mind, the significance of this rewriting is that it moves us away from the inevitable, predictable ending where the illegitimate is rejected in favor of the legitimate. It points us to a situation in which Falstaff has a place within Hal's kingship. If this rewriting were a clear rejection of order, then Prince Hal would have turned his back on his father and his role as king; he would have continued in his carnivalesque life with Falstaff. But such a move would have done nothing to disrupt power structures. The legitimate and the illegitimate would have existed in their separate spheres, and though Hal would not have taken his rightful place as king, someone else would have, and order would have remained intact. If, on the other hand, Hal had given Falstaff a job, he would have symbolically allowed for the mixing of the legitimate and the illegitimate. He would have maintained a certain type of order by accepting the kingship, but he would have changed the very nature of that order by giving Falstaff a place within it. The use of this example by Dora in describing what might happen if she and her uncle's lovemaking brought her father's house crashing down seems to imply that such an act has the ability to change the way we order things (not perhaps to destroy order all together) but to break down the clear lines between legitimate and illegitimate. Perhaps, as Dora's example of Shakespeare rewritten seems to suggest, order need not mean endless repetition of the same.

This is not the only time that the novel employs narrative symbolically to explore the idea of order. In describing her inability to narrate linearly, Dora states: "There I go again! Can't keep a story going in a straight line, can I? Drunk in charge of a narrative" (1991, p. 158). Dora's statement here highlights her position as a teller of the tale who deviates from conventional storytelling methods. Her story doesn't go in a "straight line" (might there be a pun on "straight" here?), and her labeling of herself as a drunk certainly positions her as a deviant storyteller. I would argue that Dora's comment demonstrates a form of telling that depends upon a specifically avuncular form of time. This is a story that doesn't go in a "straight line" and thus avoids the necessity of moving conventional plots to their necessary conventional and "logical" endings. Without a progressive, linear temporality, there can be no "inevitable" ending.

What is perhaps even more interesting about Dora's description of herself as "a drunk in charge of a narrative" is the way it anticipates a later statement that she will make, a statement that serves to connect narrative and reproduction, if not directly then implicitly. At the very end of the novel, when Dora and Nora are taking home the twin babies they have been given to raise (their niece and nephew), a man says to them: "Drunk in charge of a baby carriage, at your age" (1991, p. 231). In the repetition of "drunk in charge," there is a clear connection being drawn between constructing narratives and parenting children. In a genealogical narrative, time flows linearly, but here the narratives don't go "in a straight line" (1991, p. 158). This avuncular narrative produces a different trajectory, one in which aunts raise the children. These aunts, as Webb states, are "unmarried, non-biological and overage mothers" (2000, p. 288). They disrupt quite clearly the normal timeline for child rearing (just as their singing in the streets as they toddle home contrasts with the behavior expected of old women). They are signaled also as deviant parents by the man who yells that they are "drunk in charge of a baby carriage."

In this way, the Chance's story interrupts a developmental life narrative–the women become parents for the first time at the age of seventy-five, not through an act of reproduction, but by chance. This is thus a family line (and a narrative line) that does not reproduce itself in a predictable way. It is also worth noting the biracialism of the twins that Dora and Nora are given to raise. While racial otherness tears down the attempt at an alternative form of time in *Absalom, Absalom!*, it seems absolutely imperative in *Wise Children* that racial hybridity be part of the "invented families" that Nora and Dora seek to produce. When an aunt is left in charge of the narrative and in charge of the child-rearing, there seems to be the opportunity for stories and life trajectories to take off in new directions.

The question that we have to ask ourselves at the end of *Wise Children*, though, is whether the reconfiguration of family narratives has produced alternate ways of conceiving of time. Though we have a different family configuration here (one not based on the biological nuclear family), we still have that ever-present symbol of the future, as Edelman would remind us—the child. The twins that Nora and Dora are given to raise are constructed as the future of both the Hazard and the Chance families. So despite the fact that Nora and Dora have led quite unconventional lives, their ultimate job is to function as women who raise children. Additionally, the story ends conventionally: with a birth. Does the ending, then, enact a type of "reproductive futurism" (2004, p. 31), in which, as Edelman states, the past is projected into the future?

In one sense, this is hard to deny, as there does seem to be a certain value placed on child rearing at the end of the novel, on the possibilities reproduction allows for. However, this ending also seems to be like

Dora's alternate ending of *Henry IV, Part 2* in which Prince Hal gives Falstaff a job instead of publicly denouncing him. While the ending of *Wise Children* does not represent a complete stepping outside of the institutions of reproduction and child-rearing, it does inject change into the normative order of these institutions. Nora and Dora are able to alter the stories that are told about child-rearing, about family configurations, by actively taking a part in these institutions. Their story therefore offers a future that is not inevitably the same as the past.

*   *   *

In *Impossible Desires*, Gayatri Gopinath suggests that the severing of genealogy allows for the recuperation of desires that had been deemed unthinkable. Though Gopinath is writing in a quite different context than I am (exploring the notion of queer diasporas in relation to genealogical national narratives), I find her theories quite useful for my own purposes. In my readings of Faulkner and Carter, I have found that the severing of genealogical storytelling does in fact allow for certain "impossible desires." In both texts, we are presented with forms of storytelling that attempt to escape the mandates of genealogy. In each case, the text lingers on moments of waiting, of anticipation, of belief in the possibility of evading the law of the Father. Interestingly, such moments often become sexually charged or strangely erotic. These queer moments, as I have referred to them elsewhere, allow us to imagine temporalities not ruled by linear succession.

And yet the queer moments of Faulkner and Carter are somewhat different from the queer moments of Woolf and Cunningham that I explored previously. In Woolf and Cunningham, we have an explicitly sexual moment (a kiss) that allows for a queering of time. In Faulkner and Carter, however, those pauses in storytelling, those moments of waiting, actually produce a space of play in which nonreproductive desires can operate. Here it is the temporality of the storytelling that opens up the moment to these desires.

The desires that emerge in Faulkner and in Carter are certainly nonreproductive, nonnormative, and perhaps even queer. If we slip back into the anthropological language of Claude Levi-Strauss, we might read these desires in relation to societal prohibitions or refer to them as specifically taboo. Indeed, across the two novels I have explored, we have a few of the most common taboos represented. *Absalom, Absalom!* not only presents us with the dream of an incestuous union between siblings, but also allows us to witness the homoerotic storytelling of two young men. And *Wise Children* gives us the image of an intergenerational incestuous coupling between an uncle and a niece. Incest, homosexuality, and intergenerational sex are some of the most common sexual prohibitions. It seems, then, that the interruption of genealogical time in each of these authors is an attempt to evade the law of exchange, an attempt to remain poised at that moment before the law of exchange rendered those desires impossible.

These desires themselves serve to threaten genealogy, as genealogy is built through reproduction. Such desires also disrupt the smooth linearity of narratives that depend on the tracing of genealogical ties. Instead of a narrative strand stretching linearly from the distant past into the future, in these queer moments of storytelling, moments heavy with desire, we see the folding or looping of narrative strands. In these moments where genealogical lines become tangled, we find not only the opening to queer desires but also the opportunity for transgressive storytelling.

NOTES

1. According to Levi-Strauss, the incest taboo is the dividing line between nature and culture. Before the institution of the incest taboo, a society does not exist as a society. He states: "[the incest prohibition] is the fundamental step because of which, by which, but above all in which, the transition from nature to culture is accomplished [...] Before it, culture is still non-existent; with it, nature's sovereignty over man is ended. The prohibition of incest is where nature transcends itself [...] It brings about and is in itself the advent of a new order" (1969, pp. 24–25).

2. According to Peter Brooks, the "question of fathers and sons" is "perhaps the dominant thematic and structural concern and shaping force in the nineteenth-century novel, ultimately perhaps constituting a theme and structure incorporate with the very nature of the novel as we know it" (1984, p. 307). The centrality of this theme to the novel itself helps to explain the trend in the British novel that "takes a child...on a journey of exploration and discovery into the past in search of a parent's true identity, usually the father's" (Hickman 1998, p. 33).

3. Though I frame my analysis through Tobin's particular work on this subject, the connection between genealogy and narrative has been noted by other scholars as well. However, this relationship often is not explicitly articulated but rather is taken for granted. Of the literary critics I could find, Tobin has the longest and most detailed analysis of the relation between genealogy and narrative.

4. Although I will not focus on this point in my chapter, I feel it is important to note that Carter's text deals not only with biological genealogy but also with literary genealogy. For example, she explores Shakespeare as a sort of founding father and analyzes the implications of his status as a cultural icon. In some ways, the relationship between Carter and Shakespeare parallels the strange relation we see between Winterson and Eliot in my third chapter.

5. Alongside the genealogy, Faulkner's novel also includes a section titled "Chronology" and a map of Yoknapatawpha county. These neatly laid out representations of the novel's events and bloodlines seems to be in tension with the complicated nature of the narrative itself.

6. The novel's title also references the biblical story when Henry murders his half-brother Bon to prevent his marriage to their sister, an event that echoes Absalom's murder of his brother for raping his sister.

7. As I will explain more fully when I come to my discussion of *Wise Children*, avuncular relations are the relations between uncles/aunts and their nephews/nieces. The dictionary definition establishes avuncular as "Of, belonging to, or resembling, an uncle" (def. 1). However, I will be following Eve Sedgwick's more capacious use of the term.

8. In Sutpen's marriage to Ellen, even the name of the bride's father is of particular importance. According to Rosa, this marriage came about because Sutpen needed the name of Ellen's father on a document of respectability: "all he would need would be Ellen's and our father's names on a wedding license (or on any other patent of respectability) that people could look at it and read" (1936, p. 16).

9. Of course, not just any son will do. His son must be white in order to carry on the genealogical line that Sutpen has in mind. He rejects Charles Bon for being racially mixed, and he might have other children from mothers who are biracial.

10. Though Bon is the last name of Charles Bon, the novel predominantly refers to him in this manner. I will follow the novel's tendency to refer to Charles Bon by his last name and Henry Sutpen by his first.

11. This is also the version of the story that is treated by most critics as the most accurate. (And in abbreviated plot summaries of the novel, Quentin's version is the one given as true.) Quentin, unlike the narrators before him, does have the greatest access to knowledge about the Sutpen family given that he listens to the stories of all of the other narrators. However, it is also important to note that much of the story that he and Shreve tell is conjecture based on the few facts that they do have.

12. It is important to note that Levi-Strauss's *The Elementary Structures of Kinship* deals with incest almost exclusively in terms of sibling or cousin incest. For example, it is always the brothers who give away sisters and

receive other men's sisters in return. It is for this reason that his work is particularly helpful for my purposes.

13. In these lines, we might also note the homoeroticism. Henry is not only offering his sister's life to his friend, but also his own life. Under Levi-Strauss's theories, one of the direct results of giving a sister in marriage is the gain of a brother-in-law. The sister serves as the link that ties the two men, but what the man is directly gaining is the companionship of another man.

14. This might explain much about the meaning of incest for Quentin, as Quentin faces incestuous feelings in *The Sound and the Fury* toward his own sister. The way in which incest might create an eternal relationship between the siblings and serve as an affront to the father appears also with great clarity in that text.

15. Charles Bon's last name is not that of his biological father (Sutpen) but rather a name given to him by Sutpen specifically to exclude him from Sutpen's dynasty. The last name Bon is thus a symbol for the very way in which names solidify the law of the father by setting up conceptions of legitimacy and illegitimacy. The use of the first name and absence of the last name from this particular description of the man deals with the character outside of conceptions of genealogy; it attempts to forget fathers.

16. Dora's explanation of her reason for relating her life story is reminiscent of Hickman's description of that common plot device of British novels, in which a child goes "on a journey of exploration and discovery into the past in search of a parent's true identity, usually the father's" (Hickman 1998, p. 33). Though this is a seventy-five-year-old woman recalling her childhood, the quest to understand her father's identity is certainly paramount in the text.

17. This is not to say that Nora and Dora never desire acceptance and recognition from their birth father. As Hegerfeldt states, "the myth of paternity and legitimacy is a powerful one, and time and again the characters fall prey to its seductive power even while recognizing it as an instrument of social hegemony" (2003, p. 358). Dora certainly falls prey to paternity's "seductive power" even while she subtly articulates a critique of this construct.

18. The chain also conjures up images of bondage. In Sedgwick's text, it might even call up the distinction between slavery and freedom.

19. The women's biological father is named Hazard, but they are given the name of Chance. It is important to note that *hazard* is the French word for chance. However, in English, the connotations of these words are slightly different. Though the two words literally mean almost the same thing, hazard connotes more danger and chance more possibility. The movement from Hazard to Chance might then be the movement from danger to possibility.

20. This is seen even in *Absalom, Absalom!* through the character of Aunt Rosa. She is constantly referred to, even by Shreve, as Aunt Rosa despite the fact that she is neither Quentin nor Shreve's aunt. She, as a spinster, seems to occupy the role of aunt in the mind of multiple characters that are not, in fact, her biological nephews.
21. The destruction of the Father's house is exactly what happens in Carter's *The Magic Toyshop*. The incestuous relationship between Margaret and her brother Francie causes Uncle Philip to set his own home on fire, destroying the house of patriarchal privilege.

REFERENCES

Boone, Joseph Allen. 1998. *Libidinal Currents: Sexuality and the Shaping of Modernism*. Chicago: The University of Chicago Press.
Brooks, Peter. 1984. Incredulous Narration: *Absalom, Absalom*. In *Reading for the Plot: Design and Intention in Narrative*. New York: Knopf.
Carter, Angela. 1967. *The Magic Toyshop*. New York: Penguin.
———. 1991. *Wise Children*. London: Penguin.
Deleyto, Celestino. 1995. 'We Are No Angels': Woman Versus History in Angela Carter's *Wise Children*. In *Telling Histories: Narrativizing, Historicizing Literature*. Amsterdam: Rodopi.
Edelman, Lee. 2004. *No Future: Queer Theory and the Death Drive*. Durham: Duke University Press.
Faulkner, William. 1936. *Absalom, Absalom*. New York: Random.
Gamble, Sarah. 2001. *The Fiction of Angela Carter*. Cambridge: Icon.
Gopinath, Gayatri. 2005. *Impossible Desires: Queer Diasporas and South Asian Public Cultures*. Durham: Duke University Press.
Hardin, Michael. 1994. The Other Other: Self-Definition Outside Patriarchal Institutions in Angela Carter's *Wise Children*. *The Review of Contemporary Fiction* 14 (3): 77–83.
Hayase, Hironori. 1990. Sibling Incest in *Absalom, Absalom! Kyushu American Literature* 31: 97–111.
Hegerfeldt, Anne. 2003. The Stars That Spring from Bastardising: *Wise Children* Go for Shakespeare. *Anglia* 121 (3): 351–372.
Hickman, Alan Forrest. 1998. It's a Wise Child: Teaching the Lessons of History in the Contemporary British Novel. *Publications of the Arkansas Philological Association* 24 (1): 31–46.
Irwin, John T. 2003. Repetition and Revenge. In *William Faulkner's Absalom, Absalom!* ed. Fred Hobson, 47–67. Oxford: Oxford University Press.
Levi-Strauss, Claude. 1969. *The Elementary Structures of Kinship*. Boston: Beacon.

Owens, Craig. 1994. "Outlaws: Gay Men in Feminism." *Beyond Recognition: Representation, Power, and Culture*. Berkley: University of California Press.

Sedgwick, Eve Kosofsky. 1993. "Tales of the Avunculate: Queer Tutelage in *The Importance of Being Earnest*." In *Tendencies*, 52–72. Durham: Duke University Press.

Tobin, Patricia Drechsel. 1978. *Time and the Novel: The Genealogical Imperative*. Princeton: Princeton University Press.

Walter, David. 2007. Strange Attractions: Sibling Love Triangles in Faulkner's *Absolom, Absolom!* and Balzac's La Fille aux yeux d'or. *Comparative Literature Studies* 44 (4): 484–506.

Webb, Kate. 2000. Seriously Funny: *Wise Children*. In *The Flesh and the Mirror: Essays on the Art of Angela Carter*, ed. Lorna Sage, 279–307. New York: St. Martin's.

Zender, Karl F. 1998. Faulkner and the Politics of Incest. *American Literature: A Journal of Literary History, Criticism, and Bibliography* 70 (4): 739–765.

CHAPTER 5

"Pure Child": The Temporality
of Childishness in Sedgwick and Stein

In his 1927 book *Time and Western Man*, Wyndham Lewis sets out to give
an account of the turn toward issues of time in the early years of the twentieth century. Lewis examines the work of a variety of writers from across
a number of different disciplines. His goal is to show how society has
become time-obsessed and critique those writers who he sees as responsible for this phenomenon. But some of the most peculiar passages (in this
already peculiar book) occur around the subject of "Miss Gertrude Stein."[1]

Lewis's subject is, of course, time. When he comes to speak about
Stein, however, his analysis of time seems to fall away or at least recede
into the background as he constructs an elaborate extended metaphor: Gertrude Stein, it seems, is a child. After Lewis quotes Stein for
the first time in the text proper, he states: "it is easy to locate in these
passages the Child, the naïf-motif" (1927, p. 55). Stein's words, we are
told about a dozen times, are "pure 'child'" (1927, p. 55).[2] Indeed, the
chapter that is meant to prepare the reader for Lewis's analysis of Stein is
titled "A Brief Account of the Child Cult."

Lewis's critique of Stein is clear: her writing is childish; it imitates a
child. For Lewis, there is something false in this. He describes her work as
a "sham" and even titles one of his chapters on her "Tests for Counterfeit
in the Arts" (1927, pp. 49–50). What is less clear however is how the
childishness of her style relates to Lewis's topic—Time. Why does an analysis of the treatment of time in early twentieth-century writing break down
into an elaborate demonstration of how Stein's writing is "childish"?

© The Author(s) 2019
K. Haffey, *Literary Modernism, Queer Temporality*,
https://doi.org/10.1007/978-3-030-17301-2_5

145

While I agree that the characteristics of Stein's work that Lewis describes as "childish" do have a great deal to do with a particular theory of time, I find it quite difficult to parse out the connection between these two topics that his chapters on Stein are meant to elucidate. Lewis's strategy seems to be to quote a Stein passage that deals with time and then follow the quote with an explanation as to why it is childish. Lewis's exposition makes clear the distrust he feels (and that we too should feel) at her style. But precious little beyond this is achieved by his remarks on Stein.

While Lewis seems to use "childishness" as an epithet to insult an author whose writing he doesn't like and with whose politics he doesn't agree, I want to take his suggestion as a starting place for serious theoretical inquiry about the relation between childishness and temporality. In this chapter, I would thus like to think through the connection that Lewis's text suggests between Stein's writings regarding time and childishness. I will focus specifically on Stein's notion of the "continuous present," a concept that is introduced in her 1926 lecture "Composition as Explanation" and which reappears in her later theoretical writings. The "continuous present" is a form of time that Stein theorizes in opposition to a temporality defined by linear succession. It is my belief that "the continuous present" represents a strange relation to narrative temporality—a relation that caused much discomfort in certain of her contemporaries, as Lewis's comments demonstrate. While I am far from the first to describe Stein's concept of the "the continuous present" as representative of a temporality that undermine the linear trajectory of conventional narrative, I would like to focus on the more underexplored relationship between the continuous present and the temporality of childishness.[3]

This relation between temporality and the child that is called up by Lewis's book reminds me of another writer who theorized time more than half a century later: Eve Sedgwick. When reading Sedgwick's words that "queer is a continuing moment," I hear a faint echo of the phrase "continuous present" (1993b, p. xii). Like Stein, Sedgwick is interested in describing a particular form of time. And like Stein, Sedgwick is also criticized as a radical, a sexual deviant, and a thoroughly impenetrable writer. But what I find most interesting about the connection between these two writers is the way in which their theorization of narrative temporality intersects with a rethinking of "the child" or the "childish."

Though Stein and Sedgwick's writings stand at opposite ends of the twentieth century, I believe reading their works in relation to one another will allow us to see the continuities and discontinuities between Stein's sense of "the continuous present" and Sedgwick's work on "queer moments." In Sedgwick's writings we can locate the reemergence of certain modernist literary temporalities as a way to theorize queer time. In reading Stein's descriptions of the "continuous present," I will attempt to unpack one such literary temporality, a temporality that is inextricably connected to a particular imagining of "the child." After dealing with Stein (and Lewis's critiques of her) at length, I will turn to examine Sedgwick's *A Dialogue on Love*, her 1999 memoir in which she speaks literally about her own childhood. I see this text as the space in which Sedgwick most clearly theorizes the relation between the child and the adult, a relation that is at the heart of her definitions of the "queer moment." In reading these two authors who are each invested in thinking against the normative temporalities they find restrictive, a similar image emerges—an image of a queer child. It is this image that allows for a rethinking of the present moment that displaces it from its position in a chronology.

*   *   *

The image of the child that emerges in Lewis's critique of Stein's work is a very specific one, and one that is described in detail from the beginning. "She writes so like a child," Lewis says, "like a confused, stammering, rather 'soft' (bloated, acromegalic, squinting and spectacled, one can figure it as) child" (1927, p. 49). This is not the typical image of childhood. In this description, we hear nothing of the child's stereotypical innocence or purity. Instead, the image highlights this child as abnormal, speaking with a strange rhythm ("stammering"), diseased ("acromegalic").[4] The child Lewis describes seems to be bigger than a normal child ("bloated") and perhaps even older than a normal child, with its need for spectacles, an object usually associated with age. It is not so much to children in general that Lewis is comparing Stein's writing, but to a certain type of child, a strange child, a child characterized by abnormal growth and abnormal speech.

Lewis's "child" comes into greater focus later when he describes how "the demented also holds hands with the child" (1927, p. 54). He claims that Stein "is heavily indebted to the honest lunatic for her mannerisms" (1927, p. 63). There is a relation, according to Lewis, between a childlike style and certain types of madness.

Lewis's critique of Stein's writing employs some of the most dominant tropes for homosexuality. Lewis depicts her as childish or as immature, and in doing so plays on the conventional use of arrested development as an explanation for sexual deviance. When he talks of her in terms of the demented, he connects her (and her writing) to a form of pathologized sexuality. Not that Lewis is unaware of these connections either. As he states in *Time and Western Man,* he has written another book (*The Art of Being Ruled* 1926) that deals with this topic at length:

> How the demented also holds hands with the child, and the tricks, often very amusing, of the asylum patient, are exploited at the same time as the happy inaccuracies of the infant; how contemporary inverted-sex fashions are affiliated to the Child-cult; and in fact all the different factors in this intricate sensibility, being evolved notably by such writers as Miss Stein, will be found there. (1927, p. 54)

As Lewis's words demonstrate, he is clearly aware of the connections between the child-cult and "contemporary inverted-sex fashions." Indeed, *Time and Western Man* is only one of a number of his polemical books that mention the connection between "inverted-sex fashions" and "the child-cult."[5] When he calls Stein a child, therefore, his accusations deserve to be considered with attention to sexuality.

Before I consider that topic at length, I would like to return to a question I broached in the introduction to this chapter: why does Lewis mount such an attack on Stein's writings? It can't merely be that he finds her writing bad or even childish, as such writing would be dismissed without a second thought. I would argue that Stein functions symbolically in a larger argument that Lewis is sketching out in a series of conservative polemics he wrote between the late 1920s and early 1930s. In these books, Lewis bemoans the "disintegration of the western consciousness," to use Hugh Kenner's words (1954, p. 71). Part of Lewis argument concerns the role that the "Child-cult" plays in this disintegration. In this context, Stein functions as the quintessential female example of the danger of "inverted-sex fashions" (her male counterpart, according to Lewis, is Marcel Proust).[6]

As Lewis concludes his chapter entitled "A Brief Account of the Child-Cult," his words suggest that he finds Stein's work dangerous, one component of a larger, more pervasive danger. He encourages readers to begin to uncover the secret of the "Child-cult," writing: "Not to seize on the secret of these liaisons is totally to misunderstand the nature of what is occurring around you today" (1927, p. 54). Lewis's sentence shows a sense of paranoia about the "liaisons" he associates with the child-cult. His use of the word "secret" and phrase "occurring around you today" depict a situation in which readers are surrounded by covert (and seemingly sinister) things they do not know about.

This paranoia is even more visible in earlier passages when Lewis stresses to his readers:

> it is essential, if you wish to understand at all a great deal of contemporary art and thought, even the developments of positive science, not only to gather up all the dispersed manifestations of this strange fashion ["the child-cult"], but—having done so—to trace this impulse to its source in the terrible and generally hidden disturbances that have broken the back of our will in the Western countries, and have already forced us into the greatest catastrophes. (1927, p. 53)

Like the earlier passage I excerpted, this quotation emphasizes the need to "understand" the society around you. But here Lewis also articulates the connection between "this strange fashion" (notice the repetition of fashion from the earlier phrase "contemporary inverted-sex fashions") and "the generally hidden disturbances" that have "broken the back of our will" and "caused the greatest catastrophes" (1927, p. 53). Thus, the child-cult is not only dangerous but also has already been responsible for terrible events.[7]

It is perhaps for this reason that the child that Lewis compares to Stein is abnormal or strange. If the dominant feature of the discourse of childhood is an association with innocence, then Lewis would need to depict Stein's "childish" style in a way that highlights it as dangerous and cunning rather than innocent. Indeed, one of Lewis's largest criticisms of Stein is that her style is a "sham" or a "trick." He calls her "childish" language a form of "making believe," claims that she is "just pretending" (1927, p. 49). His description positions Stein as an adult playing at being a child. Interestingly, this is a common description of homosexuality: "homosexuality is childhood, played out in another place but still enacting the desires generated in infancy" (Bruhm and Hurley 2004, p. xx).

The image of the child that emerges in *Time and Western Man* is, in fact, the queer child. It is a child who does not conform to the mandate for innocence. But at the same time, Lewis's image is also that of the queer adult—a grown-up who can never quite escape being characterized as a perpetual child. It is perhaps in this image of the child that temporality enters the equation. As Kathryn Bond Stockton has shown, the queer child represents a particular problem for chronological imaginings of time. Over the past decade, Stockton has produced a wealth of scholarship on "the queer child," culminating in her 2009 book by that title. Since the child that Lewis describes is indeed a queer child, I will spend some time unpacking his dense metaphors with the help of Stockton's work on queer children. Because Stockton has considered at length the relationship between temporality and "the child," I would like to lay out some of her claims and read them in relation to Lewis's images before I return to examine the temporality of Stein's work more closely.

According to Stockton, "Embedded in 'the child' are perplexing issues surrounding the ways we speak of growth" (2004, p. 283). Recall that the child Stein is compared to is "a confused, stammering, rather 'soft' (bloated, acromegalic, squinting and spectacled, one can figure it as) child" (1927, p. 49). Part of what is so interesting about this figure is its depiction of the child characterized by "abnormal" growth. Specifically, this is a fat child, as demonstrated by the adjectives "soft" and "bloated." At one point, Lewis will even refer to Stein's work as "all fat, without nerve" (1927, p. 61). As Stockton has shown, fatness often serves as a figure for abnormal growth as it depicts a growing out rather than a growing up, or as she calls it "sideways growth" (2004, p. 287).

In her work on the film *The Hanging Gardens*, Stockton shows how fat "is the visible effect...of a child who cannot grow 'up' in his family as his preferred self. So he grows sideways—literally, metaphorically" (2004, p. 288). While Lewis might not have had this in mind when describing Stein as a child, his description of fatness is a metaphor for an abnormal, even diseased form of growth. Lewis makes this clear when he follows the words soft and bloated with "acromegalic." The term "acromegaly" refers to the enlargement of certain body parts, including the head, hands, and feet, due to excessive secretion of growth hormone by the pituitary gland. The child to whom Lewis refers, therefore, is one who is out-of-sync with a "normal" process of physical growth.

The concept of "growing up" is also connected to particular forms of narrative growth. As I demonstrated in my introduction and first chapter, individuals are said to move through a set of life stages in their progression from childhood to adulthood. In calling Stein a child, Lewis is drawing on the discourse of "arrested development," implying that she has ceased to develop or progress past childish things. But he makes this point more explicit when he refers to the "cult of childhood, and of *the Child*" as an "irresponsible, Peterpannish psychology" (emphasis in text; 1927, p. 53). As Stockton points out, "The grown homosexual has even often been metaphorically seen as a child" (2004, p. 289). Homosexual adults are often described in terms of their "immaturity," their inability to progress through childhood stages of sexual development. The phrase "arrested development" makes visible queers' "presumed status as dangerous children, who remain children in part by failing to have their own" (2004, p. 289).

The adult who is a child, then, is a dangerous child, as Lewis's paranoia about Stein's work shows. But how, we might now ask, is this dangerous childishness that he finds in Stein connected to the "time-obsession" for which he initially sets out to criticize her (1927, p. 49)? While Lewis is quite vague about the relation between the child-cult and time, he does offer one connection—a certain "Utopia of childhood" (1927, p. 54). He claims that a "romantic person of to-day" may have "the Heaven of Childhood inside himself (it is a *time-paradise*)" (italics in text, 1927, p. 54).[8] This time-paradise seems to take the person back to the time before something—here, perhaps, before original sin, as the word "paradise" might suggest.[9] The connection of childhood to a utopia or a "time-paradise" is well established. As Bruhm and Hurley claim, "Utopianism follows the child around like a family pet" (2004, p. xiii). This is partly because "the child exists as a site of almost limitless potential (its future not yet written and therefore unblemished)" (2004, p. xiii).

But while this utopianism is usually figured as positive, Lewis relates this "time-paradise" with something he sees as sinister. He claims that the cult of childhood "is connected with the cult of the primitive and the savage" (1927, p. 53).[10] In this way, Lewis is drawing on a sense of time specifically before society or before the law. The danger of the adult-as-child, then, is its regressive nature, its relation to the desire to return to a "primitive" moment.

Lewis's work with the metaphor of the child attempts to empty childhood of the positive, utopian, nostalgic meanings that have often been associated with it. In this sense, the utopia of childhood is shown to be connected to the primitive or savage. The child itself is connected to the lunatic. And the innocence of the child (or the voice of the child that he claims emerges in Stein's writing) is shown to be a trick or a sham—a form of cunning. If we put all this together, what Lewis is reacting to in

Stein's writing is a nonnormative sense of growth or development. His criticisms of her all seem to stem from his sense that her work upsets a progressive sense of time: she is an adult who writes as a child; her work stammers or stutters; her prose seems to be derived from an earlier primitive moment.

I would be remiss in not noting that Stein herself associates her work with children in her famous 1946 "Transatlantic Interview." In response to the question "How and when are poetry and prose separate things?" (a question which Stein hardly attempts to answer), Stein says: "Somehow or other in war time the only thing that is spontaneous is children. Children themselves are poetry. The poetry of adults in wartime is too intentional. It is too much mixed up with everything else. My poetry was children's poetry, and most of it is very good, and some of it is as good as anything I have ever done" (1971, p. 23). Unlike Lewis, whose images of "the child" deviate from the norm, Stein's images seem to conjure up an innocent idyllic child, a child who is untouched by the war, who is spontaneous. We can hear in Stein's words a certain nostalgia for childhood, or a vision of childhood that is perhaps shaped by adult desires (Bruhm and Hurley 2004).

Stein's depiction is pretty stereotypical and would actually line up with those understandings of childhood that imagine it as a utopian space. But what is interesting about this passage is that Stein has essentially claimed to be a child, or at least to write as one. Stein tells us here that her poetry "was children's poetry" and that it was "very good." She notes that poetry written by adults is "too intentional." Stein's poetry, then, is not poetry written by an adult. She claims for her writing that same thing that Lewis accuses her of. The only difference is the value judgment placed on this type of writing.

What I have left out up until now are the passages from Stein that Lewis quotes in his book. While he quotes from a number of her different works, including novels, poetry, and essays, the majority of the passages that Lewis uses are from "Composition as Explanation." This rather short lecture written in 1926 is one of Stein's most direct treatments of time, and it is where she first explains the phrase "continuous present." Lewis states: "*Composition as Explanation* is a little pamphlet just published by the Hogarth Press. In it you have the announcement that 'The time of the composition is the time of the composition.' But as simple as that sounds, it is only roguishness on the part of its author-ess...She is just pretending...She will disarm you and capture you by her absurdity" (1927, pp. 49–50). Here Lewis moves directly from the quotation not to any reading or analysis but straight into accusations of "roguishness." Lewis's work on Stein continues in this manner, and thus we never get a clear explanation of what he thinks Stein is saying about time.

In order to sketch out my own reading of the temporalities of Stein's work, I would like to look more closely at "Composition as Explanation" as well as Stein's later theories of time and narration in both her lecture series and her interviews. It is in these texts where we can come to a better understanding of what Stein might mean by "continuous present" and begin to connect this term to her own theories of narrative time. This work will allow us to return eventually to Lewis's accusations and understand them in a new light.

Within "Composition as Explanation," Stein refers specifically to her own texts to demonstrate some of her theories. Stein's idea of the "continuous present" is not only something she theorizes but also a style that she works to develop in her novels and autobiographies throughout her entire life. According to Catherine Parke, Stein sought to create "a new language and new literary forms that anybody could understand but that were also distinctively one's own, both based fundamentally on a new notion of time which she called the 'continuous present'" (1988, p. 556). In "Composition as Explanation," Stein approaches the concept of the "continuous present" over and over again and from many different angles. The work seems to enact a "continuous present" more than attempt to describe it, a move that mirrors the title of the piece "Composition *as* Explanation" (emphasis added). The text repeats and restates in a manner that is meant to keep the reader in the moment. It seeks to bar the reader from moving forward from beginning to middle to end. The repetitions of this piece and its attempts at "beginning again and again," as Stein calls it, are perhaps what Lewis was reacting to when he referred to the text as "stuttering" or "stammering" (though these types of repetitions are, of course, characteristic of much of Stein's work).

In discussing her story "Melanctha," Stein first mentions the idea of a "prolonged present" stating: "In that there was a constant recurring and beginning there was a marked direction in the direction of being in the present although naturally I had been accustomed to past present and future, and why, because the composition forming around me was a prolonged present" (1967a, p. 25). Stein places the idea of a "prolonged present" in opposition to "past present and future." "Past present and future" is what she is "accustomed to," but as Stein states two sentences later, "continuous present" is what came naturally to her: "I created then a prolonged present naturally I knew nothing of a continuous present but it came naturally to me to make one, it was simple it was clear to me and nobody knew why it was done like that, I did not myself although naturally to me it was natural" (1967a, p. 25). There is a movement away from what one had been "accustomed to" and toward what feels "natural." What comes along with the creation of a "continuous present," according to Stein, is "beginning again and again" and "using everything." The "continuous present" is thus a time sense connected more to beginnings than to endings or destinations. We do not see a beginning followed by a middle and end in this style, but instead a constant need to begin again rather than to bring things to conclusion.[11]

The other concept that Stein mentions, "using everything," seems to be related to ideas about composition that Stein learned from Cezanne. In Cezanne's cubist paintings, according to Stein, there is a sense that no one element is more important than any other element. As Stein says, "Cezanne conceived the idea that in composition one thing was as important as another thing. Each part is as important as the whole" (Haas 1971, p. 15). Stein claims that her work was the first time that "anyone had used that idea of composition in literature" (Haas 1971, p. 15). What Stein calls "using everything," then, is a conscious decision to include all in the making of a piece of art and give it equal value. It consists of "beginning again and again" in a way that accumulates details that are all equally valued. This seems to be in opposition to narrative conventions that would place more importance on certain aspects of a story. Stein is thus moving away from those things to which she had been accustomed (like a composition composed of "past present future") and toward a certain form of literary cubism.

Because Stein was moving away from more traditional forms of narration, the composition she produced was unfamiliar, or so she claims. It didn't look or read like those texts that were already known. Indeed, Stein describes how the writing that she produced was unfamiliar even to herself: "Having naturally done this I naturally was a little troubled with it when I read it. I became like the others who read it" (1967a, p. 26). The text written in "continuous present" is troubling and unfamiliar even to its author, who when reading is not its creator but rather becomes the same as others who read it. This point is integral to Stein's idea of "continuous present." The author writing from the continuous present does not express an identity, but only tells what she knows in that present.

As critics have described it, and as Stein will elaborate in her later writings, producing a "continuous present" in a text requires the author to refrain from relying on memory and speak only from the present position. As S. C. Neuman says,

> Telling only what it "knows" in the "continuous present," unconcerned with thematic continuity or consistency, the "human mind" approximates more closely than does conventional narrative the actual living of a life, the experience of something-happening which, in the "present" of its occurrence, is without casual connections across time. (1979, p. 75)

Stein's continuous present is an attempt to account for a particular moment without, as Neuman says, "regard for possible inconsistencies with past or future moments" (1979, p. 76). "Using everything" and "beginning again and again" are thus important because they do not rely on cause–effect connections across time. They are methods that allow for the inhabiting of the present. This mind "telling only what it 'knows'" can be connected to a phrase that Stein employs in *Composition as Explanation*: "make it as it is made" (1967a, pp. 22–23). When "telling only what it 'knows,'" the mind can only rely on the present moment to relate what its knowledge. Likewise, when Stein refers to those who "make it as it is made," it is in contradistinction to those who write things that have been prepared and decided ahead of time. Those who "make it as it is made" seem to occupy a continuous present because they create in the moment, without reference to what came before and what will come after. They do not rely (as Stein will establish in later writings) on remembering.

Stein's work on this topic continues in her 1935 lecture series *Narration,* and as Thorton Wilder claims in the introduction, her discussion leads to the development of "a theory of time" (1935, p. vi). In these lectures, Stein is struggling against the feeling "that anything that everything had meaning as beginning and middle and ending" (1935, p. 25). She attempts to think about "the narrative of to-day" in opposition to the writing of the last "many hundred of years." The difference, according to Stein, is that "the narrative of to-day is not a narrative of succession" (20). Whether or not this is an accurate depiction of the literature of Stein's "to-day," she appears here to be making a claim at least about her own writing—about a desire to eschew succession in favor of continuous present. She even describes her desire to escape from "the inevitable narrative of anything of everything succeeding something" (1935, p. 25).

In Stein's story of how narrative is written in her day, the "progressive happening of things" seems to have broken down. As she says, "When one used to think of narrative one meant a telling of what is happening in successive moments of its happening...But now we have changed all that we really have. We really now do not really know that anything is progressively happening" (1935, p. 17). Stein seems to be describing a situation in which she and her contemporaries have seen through the guise of progressive storytelling as a convention. Since she (and others) do not know if anything is progressively happening, there seems to be a need on her part to revisit narrative in general, to figure out how to tell stories without succession, beginning-middle-ending, progression.[12] As Cynthia Merrill puts it, "Stein judged that narration depended upon a belief in existence as linear succession, as beginnings, middles, and ends, a belief she considered no longer tenable in the twentieth century" (1985, p. 13).

Stein works quite hard in this lecture series to differentiate the time sense of narrative (or literature) and history (which she associates with the newspaper). If we follow Stein's reasoning to its conclusion, the problem with the newspaper seems to be that it destroys the present, the now. As Stein says:

> That is really what the newspaper has to say that everything that has happened has happened on that day but really this is not true because everything that has happened on the newspaper day has really happened the day before and that makes all the trouble that there is with the newspaper as it is and in every way they try to destroy this day the day between the day before and the newspaper day. (1935, p. 36)

If we are reading yesterday's news written as if it happened today and we will read today's news tomorrow, then the present, what Stein here calls "this day," has disappeared. The past has been projected into the future, and there is essentially no room for the now in the world of newspaper writing. As Steven Meyer claims, "The news is written up as if 'one had known it all beforehand' instead of as something that actually differs from moment to moment. This effect of authoritativeness is achieved through a process of rewriting that requires, for the news to fit into the reader's present, the concurrent removal of all traces of the actual writing and thus of the writer's own continuously changing present" (1992, p. 18). So although the newspaper does seem to do away with beginning and ending in Stein's eyes ("That is a very interesting thing in writing in a newspaper in a newspaper being existing there is no beginning and no ending and in a way too there is no going on"), it is problematic in that it erases the now and does not allow for a mode of existing in the continuous present (1935, p. 37).

Interestingly, when she attempts to describe the time sense of narrative or literature (in contradistinction to the newspaper or history), she provides us with a semi-cryptic love note for Alice B. Toklas. For example, she writes: "I love my love with a b because she is peculiar" (1935, p. 37). We might here take notice of the present tense of this statement. We might also take notice of what occupies this present moment: queer love, or "peculiar" love, to use Stein's phrase. Stein goes on to say, "One can say this. That has nothing to do with what a newspaper does and that is the reason why that is the reason that newspapers and with it history as it mostly exists has nothing to do with anything that is living" (1935, p. 37). Stein's statement comes to rest on the concept of "living"—something we might connect to her ideas about the present. "Living" is what happens in the present, in the now. Newspapers cannot describe "anything that is living" because they are not written in the "continuous present." They have no way of accessing the living.[13]

Later in Stein's career, she begins to talk directly about how the problem of time intersects with the problem of narration. In "Transatlantic Interview," she explains:

I found out that in the essence of narration is this problem of time. You have as a person writing, and all the really great narration has it, you have to denude yourself of time so that writing time does not exist. If time exists, your writing is ephemeral. You can have historical time, but for you the time does not exist, and if you are writing about the present, the time element must cease to exist....There should not be a sense of time, but an existence suspended in time. That is really where I am at the present, I am still largely meditating about this sense of time. (1971, p. 20)

This idea of "an existence suspended in time" is key to what Stein is try-ing to accomplish with the "continuous present." She insists, "the time element must cease to exist." If time enters the equation, then succession begins to dominate and the present cannot be recorded. For Stein, cause and effect do not come into play in the present; they only come into play when something is prepared beforehand, not when artists "make it as it is made" ("Composition as Explanation" 1967a, p. 22). To be "suspended in time," then, is not to account for this moment as part of something larger (as part of a chain) but as equally important to all other moments.

To be "suspended in time" also concerns casting off both the past and the yearning toward a future. For Stein, casting off the past is connected to stripping words of their histories. She does this by placing words in unfamiliar sentence structures and through repetitions. Her word choice is all part of bringing the reader into a "continuous present" and away from past associations with words. As William Carlos Williams says of her work, "having taken the words to her choice, to emphasize further what she has in mind she has completely unlinked them...from their former relationships in the sentence" (1970, p. 349). For Williams, this strategy functions to erase stories that have been told before, to turn them off and do without "their logic...which is supposed to transcend the words" (1970, p. 350). William Carlos Williams, a great supporter of Stein when other modernists were criticizing her, sees in Stein an attack on certain forms of what he calls "that paralyzing vulgarity of logic" that has seeped into literature from other disciplines (1970, p. 349). Part of this logic seems to be connected to a cause–effect mentality or a logic of succession where one element must necessarily follow another.

While some might see her use of the "continuous present" as an attempt to transcend time, Stein's need to connect to the now, to the present, seems to run counter to a desire for transcendence. Cynthia Merrill has claimed: "Stein, in her advocacy of a 'continuous present,' disparages both the linear succession of history and the timelessness of transcendence" (Merrill (1985, p. 4). While it is quite clear through her writings that Stein "disparages...the linear succession of history," I think Merrill's second point is the more significant one. Stein does not seek access to the present in order to transcend time and connect with some "eternal present" (to use a phrase from my third chapter). She actually stands in opposition to such an idea. The eternal present would connect the present to all time, allowing access to a common past and future. But, like those things that Stein critiques, it would erase the specificity of that present. For example, Stein critiques Joyce for "lean[ing] toward the past," an attribute that she claims has led to his greater acceptance by the general public (Haas 1971, p. 29). Joyce's depiction of a temporality in which mythic events play out in the present is quite different from Stein's "continuous present," which attempts to empty the present of the weight of what has come before.

Stein's notion of a continuous present also seems dependent on the distinction she draws between identity and entity. In her lecture "What Are Master-pieces and Why Are There So Few of Them?" Stein discusses identity as a thing "in relation" and entity as "a thing in itself" (1967b, p. 149).[14] She aligns the masterpiece with entity because it is "something that is an end in itself" (1967b, p. 149). Identity, conversely, is connected to memory. As Stein says, "Identity is recognition, you know who you are because you and others remember" (1967b, p. 146). Throughout the lecture, Stein stresses that identity is antithetical to the creation of a masterpiece. Likewise, identity is antithetical to her conception of "continuous present." As James Breslin states, Stein rejects the notion of identity altogether (1986, p. 150). Identity, according to Breslin, carries "the past over into the present" and functions to "familiariz[e] the strangeness, the mysterious being, of others" (1986, p. 150). The problem with identity lies in its relationality as well as its dependency on chronological time. For identity to exist, there must be memories of the past applied to the present.

The "continuous present," then, consists of a few different components. First off, it attempts to uncouple the present from its position in the logic of succession, of chronology.[15] Stein's strategies of "using everything" and "beginning again" seem connected to this goal. "Using everything" seemingly allows Stein to accumulate words and ideas such that her texts cannot be seen as stories of growth or development. And because of her tendency to continually "begin again," she never reaches any form of closure, thesis, or main point. Second, the "continuous present" is formed by the mind telling what it knows in the present, without relying on past knowledge or memory. This includes the attempt to empty even words and sentences of their prior histories, to use them in ways that defamiliarize their former meanings and connotations. Lastly, the continuous present favors a notion of what Stein calls "entity" over "identity."

To return once again to Wyndham Lewis, perhaps Lewis sees "the child" in Stein's style because it lines up with one of the most dominant images of the child. As Stockton has shown, one of the quintessential characteristics of our cultural vision of children is that they are without a past: "The child is the specter of who we were when there was nothing yet behind us" (2004, p. 296). If a child is a person without a past, they are individuals for whom words might not have the same weight of history.[16] If Stein's writing has "unlinked [words] ... from their former relationships in the sentence," as William Carlos Williams claims, then her prose might mimic a child's relationship with words. If she does not rely on the logics that are meant to order words in a sentence and order events in story, then her text might seem "child-like" to Lewis and others who accept this view of childhood.

But beyond this, those elements listed above as antithetical to a concept of "continuous present" (succession, cause/effect, memory, identity) are also all components central to developmental stories. As I demonstrated in my second chapter, stories of development rely on a concept of time that connects the past and the future (by way of the present) in a successive relationship. They also rely on a concept of identity in which things change over time and move in a predictable direction. Perhaps this is why Stein twice uses developmental narratives as counter-examples to the time sense that she is trying to produce in her texts.

Stein's time sense is ultimately connected to a desire to find and describe movement that is not succession, that is not linear growth. And this point is figured, on at least two occasions, through a metaphor of childhood. The growth of the child (or adolescent) into adulthood is presented in Stein's writing as the most normal and dominant example of this type of growth. As she says in her *Narration* lectures:

> I think one naturally is impressed by anything having a beginning middle and an ending when one is beginning writing and that is a natural thing because when one is emerging from adolescence, which is really when one first begins writing one feels that one would not have been emerging from adolescence if there had not been a beginning and a middle and an ending to anything. (1935, p. 23)

Stein demonstrates that the idea of "emerging from adolescence" doesn't make sense outside of a narrative framework that deals in beginnings, middles, and endings—a type of succession or progression with a specific destination. One would not emerge from adolescence if this framework did not exist. Indeed, adolescence by definition is a certain kind of middle in the narrative of a life—"the transitional period between puberty and adulthood in human development, extending mainly over the teen years and terminating legally when the age of maturity is reached" (*Random House Dictionary* def. 1).

Stein's comment about adolescence also resonates with a statement she makes in "What Are Masterpieces?": "What is the use of being a boy if you are going to grow up to be a man" (1967b, p. 152). The point of Stein's statement (and I call it a statement because she ends it with a period and not a question mark) seems to hinge on the notion of growing up. "Being a boy" has little "use" for Stein if it is only seen in relation to that which it will become, "man." What Stein is hinting at here is the difference between "identity" and "entity." As Stein establishes in this lecture, identity is relational, just as boy is seen as a relation to man. Stein goes on to say, "There is really no use in being a boy if you are going to grow up to be a man because then man and boy you can be certain that that is continuing and a master-piece does not continue it is as it is but it does not continue" (1967b, p. 153). The problem with the boy who "is going to grow up to be a man" seems to be that he is caught up in the act of "continuing"—a form of time that is counter to the masterpiece. The temporality of the masterpiece (or of what Stein calls "entity") is defined by a thing being "as it is" rather than continuing. As Breslin puts it, "Like remembering and identifying, narrating—telling, say, the story of a girl becoming a woman— such narrating represents a linear sequence of time, not an ongoing present" (1986, p. 150). These stories of children becoming adults need a progressive sense of time and thus remove one from the "continuous present." Stein's statements here show her investment in breaking away from a narrative based on succession, development, a form of movement figured as growth.

Stein seems to wish for this boy an experience other than linear growth, a reprieve from the need to "grow up." Perhaps part of Stein's problem with this notion of growth is that it is predetermined. The boy will inevitably become a man, as the girl will inevitably become a woman.[17] The space of the child in this configuration, then, hardly seems to matter. There is no use in "being" a boy because that is not one's final destination. The child thus has no meaningful present, it is merely waiting to become what it will be, a man. Just as the "continuous present" seeks to hold onto a now that succession wants to erase, the child occupies a space that is erased by normative growth.

It is in this way that the continuous present is connected to the notion of the child. In her insightful essay on the connections between Stein and Virginia Woolf, Rachel DuPlessis comments that Woolf's *The Waves* "is written (say it again in Stein's way) in the continuous present" (1989, p. 111). Her claim is connected to the fact that "*The Waves* seems to be a book about children, not adults—about children perpetually children despite the passage of time" (1989, p. 110). DuPlessis shows that this is a novel that disavows the oedipal story and is without traumatic events of the past "which may be recalled or healed" and "without relation to any future which these might cause" (1989, p. 11).

I mention DuPlessis's comments because they make visible the types of stories that can be told if a narrative temporality like the "continuous present" is employed. And while we might not want to conflate the writings of Stein and Woolf, DuPlessis's comments here make visible the connections between the continuous present and a particular depiction of the child. The child often perceived in relation to a future that has not yet come. In a "normal" growth narrative, the child will become an adult. But a queer child will never become an adult, at least not from the perspective of narrative (since adulthood is often defined in terms of heterosexual maturity). The "continuous present" allows for a form of movement that is not a growing up or development toward some predetermined form of maturity. Within Stein's configuration of the "continuous present," the child is not a relation to the adult, but an entity, "a thing in itself."

*   *   *

If Stein's work is related to the concept of the child in a somewhat indirect way, in Eve Sedgwick's work we find a much more direct and literal treatment of the subject. While Sedgwick's queer or "continuing moment" is far from a stand-in for Stein's "continuous present," I believe the two concepts are related, especially because they pertain to a particular way of conceiving nonnormative growth. The image of the child is the key to unlocking the intricacies of each writers' complex theorization of temporality. What we come away with is not only a new way of conceiving of time, but also a way of thinking about the relation between the child and the adult.

The child pops up all over Eve Sedgwick's critical work. Queer kids who have committed suicide haunt the introduction to *Tendencies*, and she writes essays with titles like "How to Bring Your Kids Up Gay." As

Stockton says, "Eve's work […] has fostered queer kids" (2002, p. 185). Throughout this book, I have used Sedgwick's theories to read various other texts in terms of their temporalities.[18] But here in my last chapter, I would like to turn to Sedgwick's depiction of herself as a child, to the stories she tells concerning her childhood in order to understand the queer forms of growth that become visible across her body of work. This will not only allow me to analyze the temporality of childishness in her work, but also demonstrate the ways in which I see modernist temporalities (like Stein's) as formative to the concepts of temporality produced by the queer theorists of the late twentieth and early twenty-first century.

To examine this topic, I will focus primarily on Sedgwick's 1999 memoir, *A Dialogue on Love*. While Sedgwick's critical work contains autobiography and she often crosses the traditional boundaries between literature and criticism, this is Sedgwick's most lengthy and sustained piece of autobiographical writing. In this text, Sedgwick recounts her experiences in therapy during the time surrounding her diagnosis with breast cancer. The memoir contains not only Sedgwick's writing on the experience but also the notes of her therapist, Shannon. Though *A Dialogue on Love* is most definitely a memoir, I believe that it is also theory told through narrative form, or as Jane Gallop might call it, "anecdotal theory" (2002). The text is concerned not only with narrating a particular life, but also with theoretical questions like "how does one narrate a life?" Likewise, in Sedgwick's stories about her childhood, she not only paints an image of a girl but also theorizes through narrative about the connection between the child and the adult. As Barber and Clark claim, queer temporality is comprised of an "energy that dissolves the difference, chronologically conceived, between the queer adult that one *is* and the queer child that one *was*" (2002, p. 5; emphasis in original).[19] Because I believe that *A Dialogue on Love* offers Sedgwick's most detailed theorization of this child/adult divide, I will read the text specifically from this angle.

From the beginning of the text, we get a plethora of descriptions of Sedgwick as a child. These descriptions are good examples of what Kathryn Bond Stockton is referring to when she describes the queer child. Stockton breaks queer children down into four separate categories: "(1) the ghostly 'gay' child, (2) the grown 'homosexual,' (3) the child queered by Freud, and (4) the child queered by innocence" (2004, p. 283). Sedgwick's descriptions of herself would allow her to fit into each of the first three categories.

One of the metaphors for the queer child is often the ghost, that child who haunts the family in "shadowy form" (Stockton 2004, p. 285). At times, Sedgwick describes herself in such a way, using words like "creepier" and "spookiness" (1999, p. 30). This is even an image others who knew her as a child confirm. Her husband Hal, for example, "takes the uncanniness quite for granted" (1999, p. 29). After Sedgwick's parents meet with Shannon, her therapist, Shannon tells Sedgwick that their descriptions give a sense of "this kid being uncanny or a changeling," and Sedgwick wonders if her parents had any worries about her "that weren't organized around the supposed strangeness of this presence" (1999, p. 147). Part of what seems so strange and uncanny about this child is her relation to time. A ghost itself is a representation of a strange temporality; it is an entity left over from a previous time. In Sedgwick's case, this temporal contradiction seems to be slightly different. She is out of sync with time because she seems to be (both to herself and to others in her family) an adult in a child's body. She is, as I will elaborate upon later, a child who seems to know too much.

Sedgwick's described fatness also embodies the "sideways growth" that Stockton claims is often "the visible effect…of a child who cannot grow 'up' in his family as his preferred self" (2004, p. 288). She refers to herself as "a dorkily fat, pink, boneless middle child," remarking "one of my worst nicknames is marshmallow" (1999, p. 19). Sedgwick's description of herself here resonates with Lewis's description of the child in *Time and Western Man*: "rather 'soft' (bloated, acromegalic, squinting and spectacled)" (1927, p. 49). Her nickname "marshmallow" is perhaps the perfect image of soft and bloated. Within her family, Sedgwick has been issued the position of "THE FAT KID" (1999, p. 67).[20] Upon seeing pictures of Eve as a child, Shannon says that he sees this label as "verg[ing] on delusional," calling her at most "chubby" (1999, p. 67). Her position as the fat kid thus seems to function as a mark of difference from the rest of the family. If we follow Stockton, Sedgwick's fatness might be a physical manifestation of a type of growth that is visible but has no real function within the developmental narrative that moves individuals through childhood to adulthood (i.e., it seems unrelated to progression).

Though the adult Sedgwick might not fit neatly into the category of homosexual, her descriptions of herself as a child place her squarely within Stockton's second category, "the grown 'homosexual,'" because of how they depict a state of "arrested development." This category of

Stockton's does not refer to a literal child but rather to an adult who is metaphorically a child because she has not developed beyond "childish things." Throughout her memoir, Sedgwick is continually drawing attention to the fact that her adult self is "fastened," as Stockton would say, "to the figure of the child" (2004, p. 289). It is for this very reason that she appears uncanny to herself and to her family members. She has trouble separating her child and the adult selves, and the relation of these two is a large part of what she examines throughout her therapy.

Sedgwick's depiction of herself in a state of arrested development is also linked to Stockton's third category: "the child queered by Freud." This child is "the not-yet-straight child who is, nonetheless, a sexual child with aggressive wishes" (2004, p. 291). In some ways, this category seems to be the most helpful in thinking about the images of Sedgwick as a child. She describes at length the sexual experiences of her childhood, the spankings, the long hours spent masturbating. In Sedgwick's descriptions we see a sexual child—but we also see Sedgwick as an adult in the state of arrested development. Indeed, these moments of sexual play, of masturbation, form the core of her adult sexuality. At one point she says: "it's awfully striking how much the thread of a self, for me, seems to have been tied up with all this masturbating" (2004, p. 75). Sedgwick seemingly has not moved past the queer desires that make up childhood sexuality, those desires that one is said to move past in order to enter adult sexuality. Thus, if the adult and child are connected for Sedgwick, one of the ways in which they are connected is through their sexualities.

For the rest of this chapter, I will examine the connections that Sedgwick sketches out between the child and the adult specifically in relation to sexuality. I would argue that part of Sedgwick's project in preserving queer children is also the preservation of certain forms of sexuality that have been associated with childhood (especially by Freud). We see Sedgwick's thinking about the adult/child divide play out in a series of conversations with Shannon, conversations in which Sedgwick attempts to push the boundaries of his thinking (especially his treatment of childhood and adulthood sexuality). Through reading these specific moments in *A Dialogue on Love*, I believe we gain a fuller sense of Sedgwick's queer temporality—a notion that depends on the inextricable connection between the child and the adult in the present moment.

Sedgwick is quite conscious that what she is trying to do with Shannon is to construct a narrative of her life. She even asks Shannon, "What kind of a narrative...are we trying to construct—or do we think we need to construct—about Eve's history? I mean, what is the purpose of it, what do we want from it?" (1999, p. 60). This is a narrative meant to say something about her life, but it is also a narrative that is meant to do a certain type of work, that has other purposes. This two-voiced discussion about Sedgwick's life seems to set up a pedagogical framework. In some ways, Shannon seems to be the foil against which Sedgwick describes her particular ways of thinking—he asserts his viewpoint in visible contrast to what she is saying. At a few points in the text he seems to be the voice of the norm—he is after all literally and metaphorically the straight white guy. Indeed, she refers to him as "complacent in ways [she's] prone to associate with straight male presumption" (1999, p. 103). In other ways, he is perhaps the stand-in for the reader or for those whom Sedgwick has made it her own personal project of making smarter (she refers to this "making people smarter" project throughout the text). For instance, when Shannon says, "it's just so easy for me to envision things in discrete parts. But then you come along and smudge up the barriers, and it's really different. It's important for you to keep doing that," we hear not only an admission that Shannon is learning, but also a description of Sedgwick's storytelling strategy (1999, p. 31). Sedgwick recognizes herself in the role of teacher here when she follows Shannon's comment with the statement: "Deconstruction 101, I do *not* say impatiently" (1999, p. 31; emphasis in original).

Within such a framework, it is easy to see different ideologies come into conflict with one another. We can see the ways in which Shannon and Eve seem to have different desires for Eve. Specifically, Shannon seems to have particular ideas for how Eve should experience time. Early on in the memoir, Sedgwick admits that she is "a bit surprised [Shannon] admit[s] to keeping a list of how he wants [her] different" (1999, p. 60). After this comment, she breaks in and out of verse:

> But he also says
> he wants me to have
> a more continuous sense
> of moving through time.

"Less spastic" is his gracious description. "To see yourself being more of
the same person."
> not identical,
> not grappled tight to myself,
> just floating onward. (1999, p. 60)

Shannon desires for Eve a different time sense ("a more continuous
sense / of moving through time") and a different sense of identity ("To
see yourself being more of the same person"). Shannon is perhaps correct in noting that she does not experience herself as "the same person"
moving "continuously" through time. But it is precisely this way of
experiencing time that allows Sedgwick to develop a concept of a queer
temporality. Shannon's desire for Sedgwick is that she develop within a
certain framework, that she experience time as something that develops
her in a particular direction. He seems to want for her a coherent narrative in which a singular person changes over the course of time—indeed
this quotation comes within a conversation about the narrative they are
trying to construct for Eve. Conversely, Sedgwick's sense of her self is
much more double, or even multiple, not one person who changes and
develops, but something "identical," something "grappled tight" to
itself. Sedgwick's use of "identical" here seems to imply a doubleness
(rather than sameness) because she is "grappled tight" to herself.

This idea of a double identity plays out in Sedgwick's other descriptions of herself—namely in her descriptions of herself as a child and an
adult simultaneously. In some instances, she merely expresses confusion—at one point she says: "I wonder what age Shannon perceives me
as being, I mean, I wonder what age I am?" (1999, p. 178). In other
moments, she outright names this double identity. For instance, she discusses how as a child she felt as if she were acting out a role, that she was
somehow an adult forced to play the role of kid:

> So it was as if I were a method actor: it was my job to propel myself into
> 'kid' by the very force of my sincerity, I would have to want to be 'kid.'
> But for the same reason I wasn't very good at it—my child-likeness was
> always too much, too insistent or off in some way or another. And because
> of this, of course, I could never be anything like centered; I just got so,
> so flung around. My being was always hollowing out, or whirlpooling, or
> flooding. (1999, p. 32)

This description shows the simultaneous existence of the adult and the child. The adult seems to exist inside the child, just as later, we will see, the child exists within and alongside the adult. But when Sedgwick comes to the end of this description we get some very specific images for the type of identity that is being described. Specifically, I would like to focus on the word "whirlpooling" because it is a trope that appears a few times in *A Dialogue on Love*, often hovering around the descriptions that Sedgwick gives of herself as a child.

When Sedgwick tells us "I could never be anything like centered... My being was always hollowing out, or whirlpooling, or flooding (1999, p. 32), she focuses on an identity without a center or a core. She could not be "centered"; her being is "hollowing out." Likewise, a whirlpool conjures up an image in which water is swirling around a center that is empty. There is also an image of excess when Sedgwick uses the word "flooding." She could not perform the role of "kid" properly and ends up only circling around her perception of that identity.

Sedgwick's childhood self also is defined by the fact that it consists of multiple parts existing simultaneously. There is no one unifying core, but particular parts that endure over time. This is evidenced by something she says slightly earlier. In trying to describe to Shannon the two parts of herself as a child (the one that was a child and the eerily adult-like one), she says:

> But...what you completely do not seem to catch on to about these two parts of the kid is that they are not separate. They are constantly whirlpool-ing around in each other—and the basic rule is this: that each one has the power to poison the other one. So what being a kid was like for me was, at the same time, like being an adult in bad drag as a child, and being a child in bad drag as an adult. (1999, p. 30)

Sedgwick's comparison of childhood and adulthood to "bad drag" seems to dramatize the situation of the queer child—the child who recognizes her abnormality.[21] She cannot be innocent because both she and those around her recognize that she knows too much. This seems to create a double identity in which the child is both child and not-child at the same time.[22] And it is perhaps knowledge that is at the root of this divide. Part of what seems so adult-like about this child to her parents is her knowl-edge; they reportedly tell Shannon: "Eve always knew what / she knew, and knew she knew it" (1999, p. 148). So when Sedgwick says that the two parts are "constantly whirlpooling around each other," that "each one has the power to poison the other one," it seems possible that she might be talking about innocence and knowledge. One part of Sedgwick is seen as innocent, the other as having knowledge. The innocence is poisoned by the knowledge and vice versa. If knowledge is perceived as the dividing line between childhood and adulthood, then the child with knowledge poses a semantic and a temporal problem.

The whirlpool itself is a temporal image. One of the most dominant metaphors for the flow of time is the image of a river. It imagines time as flowing in one direction, but as an image it also has its idiosyncrasies. Rivers have snags, eddies, and do not always flow at the same rate. A whirlpool, then, can be seen as an image for time that flows in a circle or swirls. Indeed, as I have already indicated in the introduction, the eddy (one form of which is the whirlpool) is a figure for what Sedgwick in *Tendencies* calls "the queer moment"; she refers there to the queer moment as "recurrent, eddying" (1993b, p. xii). I find it interesting then that this related image returns so often in *A Dialogue on Love* when Sedgwick is talking about a childhood that seems to defy particular temporal boundaries. The whirlpooling that Sedgwick describes is related to an out-of-sync-ness she feels at being forced to play the role of child when she feels too old for such a role.

I have examined images of the child as an adult, but Sedgwick also depicts the adult as a child in number of rich moments. These moments in which the adult Eve is cleaved to her childhood self are very often connected to sexuality. For example, she tells Shannon: "Up until recently, from as far back into childhood as I can remember, I was somebody who, given the opportunity, would spend hours and hours a day in my bedroom masturbating. Really. Hours and hours." To which Shannon replies, "Well, don't most kids do that?" And Sedgwick thinks, "Do most adults? I feel quickly foreclosed" (1999, p. 45). Sedgwick's behavior, which she locates not only in her childhood but "up until recently," is characterized by Shannon as a childhood behavior, a thing "most kids do." Sedgwick feels "foreclosed," acknowledging that her masturbatory sexuality—which, as she says a sentence later, is "what feels like sex" to her, is associated with the child rather than the adult. As Sedgwick says in "Jane Austen and the Masturbating Girl," contemporary "views of masturbation tend to place it firmly into the narratives of all-too-normative individual development" (1999, p. 109). Even when it is seen within the framework of adulthood, masturbation is often as a means to an end, as the means to help develop a normal sex life, not as the sex life itself. Sedgwick discusses how masturbation has been "conclusively subsumed under that normalizing developmental model" in which it "represents a relatively innocuous way station on the road to a 'full,' i.e., alloerotic, adult genitality" (1999, p. 117). But it is in this "childhood" form of sexuality that Sedgwick seems to derive the most pleasure. In Shannon's notes, we learn that Sedgwick "FINDS IT PLEASURABLE/SATISFYING TO BE THINKING ABOUT HER [SEXUAL FANTASIES] AS SHE HAS NOT FOR SOME TIME, ESP FROM THE PERSPECTIVE OF A CHILD" (170). Sedgwick shows childhood as the site of rich sexual pleasures, pleasures that are and should be accessible to the adult—not moments of sexual immaturity that pass as the child develops into the adult.

It is on this topic of child sexuality that we see Sedgwick's perspectives in opposition to Shannon's. Shannon seems to view children as primarily sexually innocent. While he does at times acknowledge them as sexual, his envisioning of this childhood sexuality seems quite different from Sedgwick's. For example, when Sedgwick describes the experience of being at Girl Scout camp as "lusciously homosocial space," Shannon replies that "it doesn't sound as if there was anything sexual about this Girl Scout camp space…I mean it wasn't coed or anything, not like your school…What you're describing about the camp, it sounds like that has to do with nurturance, really, not with sexuality" (1999, p. 72). Shannon's conception of sexuality here is undoubtedly heteronormative as he sees the Girl Scout camp as nonsexual in contrast to her school, which is "coed." Sedgwick describes her reaction to Shannon's comments as "unmistakable manifestations of impatience" and attempts to challenge his easy separation of sexuality and nurturance by stating, "Like these have nothing to do with each other." This is another instance of Sedgwick "smudg[ing] up the barriers" of Shannon's neat "discrete parts." But it also demonstrates the difference between envisioning and acknowledging children as sexual (and queerly so) and dismissing their sexual energies by referring to them as something else, characterizing them as "nurturance" rather "sexuality."

This fundamental difference between Shannon and Sedgwick's view on childhood sexuality becomes even more visible in a heated discussion between the two regarding Shannon's characterization of Eve's parents' behavior as "neglect" for letting her spend so much time alone in her room masturbating. She says: "I can't bear the thought that you want this kid constantly haled out of her room, back into the space of the family, in the name of togetherness and mental hygiene. I think it's just plain true that I would not have survived. I really wouldn't" (1999, p. 81). Sedgwick makes clear here that masturbation is completely tied up in this child's survival. It is at this moment that we can hear what is at stake in the conversations between Shannon and Sedgwick—the survival of a queer child. This discussion seems to pit a certain type of psychology reliant on "togetherness and mental hygiene" against the queer sexuality of the child. Sedgwick's insistent tone ("I can't bear the thought," "it's just plain true") conveys just how deep the ideological rift between Shannon and herself is on this issue. The "space of the family," while healing from Shannon's perspective, represents a site of extreme danger for the masturbating Eve. While the child's rightful place is in the family, the family threatens to sanitize or force conformity onto the queer child. The survival of Eve as a child is tied up in this constant masturbation, this "childish" form of sexuality. This is perhaps one way that Eve, the child, survives into Sedgwick's adulthood.

The intense need of this child to survive across time becomes even more visible later when Eve as a child makes her presence known by projecting herself across time into the future. Sedgwick says: "I'm suddenly in mind of the many childhood moments when, for one reason or another, I vowed to myself to remember something or willed to remember it. Specifically: to remember it into adulthood. Whether to bear witness to the pains of childhood, or to make myself behave differently towards kids when I was a grown up, or just—to remember" (1999, p. 116). This child needs to be remembered, insists on being present in the adult.

Here we might note the very different valences given to memory for Sedgwick and Stein. For Stein, memory is quite negative; the mind that remembers is a mind that is unable to experience the "continuous present." For Sedgwick, memory is part of what makes possible the child's survival across time. Though these positions might seem to be diametrically opposed, I would focus our attention on the way in which Sedgwick's desire "project" the present "forward into the future" resonates with Stein's desire that a thing remain forever "as it is." Sedgwick's child may function as a type of entity that endures, something that remains "as it is" despite the passage of time.

For Sedgwick, it seems, the queer child is always under threat; its survival is always at stake. But the child's insistent desire to endure over time reveals the child as something other than simple and innocent.

As the young Eve conveys to the adult Eve, "This may look like just another little kid, looking back—you may wonder if she has an inner life at all!—but, here's proof: her inner life was powerful enough to conjure you up, long before you existed, and install an...imprint in your memory" (1999, p. 117). What Sedgwick highlights here is the inner life of the child; she gives evidence of a child who knows that her days are numbered, a child who does not want to grow up and out of existence. And in a sense this child does survive, her presence in Sedgwick's life is made clear throughout the memoir, both as an uncanny adult-like child and as a space where queer desires and pleasures played out.

This is perhaps why Sedgwick is seen as a threat to her parents within the space of the family. Shannon is quite skeptical about the ability of Eve as a child to be threatening to her parents. "This is one I'll need convincing on," he says. "Because I don't know how to take it for granted that a child can be that threatening to a grownup" (1999, p. 29). Why, we might ask, is Shannon unable to imagine feeling threatened by a child? Why can he not imagine such a threat? It might be easy to answer that in a society that predominantly views children as innocent, an adult is much more likely to view children as those who need to be protected than those who could pose a threat themselves. But Sedgwick seems to recognize what Shannon does not, that certain children are perceived as dangerous. And queer children specifically are both a threat to the norm of childhood innocence and a temporal contradiction. For Sedgwick, it is for precisely this reason that the queer child needs to survive.

The child that Sedgwick needs to survive embodies something quite different from innocence. She actually embodies a queer form of sexual knowledge. It is this sexual knowledge that comes out in bits and pieces as Sedgwick attempts to narrate her sexuality to Shannon. In Shannon's notes, we learn: "PART OF THAT IS THE FACT THAT, WHILE SEX IS A PRESENCE IN E'S LIFE IN MYRIAD WAYS, THESE WAYS ARE SO DISCONTINUOUS. THIS MAKES IT HARD FOR HER OR US TO FORM A COHERENT NARRATIVE UNDERSTANDING OF IT" (1999, p. 158). This description of Sedgwick's sexuality as "discontinuous" appears a number of time in the text. It seems to be related to the ways in which sex intersects the various aspects of her life, at times in contradictory ways. What is clear from Shannon's notes, however, is that sex as a "presence" in Sedgwick's life will not conform to a "coherent narrative." The impossibility of making her sexuality fit into a coherent narrative is connected to the fact that her sexuality whirlpools around desires and pleasures rooted in her childhood, that her sexuality has not "developed" or moved past what some would describe as adolescent sexuality, that she is in a state of arrested sexual development. To construct a "coherent narrative" of such a state would risk erasing those aspects that Sedgwick sees as most central to her sexuality. Perhaps the story of queer sexuality can only be told in bits and pieces that don't conform to familiar narrative timelines. And perhaps the queer child stands as a figure for this incoherent narrative temporality. The queer child cannot be a child because it has sexual knowledge that disqualifies it for this category. The queer adult has not properly grown up and can thus never fully be an adult. The queer is forever both and neither.

For Sedgwick, this can be a productive configuration. As Barber and Clark have shown in their introduction to *Regarding Sedgwick*, the "adult-child cleaving" that can be seen across her body of work "leaves it undecidable where one subjectivity begins and the other ends" (2002, p. 6). Sedgwick's tendency to "smudge up the barriers" leaves us with a situation in which we must think the child and adult together. We cannot leave childhood sexuality in the past. As Sedgwick says in her critical work: "If queer is a politically potent term, which it is, that's because, far from being capable of being detached from the childhood scene of shame, it cleaves to that scene as a near-inexhaustible source of transformational energy" (1993a, p. 4). This "childhood scene of shame" reverberates through the adult in the same way that Sedgwick's own childhood spankings come to figure in her adult sexual fantasies.

This is perhaps Sedgwick's most meaningful contribution to the theorization of queer temporality, to devise a way of talking about how childhood, time, and sexuality come together. The image of the whirlpool is particularly helpful here. A whirlpool is created by the meeting of opposing currents. This image comes to represent a space in which the child and the adult can coexist. This is a space in which there is not forward or backward movement but a swirling of two (or more) different forces. Sedgwick's images of two identities whirlpooling around each other present us with a queer moment, a moment that allows for the preservation of the queer child in the adult. For Sedgwick, there is so much tied up in this image of the queer child—a pleasurable sexuality, promises made across time, a "transformative energy" (1999, p. 210). It is for these reasons that the queer child must survive.

*   *   *

The central connection between Stein's "continuous present" and Sedgwick's "continuing moment" is that they are both counter to the conventional narrative of adulthood. These two temporalities find common ground in their commitment to a form of movement that is opposed to normative development or a concept of growing up that follows conventional narratives. With that said, it is important to note that the "continuous present" and the "continuing moment" are not the same thing. For one, the "continuing moment," as described by Sedgwick, is much more open to the past than is Stein's "continuous present," which seeks to empty the present moment of its associations with what has come before and what will come after. Despite their differences, however, there are some major similarities between these two temporalities, similarities that I believe have important theoretical consequences. In order to draw out the connections between these two temporalities, I would like to compare a short passage from Stein to a short passage from Sedgwick. These two passages (both of which I have already briefly examined in this chapter) will allow me to show the modernist thread of Stein that seems to run through Sedgwick's work.

Shortly following Stein's statement: "What is the use of being a boy if you are going to grow up to be a man," she goes on to say, "There is really no use in being a boy if you are going to grow up to be a man because then man and boy you can be certain that that is continuing and a master-piece does not continue it is as it is but it does not continue" (1967b, p. 153). As Stein deals with the growing up required for a boy to become a man, she uses the words "continuing" and "continue" to describe this type of growth. She places this "continuing" in opposition to something that "is as it is." Part of what is objectionable for Stein about the growth of the boy into the man is that it represents for her a form of "continuing" that destroys the thing (in this case, a boy) "as it is." "Continuing" is connected to a progressive movement through time that turns one thing (a boy) gradually into something else (a man). This opposition is at the heart of Stein's preference for entity over identity. Identity moves the boy through time to develop him into a man. Entity denotes something that "is as it is."

Stein thus uses Sedgwick's preferred term, "continuing" (as in "continuing moment"), in opposition to her own preferred term, "continuous." She sees "continuing" as connected to a rather negative form of progressive movement, a form of temporality opposed to the "continuous present." As we follow this concept into Sedgwick, I need to point out that the word "continuing" has quite different connotations in Sedgwick's work. As I have demonstrated previously, Sedgwick's "continuing moment" runs counter to a form of development that would progress individuals from child to adult (or boy to man, as Stein says). The central aspect of Sedgwick's "continuing moment," as I have described it, is that it allows something to remain "as it is" and yet survive into the future.[23] In fact, Sedgwick uses the word "continuing" to mean almost the same thing that Stein means when she uses "continuous."

Likewise, Sedgwick uses Stein's word "continuous" in a different manner than Stein uses it. When relating Shannon's desires for her, Sedgwick writes "But he also says / he wants me to have / a more continuous sense / of moving through time" (1999, p. 60). Shannon wants Sedgwick to experience time in a way that would give a more coherent sense of her own identity or allow her, as he says, "To see [herself] as being more of the same person" (1999, p. 60). Sedgwick uses "continuous" to represent a very conventional view of temporality, one seemingly connected with a certain type of developmental psychology. This temporality is in opposition to how Sedgwick views herself, as multiple, as "grappled tight to [herself], / just floating onward" (60). A "continuous sense / of moving through time" seems to represent a certain type of developmental temporal movement, a form of linear movement that describes an uninterrupted identity.

Each of these authors thus seems to use "continuing" as the opposite of "continuous." One of these terms denotes a progressive developmental temporality and the other refers to a preferred temporality, a temporality that allows something to remain permanently "as it is." The difference is that Stein uses "continuous" as the preferred term, and Sedgwick uses "continuing." They are both, however, opposing the same thing, a temporality of succession that registers a form of normative growth. And for both authors these temporalities are tied up with issues of identity.

In fact, in a particular passage of Sedgwick's, we can see a distinction set up that is quite similar to the distinction that Stein sketches out between identity and entity. This occurs when Sedgwick is describing what she calls "object permanence":

MY WAY OF PAYING ATTENTION TO PEOPLE IS ADDITIVE, NON-NARRATIVE. THUS I DON'T HAVE A SENSE OF CHANGE IN PEOPLE, I.E., IF I NOTICE SOMETHING NEW I DON'T THINK "THEY'VE CHANGED." INSTEAD, I THINK, "THIS IS AN ADDITIONAL WAY X IS"—GROWS OUT OF SOME KIND OF STRESS ON OBJECT PERMANENCE, HOW TO KEEP THE SAME PERSON, A KIND OF CUBIST THREE-DIMENSIONALITY. (1999, p. 109)[24]

This is perhaps the moment in which Sedgwick sounds the most like Stein, specifically in her invocation of cubism in relation to temporality. In her placement of "change" in opposition to "object permanence," Sedgwick pairs these two terms in much the same way that Stein pairs "identity" and "entity." Sedgwick's "object permanence" is a conception of people that is not about growth, or at least not growth that registers change. This is quite similar to Stein's notion of entity, which she refers to as "a thing in itself" and something that "does not begin and end" (1967b, p. 149). Likewise, the notion of "change" is something that both Sedgwick and Stein have linked to identity (the person who becomes something new, the boy who changes into the man).

Sedgwick also describes "object permanence" as specifically "additive." This is because it relies on an accumulation of detail rather a sense of development that registers change and loss. In my discussion of Stein, I highlighted her use of accumulation in her various texts. Stein builds multiple partial images of her characters that add up like a cubist painting to a whole picture. For Stein, this was connected to "using everything," to producing a narrative in which all parts had equal importance, as Cezanne had done in painting. As Varghese John says, Stein's manner is "comparable to the dissected planes of a cubist painting adding up to make a vaguely defined total image of its subject" (1998, p. 131). Stein's notion of the whole character and Sedgwick's "object permanence" both eschew an idea that individuals develop, but instead see them as comprised of a variety of parts, parts that exist permanently.[25] As a component of this notion of "object permanence," we might include the child. In such a framework, the child does not develop into the adult but rather forever endures as it was.

We could thus say that Sedgwick's temporality is based on "a kind of cubist three-dimensionality," a dimensionality brought into prose, many would argue (including Stein herself), through the work of Gertrude Stein. Quite often Stein's work is described as a form of literary cubism. When we imagine Sedgwick's work in this way, as "a kind of cubist three-dimensionality," we can see the connection between a certain critique of identity, one carried out on a large scale by Sedgwick and other practitioners of queer theory at the end of the twentieth century, and a queer theory of time. Sedgwick's "queer moment"—her "continuing moment"—reimagines in a new context a Steinian temporality, a temporality that searches for enduring permanence in the face of meaningless change.

*　*　*

As I close this chapter, I want to return to one last phrase, a phrase I barely touched upon in constructing my argument: "I love my love with a b because she is peculiar" (1967a, p. 37). Stein uses this phrase to describe what *can* be said in the "continuous present" and *cannot* be said in the newspaper. In this claim, we can hear the temporality of the "continuous present" pitted against the perhaps linear temporality of the newspaper. Stein can say "I love my love with a b because she is peculiar" in the continuous present because it has "nothing to do with what the newspaper does"—which is to destroy the present moment (1967a, p. 37). The "continuous present" thus fosters queer desires. It functions like those queer moments that I have been describing throughout this book and destroys the chronology that requires the movement from one word, event, or idea to the "logical" next thing.

Across this book, we have seen various instances in which queer moments have been placed in opposition to more normative conceptions of time. In a number of instances, these moments produced or made visible queer forms of desire. In my second chapter, we saw this in the kiss that endured and remained present across many years. In my third chapter, nonnormative desire emerged as Winterson sought to touch Eliot across a temporal divide. The connection between temporality and desire became perhaps the most clear in my fourth chapter as I showed the way in which the severing of genealogical storytelling made visible nonreproductive desires in both Faulkner and Carter.

These queer literary moments are, for the most part, made possible through modernist experiments with temporality. Woolf, Eliot, Faulkner, and Stein are all authors who have made major contributions to the rethinking of literary temporalities. Even the contemporary novelists whom I explore consciously depend upon literary modernists as they perform their own work on temporality (Cunningham relies explicitly on Woolf, and Winterson depends upon Eliot). My work on the relationship between these two sets of texts shows that there is something queer about the temporalities of modernism. They constitute a form of temporality that not only upsets chronological times lines but also produces peculiar desires. These modernist literary moments need to be reread as the vehicles through which we consider the possibilities for a queer temporality.

NOTES

1. This book's peculiarity arises in part from its strange tone, a tone that Hugh Kenner calls "violently partisan" (1954, p. 75). *Time and Western Man* is, to be sure, a polemic, and it numbers among the many polemics that Lewis wrote in the late 1920s and early 1930s.
2. Wyndham Lewis is not the only critic to comment on the childishness of Stein's work. In *Testimony Against Gertrude Stein*, a statement issued by a number of artists angry at how Stein had depicted them in *The Autobiography of Alice B. Toklas*, Tristan Tzara calls Stein's device of speaking as Toklas "a childish subterfuge" (Braque 1935, p. 12).
3. Many critics have described the continuous present as in opposition to linear notions of time. For example, Cynthia Merrill has pointed out that Stein, in "her advocacy of a 'continuous present,' disparages both the linear succession of history and the timelessness of transcendence" 1985, p. 14).
4. The term "acromegaly" refers to "a disease characterized by hypertrophy and enlargement of the extremities," especially "the enormous enlargement of the feet, hands, face, and chest." This condition is caused by "an excessive production of growth hormone" (def. 1).
5. *Doom of Youth*, for example, mentions how male homosexuals seek "[t]o be eternally 'children'—never to enter the category of 'fathers'" (1932, p. 218). According to Lewis, such a desire is "an attack upon the Father-principle" (1932, p. 219). Lewis's words here resonate quite strongly with my chapter on genealogical time.
6. In the chapter summaries for *Doom of Youth*, we come across these telling sentences: The "roman homosexual is related to the modern European, postproustian, homosexual; and that, in its turn, is related to the *Child-cult*. The gigantic figure of Miss Gertrude Stein is (temperamentally) married to the chétif silhouette of Marcel Proust" (1932, p. xxvii).
7. Lewis's analysis of the dangerous nature of the "Child-cult" is strikingly similar to arguments that are still being made. For example, in 2007, St. Martins Press released *The Death of the Grown-Up: How America's Arrested Development Is Bringing Down Western Civilization*. Like Lewis's polemics, in this text queers hang out in the margins as inextricably connected to the notion of "arrested development."

8. Lewis's claim here seems connected to some of the discourses surrounding incest presented in my fourth chapter. Here the invocation of childhood (like incest) takes a person back to a utopian moment before something (before the law, before the responsibilities of adulthood).

9. Although utopia is often used as a spatial metaphor (a paradise located elsewhere, often an island or hidden garden), Lewis focuses on this image as specifically temporal, calling it a "time-paradise." This is perhaps because he is invested in critiquing the contemporary obsession with time.

10. This comment resonates with T. S. Eliot's reading of Stein in his 1927 review of Stein's "Composition as Explanation" in which he considers the rhythmic nature of Stein's prose. In response to her writing, he wonders "whether the thought and sensibility of the future may not become more simple and indeed more crude than that of the present" (1927, p. 595). He concludes his review: "If this is the future, then the future is, as it very likely is, of the barbarians" (1927, p. 595).

11. This concept of a temporality ruled by beginnings, middles, and endings is something we will see Stein theorize at length in her later lectures, though it is not something she directly touches on here.

12. Stein's "we" might include some of those other writers I have discussed in this book, for as my work has shown, these writers (along with many other modernists) were certainly interested in experimenting with conventions of narrative structure and progression.

13. I think it is important to note that Wyndham Lewis's "most general objection," as he states, "to the work of Miss Stein is that it is *dead*," (1927, p. 63; emphasis in original) that "it is composed of dead and inanimate material" (1927, p. 61).

14. Though Stein does not cite him, her phrase "thing in itself" recalls Kant's noumenon.

15. Some critics have even connected Stein's notion of the "continuous present" with a dismissal of the logic of the family. As Catherine Parke states "The family, as a model of perception and of knowledge, values relation and relatedness over connection and connectedness and, by thus legislating cause-and-effect thinking, deprives us of the present" (1988, p. 563). Parke's reading is derived partly from a sentence in *Everybody's Autobiography* in which Stein states that "There is too much fathering going on just now and there is no doubt about it fathers are depressing" (1988, p. 562). Parke's reading of family relations, particularly paternal relations, as a representation of a particular form of time that emphasizes "cause-and-effect thinking" resonates quite strongly with my fourth chapter.

16. The discourse of the child as a person without a past is just one of the stories that circulate about childhood. As my previous chapter has shown, children are also born into complex familial relations that give them a

history and future. Regardless, certain discourses about childhood figure it as a blank slate or tabula rasa.

17. It might be interesting to consider the fact that in Stein's case, she was a girl who grew up to be a husband. Stein often describes herself in the role of husband to Alice B. Toklas.

18. In my second chapter, I used the introduction of *Tendencies* to talk about the link between the child and the adult that a concept of the queer moment makes possible. In my fourth chapter, I used Sedgwick's article "Tales of the Avunculate" to examine familial relations that eschew the cause-and-effect logic of paternal genealogy.

19. I used this quote in my second chapter along with Sedgwick's work in the introduction to *Tendencies* in order to understand a particular form of queer temporality in *Mrs. Dalloway*. I intend here, in this chapter, to produce a more thorough reading of queer temporality that is specific to Sedgwick's own work.

20. This phrase appears in all capitals because it is taken from Shannon's notes. Sedgwick has interspersed her own writing with sections from Shannon's notes about her. In some instances, Shannon's notes contain sections that give direct quotes from Sedgwick or seem to be written from her point of view. These notes always appear in her text in all caps, and I will continue this practice as I quote them in this chapter.

21. So much could be said about this quote and its likening of the divide between the child and the adult to "drag." For my own purposes, I have chosen to focus on this image specifically as a temporal one.

22. It might be that the word "kid" is meant to express the complexity of this situation. Given its history, "kid" is not exactly a synonym for "child" and might in fact capture a certain lack of innocence (Think: Billy the Kid).

23. One aspect of this "continuing moment," as Jane Gallop has shown in *The Deaths of the Author*, is the anachronism of the printed word. As Gallop says, while most authors are "embarrassed by the queer temporality of the printed word, Sedgwick would embrace and celebrate it" (2011, p. 13). The printed word does not change with the times but is able to continue on "as it is." We might also connect the anachronism of the printed word to Stein's comments about "master-pieces," her prime example for something that "is as it is."

24. This section is in all caps because it comes from Shannon's notes about Stein. However, this note is told from Sedgwick's perspective.

25. This view of identity reminds me very much of a description of Clarissa Dalloway that I examined in my second chapter: "That was her self when some effort, some call on her to be her self, drew the parts together, she alone knew how different, how incompatible and composed for the world only into one centre, one diamond, one woman who sat in her drawing-room and made a meeting point" (1925, p. 37).

REFERENCES

Barber, Stephen M., and David L. Clark. 2002. Queer Moments: The Performative Temporalities of Eve Kosofsky Sedgwick. In *Regarding Sedgwick: Essays on Queer Culture and Critical Theory*, ed. Stephen M. Barber and David L. Clark, 1–56. New York: Routledge.

Braque, Georges. 1935. *Testimony Against Gertrude Stein*. The Hague: Servire Press.

Breslin, James E. 1986. Gertrude Stein and the Problems of Autobiography. In *Critical Essays on Gertrude Stein*, 149–159. Boston: G. K. Hall.

Bruhm, Steven, and Natasha Hurley (eds.). 2004. *Curiouser: On the Queerness of Children*. Minneapolis: University of Minnesota Press.

DuPlessis, Rachel Blau. 1989. Woolfenstein. In *Breaking the Sequence: Women's Experimental Fiction*, ed. Ellen G. Friedman and Miriam Fuchs, 99–114. Princeton: Princeton University Press.

Eliot, T.S. 1927. Charleston, Hey! Hey! *The Nation & Atheneum* 29: 595.

Gallop, Jane. 2002. *Anecdotal Theory*. Durham: Duke University Press.

Gallop, Jane. 2011. *The Deaths of the Author*. Durham: Duke University Press.

Haas, Robert Bartlett. 1971. Transatlantic Interview. In *Gertrude Stein: A Primer for the Gradual Understanding of Gertrude Stein*, 13–35. Los Angeles: Black Sparrow.

John, Varghese. 1998. *The Autobiography of Alice B. Toklas*: A Significant American Autobiography. In *Indian Views on American Literature*, 126–134. New Delhi: Prestige.

Kenner, Hugh. 1954. *Wyndham Lewis: The Making of Modern Literature*. Norfolk: New Directions.

Lewis, Wyndham. 1926. *The Art of Being Ruled*. London: Chatto. Print.

———. 1932. *Doom of Youth*. New York: Haskell. Reprint 1973.

———. 1927. *Time and Western Man*. New York: Harcourt.

Merrill, Cynthia. 1985. Mirrored Image: Gertrude Stein and Autobiography. *Pacific Coast Philology* 20 (1–2): 11–17.

Meyer, Steven J. 1992. Gertrude Stein Shipwrecked in Bohemia: Making Ends Meet in the Autobiography and After. *Southwest Review* 77 (1): 12–33.

Neuman, S. C. 1979. *Gertrude Stein: Autobiography and the Problem of Narration*. Victoria: University of Victoria Press.

Parke, Catherine N. 1988. 'Simple Through Complication': Gertrude Stein Thinking. *American Literature: A Journal of Literary History, Criticism, and Bibliography* 60 (4): 554–564.

Sedgwick, Eve Kosofsky. 1993a. Queer Performativity: Henry James's *The Art of the Novel*. GLQ 1: 1–16.

———. 1993b. *Tendencies*. Durham: Duke University Press.

———. 1999. *A Dialogue on Love*. Boston: Beacon.

Stein, Gertrude. 1935. *Narration: Four Lectures by Gertrude Stein*. New York: Greenwood. Reprint 1969.

———. 1967a. "Composition as Explanation." In *Gertrude Stein: Writings and Lectures 1911–1945*, ed. Patricia Meyerowitz, 21–30. London: Peter Owen Ltd.

———. 1967b. "What Are Masterpieces and Why Are There So Few of Them?" *Gertrude Stein: Writings and Lectures 1911–1945*, ed. Patricia Meyerowitz, 146–154. London: Peter Owen Ltd.

———. 1971. "Transatlantic Interview." In *Gertrude Stein: A Primer for the Gradual Understanding of Gertrude Stein*, ed. Robert Bartlett Hass, 13–35. Los Angeles: Black Sparrow.

Stockton, Kathryn Bond. 2002. "Eve's Queer Child." In *Regarding Sedgwick: Essays on Queer Culture and Critical Theory*, ed. Stephen M. Barber and David L. Clark. New York: Routledge, 181–199. Print.

———. 2004. "Growing Sideways, or Versions of the Queer Child: The Ghost, the Homosexual, the Freudian, the Innocent, and the Interval of Animal." In *Curiouser: On the Queerness of Children*, ed. Steven Bruhm and Natasha Hurley, 277–316. Minneapolis: University of Minnesota Press.

Wilder, Thorton. 1935. "Introduction." In *Narration: Four Lectures by Gertrude Stein*. New York: Greenwood. Reprint 1969.

Williams, William Carlos. 1970. "The Work of Gertrude Stein." In *Imaginations*, ed. Webster Schott, 346–353. New York: New Directions.

Woolf, Virginia. 1925. *Mrs. Dalloway*. San Diego: Harcourt. Reprint 1981.

CHAPTER 6

Conclusion: Figuring the Future—Queer Time in Contemporary Literature

The majority of this book has focused on how contemporary writers and theorists have reused or repurposed modernist temporalities with a focus on the similarities between the two. However, it would be inaccurate to suggest that when modernist temporalities appear in contemporary texts they are operating the same way they did in the early twentieth century. Therefore, here in the conclusion, I would like to consider the distinctions between modernist and contemporary uses of these temporalities in order to think about how these modernist temporalities are mobilized in contemporary texts to do a particular type of work in the cultural context of the late twentieth and early twenty-first centuries. To do this, I would like to return briefly to common narratives of modernism's relation to time to consider the differences we see in the contemporary texts I explore.

It is often said that modernist literature is oriented toward the past. And certainly, such an orientation can be seen in the temporalities I've explored in this book. I would point to the way the past interrupts the present in *Mrs. Dalloway* or the way in which Quentin's family's past threatens to determine his whole future in *Absalom, Absalom!* to name a few examples. Perhaps the most famous example of this is the ending to F. Scott Fitzgerald's *The Great Gatsby*: "So we beat on, boats against the current, borne back ceaselessly into the past" (1925, p. 180). In this ending, the past eclipses the "the orgastic future that year by year recedes before us" (1925, p. 180). As Jesse Matz has said, modernist novelists "tried to break the sequence, to put things out of order, to work from

© The Author(s) 2019
K. Haffey, *Literary Modernism, Queer Temporality*,
https://doi.org/10.1007/978-3-030-17301-2_6

the present back into the past, to dissolve linear time in the flux of memory and desire" (2004, p. 62). This tendency to move from "the present back into the past" is a crucial component of modernist temporality that has allowed it to serve as a model for contemporary queer theorists, as I have show in my introduction. Carla Freccero's argument, for example, about "affective force of the past in the present, of a desire issuing from another time and placing a demand on the present" sounds very much like the temporalities developed by modernist literary experiments (Dinshaw et al. 2007, p. 184).

However, with this emphasis on the past and the present's relation to the past in modernist writing, the future is often an afterthought. The focus is the heavy burden of the past and in living in a moment that is defined by what it comes after, which for modernists is most often WWI. The future exists on the horizon, but the present is pregnant with all that has come before. This can be seen in the opening to D. H. Lawrence's 1928 novel *Lady Chatterley's Lover*: "Ours is essentially a tragic age, so we refuse to take it tragically. The cataclysm has happened, we are among the ruins, we start to build up new little habitats, to have new little hopes. It is rather hard work: there is now no smooth road into the future: but we go round, or scramble over the obstacles. We've got to live, no matter how many skies have fallen" (1959, p. 1). Lawrence's opening is loaded with references to what has come before, to living in an era after "the cataclysm," after the "skies have fallen." The future exists, but the passage seems to emphasize more the obstacles that the past has presented than to getting to that future.

While the future often appears as an afterthought, as in *Lady Chatterley's Lover*, or as something beautiful but unreachable far off in the distance, as in *The Great Gatsby*, the contemporary authors I explored in this book, Michael Cunningham, Jeanette Winterson, Angela Carter, and Eve Sedgwick, all engage more directly with the future as a concept. As I have shown throughout my various chapters, their writing is heavily indebted to the experiments with time that the modernists developed, but each of these contemporary writers differs with their predecessors' configurations of futurity. There could be many reasons for this, not the least of which is the authors positioning at the end of the millennium, in a cultural context in which futures were being cut short for many due to the AIDS epidemic. This is also the era of neoliberal economic practices championed in the U.S. by President Reagan and in the U.K. by Margaret Thatcher. Thatcher's claim that there is no alternative to capitalism imagined a future of free-market economics that was utterly inescapable. But this is also the age of increasing political activism born out of the AIDS epidemic for LGBTQ+ rights, as individuals fought politically to make the future different from the past. In that context, it is perhaps no surprise that contemporary novelists began to devote their energy to considerations of the future.

To briefly sketch out the different forms of futurity that I see in the contemporary texts that make use of modernist temporalities, I would like to return to a quote that I discussed in my third chapter and explore it from a new angle. In Jeanette Winterson's *Sexing the Cherry*, one of the novel's narrators states: "The future lies ahead like a glittering city, but like the cities of the desert disappears when approached. In certain lights it is easy to see the towers and the domes, even the people going to and fro. We speak of it with longing and with love. *The future*. But the city is a fake" (1989, p. 167; emphasis in original). Winterson's description of the future here makes clear two things about it simultaneously: (1) that the future is fake and (2) that we desire the future. Winterson's claim that the future is fake recognizes the future as a figure that often functions as an ideological tool. For Winterson, the future is a fantasy, a mirage, a compensatory fiction. Her recognition of this is in line with postmodern meta-awareness about the ideological function of narrative and history as well as the tendency of language to create rather than describe reality. This aspect of her claim about the future is in line with Lee Edelman's critique of the future in *No Future*. Conversely, along with this recognition of the future as fake, Winterson emphasizes our desire for the future, stating "we speak of it with longing and with love."[1] Winterson's ambivalence about the future is perhaps the same ambivalence we see in the contemporary queer theory's current debates about this topic. On the one side of this debate we have Lee Edelman's utter rejection of the future because what is called "the future" is often merely the endless reproduction of the past. On the other side of this debate, we have a number of queer theorists, most notably José Esteban Muñoz, who have taken up the banner of the future as a rallying point within queer theory and identify the ways in the queer longing for a future that has not yet come can be theoretically productive.

Given the centrality of these debates to the last 15–20 years of queer theory, I would like to take time to lay out the various positions that critics have taken with regard to futurity before returning to show how contemporary literature takes up such issues. This is necessary because

I believe that much of contemporary fiction, especially those texts that I have explored in this book, present an ambivalent relation to the future, both recognizing its ideological function and yet still displaying a longing for a future that might be different than the present. In other words, the anxieties about the future that are presented in the critical theory of the late twentieth and early twenty-first century are already present in the literature of the 1980s and 1990s that this book has explored. Thus, by considering these debates, I hope to show how the contemporary texts that I explore across this book are able to reconfigure modernist temporalities in order to produce queer temporalities that engage the problematics of representing the future in the late twentieth century.

In January of 1998, when Lee Edelman first published "The Future is Kid Stuff" in an issue of *Narrative*, few would have predicted the impact the essay would have on the future of queer theory itself. The article would go on to become the opening chapter of Edelman's 2004 book *No Future*, and the ideas therein continue to incite controversy more than ten years later. In his book, Edelman claims that within political discourse the image of the child serves as the emblem of the future. The correlation that Edelman points out appears everywhere in contemporary culture, from political endeavors taken up "for the children" to Whitney Houston songs. While children occupy the place of the future, queers have come to figure as a bar to that future, in many cases posing a direct threat to this metaphorical child and thus to the future itself.

If Edelman's argument had ended here it would have perhaps not been so novel. Asserting the need to protect children from queers has been one of the most predictable tactics of those opposed to LGBT rights. However, instead of arguing back against this representation and claiming for queers a more positive space in political discourse, a tactic often used by mainstream LGBT political organizations, Edelman suggests an alternate approach. He calls on queers to opt out of this brand of reproductive futurism and to embrace the negativity that the queers have come to represent. Edelman's tactic asks us to turn our backs on the future as it is always already enmeshed in this type of symbolic representation. In a particularly lively and often-quoted piece of *No Future*, Edelman writes: "fuck the social order and the figural children paraded before us as its terroristic emblem; fuck Annie; fuck the waif from Les Miz; fuck the poor innocent kid on the 'Net; fuck Laws both with capital "l"s and with small; fuck the whole network of symbolic relations and the future that serves as its prop' (1998, p. 29). Edelman's dismissal of the future becomes all the more evident later when he closes "The Future is Kid Stuff" stating "what is queerest about us, queerest within us, and queerest despite us, is our willingness to insist intransitively: to insist that the future stops here" (1998, p. 30).

While Edelman has rejected wholesale the rhetoric of futurism, in popular culture the mainstream LGBT movement has seemingly embraced precisely the reproductive futurism that he describes as part of a political rehabilitation of the image of the queer. From a political standpoint, of course, this is seemingly the only option. As Edelman states, "The image of the child coercively shapes the structures within which the 'political' itself can be thought" (1998, p. 19). Within political discourse, it becomes impossible to oppose the side fighting for the children, and thus the rhetoric allows only one option. If fighting against the children is an unthinkable political position, then LGBT groups have chosen the thinkable position and organized their arguments around the child and the rhetoric of the nuclear family. And it is to this tactic that such groups owe much of their success. Over the past decade or so, same-sex marriage has been the top priority for LGBT organizations. In that time, the U.S. has gone from having no states where same-sex marriage was legal to the achievement of nationwide legalization in 2015. Perhaps much of the success the movement has had in achieving this political goal has come from its explicit casting of queers as parts of families, as parents and children. Same-sex marriage has often been constructed as beneficial to the children of those couples whose parents' relationship is now recognized in the eyes of the law and afforded the material benefits of marriage. Such rhetoric can be been seen not only in political discourse but also in popular culture as one of the most successful gay-themed films of the last decade focused on the children of a lesbian couple and was titled "The Kids Are Alright." The fight for gay marriage has thus presented gays and lesbians as invested in the same type of reproductive futurism that has been expected of straight couples.

The type of futurism that Edelman describes is not only part of the battle for same-sex marriage but has popped up in how we approach queer adolescents. Take, for example, the "It Gets Better Project." This project was developed to combat LGBT suicide among teenagers. In hundreds of videos, LGBT adults offer personal testimonies that tell of the bright futures possible for these youths if they only stick it out a bit longer. These videos often construct a narrative of redemption in which the future itself plays the role of savior. In video after video, the speaker demonstrates how time passing resulted in a happier life and assures the viewer that the same will be true for him or her. These videos have placed the future in front of their viewers like a glittering city, always just beyond the horizon. Within the mainstream LGBT movement at least, futurism is alive and well.

Edelman's analysis in *No Future* has forced many to view this type of political rhetoric with a certain amount of skepticism. Edelman's work brings to light the many insidious effects of this brand of futurism. As Heather Love pointed out in her review of *No Future*, "Edelman is relentless and right in his exposure of the violent homophobia implicit in these sentimental paeans to gay family" (2005, p. 131). He shows time and again that it is only queers who embrace reproductive futurism who can gain legitimacy, while those who do not place family at the center of their lives remain outside the fold. In the process of legitimizing gay families, the mark of queerness is merely passed on to someone else. As Edelman says, "those of us inhabiting the place of the queer may be able to cast off that queerness and enter the properly political sphere, but only by shifting the figural burden of queerness to someone else. The *structural position* of queerness, after all, and the need to fill it remain" (2004, p. 27).[2] Beyond this, Edelman has shown that the future promised through the image of the child is not a future at all. It is instead a fantasy that reproduces "the past, through displacement, in the form of the future" (2004, p. 31). The future promises only endless repetition of the same. And the image of the child, which can never actually grow up because it is a figure and not a person, forever ensures that this is the case.

Edelman's convincing analysis of the figure of the child and his unequivocal opposition to the future have forced many academics to seriously consider the implications of his argument. Since the initial publication of "The Future is Kid Stuff," there have been dozens of responses to Edelman's argument, both in the pages of journals and in special conference sessions. Criticism of his work ranges from issues with his style and the narrowness of his archive to critiques of his uses of Lacan to the implications of his argument for the treatment of real children.[3] More important for my purposes, however, are the questions that his work has raised concerning the viability of the future as a concept. While Edelman has outright rejected the future, his work has brought the future to the forefront of queer theory as a space for theoretical thinking.

Indeed, on the other side of this debate is José Esteban Muñoz, a queer theorist who has aligned himself with the future and against Edelman. Muñoz takes issue with Edelman's utter rejection of the future as a viable concept in queer theory. In order to get a sense of the full landscape at the present moment, it is important to lay out the opposition between Edelman's queer negativity and "queer futurity," to use José Esteban Muñoz's term. Among Edelman's critics, Muñoz is perhaps the most vocal opponent of his rejection of the future. In his 2009 book *Cruising Utopia*, Muñoz specifically valorizes the future and attempts to develop a theory of "queer futurity." Muñoz criticizes what he sees as "the failures of imagination in queer critique that [he] understand[s] as antirelationality and antiutopianism" (2009, loc. 443). His reference to antirelational critiques makes use of one of the terms most often applied to the work of Lee Edelman and other theorists of negativity.[4] His theories are thus a direct response to Edelman and an attempt to correct the lack of "imagination" in Edelman's and others' antirelational theories.

Muñoz describes the relationship between queers and the future in ways entirely opposed to Edelman. While Edelman has made the bold claim that "there can be no future for queers" (2004, p. 30), Muñoz has argued nearly the opposite, stating that "Queers have nothing but a future" (Caserio et al. 2006, p. 820). Muñoz counters Edelman's antirelationality by arguing that queerness is "primarily about futurity." "Queerness," he says, "is always on the horizon. Indeed, for queerness to have any value whatsoever, it must be considered visible only on the horizon" (2009, loc. 309). The language that Muñoz employs here imagines queerness as that glittering city of the future that Winterson mentions in *Sexing the Cherry*. In Muñoz's construction, queerness becomes synonymous with the future and takes on its symbolic properties: it is utopian, optimistic, and hopeful.

But what does Muñoz mean when he says that queerness is "primarily about futurity"? In the opening sentences of *Cruising Utopia*, he makes the provocative claim that "we are not yet queer" (2009, loc. 115). From that point on, Muñoz talks of queerness in terms of ideality, potentiality, and possibility. Queerness is thus something to strive toward, to dream about, to imagine. Muñoz's concept of queerness is entirely opposed to the present, or what he sometimes refers to as the "here and now." At various points in his introduction and first chapter, the present is described in extremely negative terms, being called "a prison house" (2009, loc. 115), a "quagmire" (2009, loc. 115), "a limited vista" (2009, loc. 538), "alienating" (2009, loc. 203), "stul-tifying" (2009, loc. 325), "broken-down" (2009, loc. 325), "hollow" (2009, loc. 508), and "poisonous and insolvent" (2009, loc. 666). It is perhaps important to note here, however, that the present Muñoz is describing is a present conceived of within the realm of what he calls "straight time," a linear form of time in which the present is entirely cut off from past and future.[5] His purpose in conceiving of queerness in this way is to hold it "in a sort of ontologically humble state, under a con-ceptual grid in which we do not claim to always already know queerness in the world," to in a sense "stave off the ossifying effects" produced by assuming to know queerness in advance (2009, loc. 523). Seemingly, part of what makes the future so attractive to Munoz is its openness, its seeming formlessness, its ability to remain untethered, and its relation to the desire for what is not yet. In this sense, Muñoz is conceiving of the future in quite a different way than Edelman has. For Edelman, the future, far from being untethered to the past, is merely the past projected into the space of the future.

While he is clearly an advocate for futurity, Muñoz is no champion of the type of reproductive futurism that Edelman describes, connected as it is with "straight time," one of Muñoz's central foci for critique. "Straight time," he states, "tells us that there is no future but the here and now of everyday life. The only future promised is that of reproduc-tive majoritarian heterosexuality, the spectacle of the state refurbishing its ranks through overt and subsidized acts of reproduction" (2009, loc. 523). Like Edelman's notion of reproductive futurism, which reproduces "the past, through displacement, in the form of the future" (2004, p. 31), the future that straight time promises is one of repetition of the past through reproduction. The futurism that Muñoz describes and cham-pions is thus not the same brand of futurism that Edelman spends the majority of *No Future* critiquing. Indeed, Muñoz has as much disdain for reproductive futurism as Edelman does. Unlike Edelman, however, Muñoz believes that there are other ways of conceiving of the future and that the future can and should be recuperated as a conceptual tool.[6]

Given these debates, it is clear that queer theory grapples with the question of whether or not the future can be a useful theoretical concept. While Muñoz and others have shown its productive efficacy, Edelman points to the concept as always already enmeshed in a logic that pro-duces endless repetition of the same, a logic that takes up reproduction in both its literal and figurative forms to ensure that the future recreates the past. Though the modernist authors I explored in this book rarely directly address issues of futurity, they often seek to find their way out of temporalities that bear striking resemblances to reproductive futurism. Woolf, for example, seeks to "break the sequence" of narrative such that stories need not follow the particular trajectories that they had in the past. Likewise, Stein was looking for a way out of succession itself, a way to keep one thing from inevitably following another. And in Eliot and Faulkner, we find figures that could be associated with reproductive futurism itself. For Eliot this comes in the form of a coupled dance that represents the temporality of marriage and reproduction, and in Faulkner, we see it in his response to genealogical time, a temporality that, like reproductive futurism, works to assure the future will merely recreate the past. All of these writers were responding to narrative conventions that they believed shut down possibilities. Specifically, they sought a way out of a temporality that was predetermined, that replicated itself over and over. Like Edelman, the modernists I've explored often said no to temporalities akin to reproductive futurism.

It is perhaps in modernism's oppositions to these conventions that they provided a framework for contemporary writers to think more explicitly about models of the future that that would not fall into the trap that Edelman describes. Across this book I have focused on the concept of the queer moment, a temporality that, as I've claimed, doesn't neatly distinguish between past, present, and future. Even as modernism looks toward the past, we are able to recognize particular moments that attempt to produce new relations to time. The contemporary authors that I explore in this book make use of these moments in order to rethink the future as the twentieth century was coming to a close. This is not to say that the authors I study in this book are champions of the future in the same way that Muñoz is. Instead, we can see a rejection of the type of future associated with reproductive futurism, as well as reluctance to give up the notion of the future entirely. As such, we are left not with the dream of a predictable future somewhere out on the distant horizon, but with the tools to untether the future from the past, to create a future that can be different from the past.

I close my second chapter talking specifically about the future. In reading Cunningham's *The Hours*, I come to the notion of an open future, a future that is not yet decided. It is my claim that Cunningham is able to use the temporalities developed by Woolf in *Mrs. Dalloway* in order to rethink futurity. While the queer moment as I explored it in *Mrs. Dalloway* very rarely turns toward the future, her conception of time offers a model open to new forms of futurity. Cunningham takes advantage of this and conceives of a future that is not reproductive futurism. His model of the future depends on unpredictability, on a future that can't be known in advance. My reading of Cunningham here relies on the work of Elizabeth Grosz whose writing on time offers a critique and a reconfiguration of the future. Grosz talks of bringing about "a future we don't recognize" (2005, p. 2). For Grosz, the attempt to know the future in advance destroys it as the future. As she argues, "to know the future is to deny it as future, to place it as a given, as past" (1999, p. 6). To make such claims, Grosz relies on theorists who have "insisted on the fundamental openness of time to futurity, who have resisted all attempts to reduce time to the workings of causality," including Nietzsche, Bergson, and Deleuze (1999, p. 3). Reproductive futurism is exactly the type of futurity that relies on causality and thus reproduces the past.

The work of Grosz and others thus provide the groundwork for calling reproductive futurism out as mock-futurity and for developing a concept of the future that is open to chance and change. For example, some of the recent criticisms of Edelman have taken issue with his reading of Lacanian negativity, a concept on which much of his argument rests. According to Mari Ruti, "Lacanian negativity holds open the future as a space of ever-renewed possibility" (114). Ruti and others have shown that there are ways of reading Lacan that offer alternate forms of futurity. Likewise, Mikko Tuhkanen looks to Deleuze's delineation of becoming as a fruitful paradigm for rethinking futurity within a queer context. Whether it be Grosz, Bergson, Deleuze, or Lacan, there are models of futurity that might not fall into the trap of reproductive futurism.

When we turn to T. S. Eliot, the relation to the future becomes a bit more complicated. The division between the dance of the couple and the solitary dance in *Four Quartets* structures much of my third chapter. There I argue that the dance of the couple is connected precisely to the type of reproductive futurism that Edelman describes in *No Future*, while the solitary dance produces a temporality that is much more difficult to describe. Eliot even begins "Burnt Norton" with the description of a future that correlates with reproductive futurism: "time future [is] contained in time past" ("Burnt Norton," line 3). The future here is tamed, predestined, and utterly linked to the past. Even the ending of "Little Gidding," the last poem of the sequence, presents us with a gesture toward a future closure, a closure that seems to promise "messianic" redemption, to use Edelman's word, in a quite literal sense given its clearly Christian overtones. The lines "and all shall be well / and all manner of thing shall be well" point to a future moment "when" all things will be revealed ("Little Gidding," lines 882–883). However, there seems to be a tug of war going on between the notions of present and future elaborated throughout the bulk of the poem and the more predictable way in which the poem is closed. The image of the solitary dance that Eliot develops within the poem sequence is a temporality that makes nonsense of linear temporalities that lead toward predictable endings. So which do we give priority to? To the pat ending that offers redemption, meaning making, and closure? Or to the moments in the poem that seem to negate a forward-looking temporality that functions to make those things legible? The question is an impossible one, but it perhaps points us to the boundaries of narrative since, in this case, it is the components of narrative that force closure and give priority to the ending. Ultimately, Jeanette Winterson is able to play with the temporalities that Eliot developed in *Four Quartets* to rethink issues of narrative closure. Winterson's treatment of Eliot's time sense offers a possible way to rethink the relationship between the temporality of Eliot's solitary dance and futurity. The temporality that eschews predictability for perpetual possibility may point toward a way of conceiving of a more open and unpredictable future.

For Faulkner, on the other hand, the future is nothing if not predictable. The characters of *Absalom, Absalom!* are caught in the temporality of genealogical succession, a temporality that, like reproductive futurism, ensures the past is endlessly recreated in the future. Much of my reading of that novel focuses on various characters' attempts to escape this type of genealogical time. These attempts at escape, however, are not future-oriented. Instead, characters like Quentin and Henry try to slow down time, to prevent the future from coming. Of course, for both characters, the only future possible is a genealogical one, a future in which they take their father's place and bear the burden of his past. However, in their attempts to slow down and stop time, we might see an opening to a different type of future, one outside the rule of fathers. This plays out especially at the level of narrative, where Quentin and Shreve's storytelling allows them not to just recreate the past through retelling the stories that have been handed down to them but to create something new. Of course, in Faulkner, these respites from genealogical time seem to be only momentary, ephemeral dreams. Thus we might glimpse in Faulkner (as in Edelman) a rejection of future as anything other than endless repetition of the same. However, if we follow genealogical notions of time into Angela Carter's work, there is a more sustained consideration of futurism outside of genealogy. In Carter's *Wise Children*, we can discern an alternate temporality to genealogical time, a temporality that favors avuncular relations. In Carter's configuration this temporality, which I refer to as "avuncular time" in the fourth chapter, depends on an articulation of the future as not predetermined, as offering alternate trajectories. As I make clear in that chapter, avuncular time represents a relation to the future that is quite different from reproductive futurism, as it offers that opportunity for the future to be different from the past.

In Stein's work, like Faulkner's, the future is suspect. The future is part of the "past present future" configuration that Stein links to narratives of succession. Such narratives depend on chronology, progression, and linearity, and they create a situation in which one event must necessarily follow another. Stein's notion of the continuous present seeks to extend the present in order to prevent the logic of succession. Stein is much less concerned with anything like a future than she is with creating a present-tense experience. To think of the future, for her, is to think of what comes next, to resort to succession. But this doesn't mean that the continuous present has nothing to contribute to an articulation of the future that doesn't depend upon succession. The continuous present creates a situation in which the present is unlinked from both the past and the future that would proceed inevitably from a logical successive chain of events; it attempts to remove casual connections across time. For Stein, the problem with succession is that it causes a future that is predetermined. However, if the present is uncoupled from this type of teleology, then it offers an opportunity for the present to open onto a different kind of future, one not ruled by these logics. Stein's contribution becomes even clearer when we follow such concepts into the work of Eve Sedgwick. Like Stein, Sedgwick articulates her own theory of the present—the queer moment—but Sedgwick's configuration is much more explicitly concerned with the future. Indeed, she calls queer a "continuing moment," a configuration that upsets normative notions of succession from a present to a future. She imagines a present that endures into the future not as a form of repetition but as a remnant from the past that makes an ethical claim on the future. While her future is one that preserves the past, it is not one that merely repeats it. The queer moment thus becomes an alternative to the type of future that produces endless repetition of the same.

The questions that queer theory has recently raised about futurism are deeply enmeshed with questions concerning narrative. The future itself seemingly only becomes visible before us in the form of a narrative. Within fiction, narrative structures help to form the parameters within which the future can be thought. If narrative texts structure time so as to tell a story, they provide us with creative critical models for imagining new ways of conceiving of the future. Such is certainly the case for modernist literary texts, which sought to escape conventional methods of plotting narratives. But what is often missed when we read modernists as obsessed with the past is the ways in which their experiments with temporality provided openings for contemporary critics and novelists to rethink the future in alternate ways. It might be the case that modernism, in addition to being preoccupied with the past, was more subtly scripting blueprints for new conceptions of the future.

Notes

1. In my claim about Winterson's description of the future, I see a similarity to what Jane Gallop says about Barthes relation to the author in her book *The Deaths of the Author*. In her chapter titled "The Author is Dead but I Desire the Author," she discusses Bathes "perverse desire for the author he nonetheless knows to be dead" (2011, p. 5). This is quite similar to Winterson's narrator's desire for a future he knows is fake.

2. This criticism is not specific to Edelman. Michael Warner made similar arguments in *The Trouble With Normal* in his discussion of sexual shame.

3. In a forum in PMLA meant to summarize the events of a 2005 MLA session, Jack Halberstam critiqued Edelman's writing style and the narrowness of his archive (2006, p. 824). In the same publication, José Esteban Muñoz referred to Edelman's work on "the antirelational" as "the gay white man's last stand" (2006, p. 826). Several academics, including Mari Ruti, John Brenkman, Tim Dean, Carolyn Dever, have criticized Edelman's use of Lacan. Both Muñoz and Susan Fraiman have taken issue with how children are represented within his text and what the effects of this type of representation are for actual children.

4. The work of Lee Edelman is often referred to through the moniker of "the anti-social thesis" in queer theory. As Muñoz sketches out in *Cruising Utopia*, "antisocial queer theories are inspired by Leo Bersani's book

Homos, in which he first theorized the so-called thesis of antirelationality." Edelman's work is sometimes described as following Bersani's antirelational turn.

5. While Muñoz seems to acknowledge queer theories with more capacious understandings of the present, when he speaks of the present in *Cruising Utopia*, he seems to be primarily talking about the normative notion of it encompassed within "straight time."

6. For Edelman, even the logic of Muñoz's argument recreates the logic of reproductive futurism, dependent as it is on redemption and what Edelman calls "messianic hope" (Dinshaw et al. 2007, p. 159). Indeed, in his dismissal of Muñoz's argument in "The Anti-social Thesis in Queer Theory," he refers to queer utopians as "oblivious to their own particular ways of reproductive futurism" and suggests that they lead "a hymn to the Futurch even while dressed in heretical drag" (2006, p. 821). In this way, Edelman's argument participates in the larger discourse in critical theory that Sean Grattan identifies in his recent book *Hope Isn't Stupid* of disavowing utopian possibility, or even hope itself, "on the grounds of its naiveté or stupidity" (2017, p. 12).

References

Bersani, Leo. 1995. *Homos*. Cambridge: Harvard University Press.

Carter, Angela. 1991. *Wise Children*. London: Penguin.

Caserio, Robert L., Lee Edelman, Jack Halberstam, Jose Estean Munoz, and Tim Dean. 2006. The Antisocial Thesis in Queer Theory. *PMLA* 121 (3): 819–828.

Cunningham, Michael. 1998. *The Hours*. New York: Farrar.

Dinshaw, Carolyn et al. 2007. "Theorizing Queer Temporalities: A Roundtable Discussion." *GLQ: A Journal of Gay and Lesbian Studies* 13 (2–3): 177–195.

Edelman, Lee. 1998. The Future Is Kid Stuff: Queer Theory, Disidentification, and the Death Drive. *Narrative* 6 (1): 18–30.

———. 2004. *No Future: Queer Theory and the Death Drive*. Durham: Duke University Press.

Eliot, T.S. 1943. *Four Quartets*. New York: Harcourt.

Faulkner, William. 1936. *Absalom, Absalom*. New York: Random House.

Fitzgerald, F. Scott. 1925. Reprint 2018. *The Great Gatsby*. New York: Scribner.

Gallop, Jane. 2011. *The Deaths of the Author*. Durham: Duke University Press.

Grattan, Sean Austin. 2017. *Hope Isn't Stupid: Utopian Affects in Contemporary American Literature*. Iowa City: University of Iowa Press.

Grosz, Elizabeth (ed.). 1999. *Becomings: Explorations in Time, Memory and Futures*. Ithaca, NY: Cornell University Press.

———. 2005. *Time Travels: Feminism, Nature, Power*. Durham: Duke University Press.

Lawrence, D.H. 1959. *Lady Chatterley's Lover*. New York: Grove Press.

Love, Heather. 2006. Wedding Crashers. *GLQ* 13 (1): 125–139.

Matz, Jesse. 2004. *The Modern Novel*. Malden, MA: Blackwell.

Muñoz, José Esteban. 2009. *Cruising Utopia: The Then and There of Queer Futurity*. New York: New York University Press.

Ruti, Mari. 2008. Why There Is Always a Future in the Future. *Angelaki: Journal of the Theoretical Humanities* 13 (1): 113–126.

Tuhkanen, Mikko. 2009. Performativity and Becoming. *Cultural Critique* 72: 1–35.

Warner, Michael. 1999. *The Trouble with Normal: Sex, Politics, and the Ethics of Queer Life*. Cambridge: Harvard University Press.

Winterson, Jeanette. 1989. *Sexing the Cherry*. New York: Grove.

Woolf, Virginia. 1925. *Mrs. Dalloway*. San Diego: Harcourt. Reprint 1981.

INDEX

© The Editor(s) (if applicable) and The Author(s),
under exclusive license to Springer Nature Switzerland AG 2019
K. Haffey, *Literary Modernism, Queer Temporality*,
https://doi.org/10.1007/978-3-030-17301-2